Characterization of the Hosgri Fault Zone and Adjacent Structures in the Offshore Santa Maria Basin, South-Central California

By C. Richard Willingham, Jan D. Rietman, Ronald G. Heck, and William R. Lettis

Chapter CC of **Evolution of Sedimentary Basins/Onshore Oil and Gas Investigations—Santa Maria Province**, edited by Margaret A. Keller

Bulletin 1995–CC

U.S. Department of the Interior
U.S. Geological Survey

U.S. Department of the Interior
KEN SALAZAR, Secretary

U.S. Geological Survey
Suzette M. Kimball, Acting Director

U.S. Geological Survey, Reston, Virginia: 2013

For more information on the USGS—the Federal source for science about the Earth,
its natural and living resources, natural hazards, and the environment:
World Wide Web: http://www.usgs.gov
Telephone: 1-888-ASK-USGS

For an overview of USGS information products, including maps, imagery, and publications,
visit http://www.usgs.gov/pubprod

Suggested citation:
Willingham, C.R., Rietman, J.D., Heck, R.G., and Lettis, W.R., 2013, Characterization of the Hosgri Fault Zone and
adjacent structures in the offshore Santa Maria Basin, south-central California, chap. CC of Evolution of sedimentary
basins/onshore oil and gas investigations—Santa Maria province: U.S. Geological Survey Bulletin 1995-CC, 105 p.

Contents

Figures

Tables

Plates (separate files at http://pubs.usgs.gov/bul/1995/cc)

This page left intentionally blank.

Characterization of the Hosgri Fault Zone and Adjacent Structures in the Offshore Santa Maria Basin, South-Central California

By C. Richard Willingham[1], Jan D. Rietman[2], Ronald G. Heck[3], and William R. Lettis[4]

Abstract

The Hosgri Fault Zone trends subparallel to the south-central California coast for 110 km from north of Point Estero to south of Purisima Point and forms the eastern margin of the present offshore Santa Maria Basin. Knowledge of the attributes of the Hosgri Fault Zone is important for petroleum development, seismic engineering, and environmental planning in the region. Because it lies offshore along its entire reach, our characterizations of the Hosgri Fault Zone and adjacent structures are primarily based on the analysis of over 10,000 km of common-depth-point marine seismic reflection data collected from a 5,000-km² area of the central and eastern parts of the offshore Santa Maria Basin.

We describe and illustrate the along-strike and downdip geometry of the Hosgri Fault Zone over its entire length and provide examples of interpreted seismic reflection records and a map of the structural trends of the fault zone and adjacent structures in the eastern offshore Santa Maria Basin. The seismic data are integrated with offshore well and seafloor geologic data to describe the age and seismic appearance of offshore geologic units and marker horizons. We develop a basin-wide seismic velocity model for depth conversions and map three major unconformities along the eastern offshore Santa Maria Basin. Accompanying plates include maps that are also presented as figures in the report. Appendix A provides microfossil data from selected wells and appendix B includes uninterpreted copies of the annotated seismic record sections illustrated in the chapter.

Features of the Hosgri Fault Zone documented in this investigation are suggestive of both lateral and reverse slip. Characteristics indicative of lateral slip include (1) the linear to curvilinear character of the mapped trace of the fault zone, (2) changes in structural trend along and across the fault zone that diminish in magnitude toward the ends of the fault zone, (3) localized compressional and extensional structures characteristic of constraining and releasing bends and stepovers, (4) changes in the sense and magnitude of vertical separation along strike within the fault zone, and (5) changes in downdip geometry between the major traces and segments of the fault zone. Characteristics indicative of reverse slip include (1) reverse fault geometries that occur across major strands of the fault zone and (2) fault-bend folds and localized thrust faults that occur along the northern and southern reaches of the fault. Analyses of high-resolution, subbottom profiler and side-scan sonar records indicate localized Holocene activity along most of the extent of the fault zone. Collectively, these features are the basis of our characterization of the Hosgri Fault Zone as an active, 110-km-long, convergent right-oblique slip (transpressional) fault with identified northern and southern terminations. This interpretation is consistent with recently published analyses of onshore geologic data, regional tectonic kinematic models, and instrumental seismicity.

Introduction

This chapter follows two others on the Hosgri Fault Zone in the eastern offshore Santa Maria Basin. The Lettis and others (2004) chapter provides an overview of the Hosgri Fault Zone in the context of the regional Quaternary tectonic kinematic setting of south-central coastal California. The Hanson and others (2004) chapter provides quantitative analysis of the late Quaternary behavior of the fault zone. This chapter presents the seismic reflection data and interpretive maps used to characterize the fault zone and adjacent structures.

Setting and Significance of the Hosgri Fault Zone

The Hosgri Fault Zone trends subparallel to the south-central California coast for 110 km from north of Point Estero to south of Purisima Point (fig. 1). The fault zone is between 3 km and 20 km offshore and forms the east margin of the present offshore Santa Maria Basin. It has played a significant and continuing role in the tectonic development of the south-central California region since at least the Neogene, and possibly earlier (McCulloch, 1987).

---

[1]C.R. Willingham & Associates, Houston, TX

[2]Fugro Consultants, Oakland, CA

[3]R.G. Heck and Associates, Santa Barbara, CA

[4]Lettis Consultants International, Walnut Creek, CA

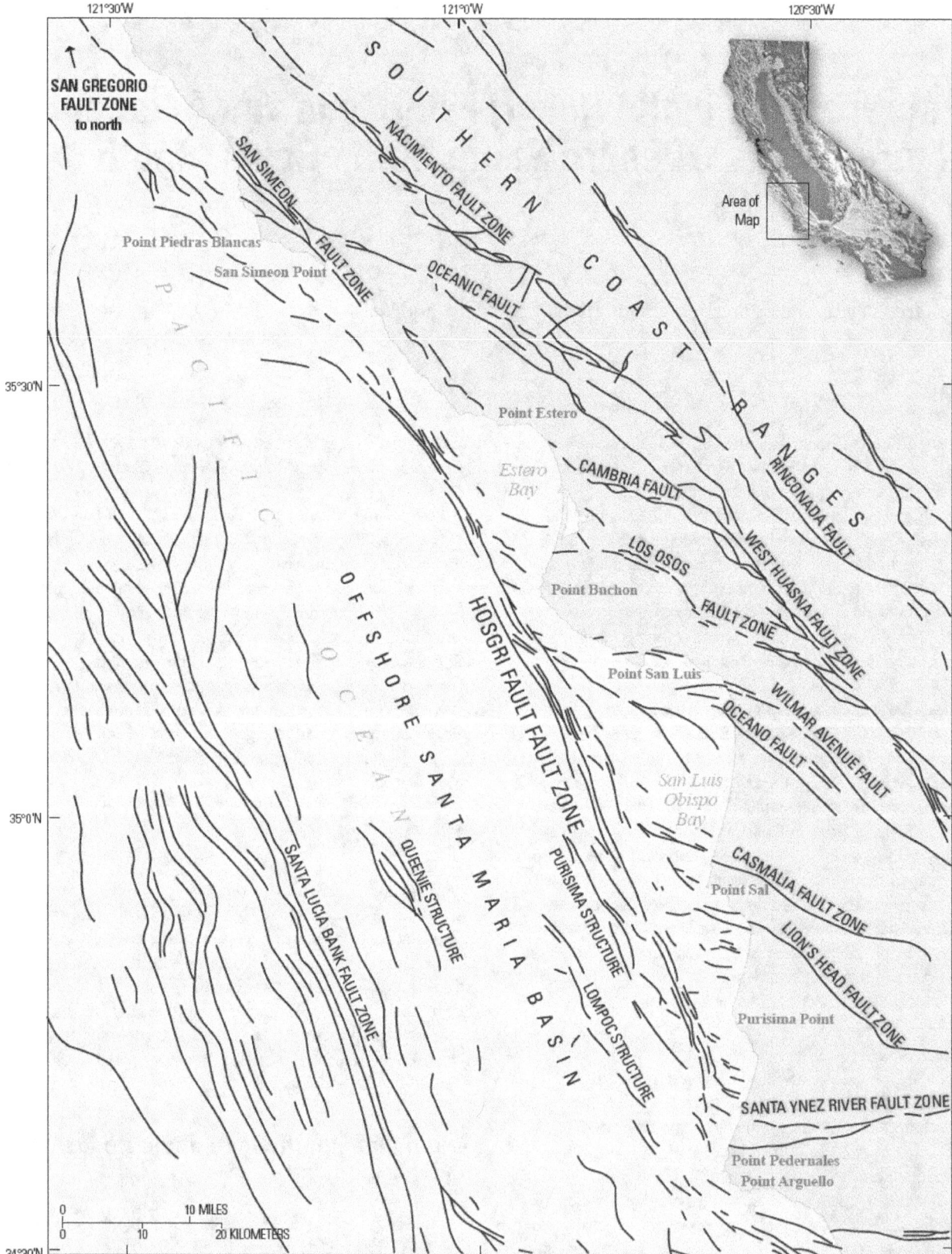

Figure 1.   Fault traces in the offshore Santa Maria Basin and adjacent coastal California. The Hosgri Fault Zone forms the eastern boundary of the offshore Santa Maria Basin; the northern part is aligned with the strike-slip San Simeon/Sur/San Gregorio Fault System to the northwest (Lettis and others, 2004). The Hosgri Fault Zone is subparallel to the north-northwest trend of faults in the offshore Santa Maria Basin. However, the west-northwest trends of faults to the east of the Hosgri Fault Zone are abruptly terminated at the fault zone.

The offshore Santa Maria Basin is one of the largest partially developed petroleum provinces in the United States, having recoverable reserves estimated to be nearly 1 billion barrels (Mayerson, 1997). The Hosgri Fault Zone is a major structural element in the tectonic regime that formed the structures responsible for hydrocarbon entrapment. Knowledge of the attributes of the Hosgri Fault Zone is important not only for petroleum exploration and development but also for seismic engineering studies and environmental planning that are necessary for locating and building critical facilities in the offshore basin and coastal region.

The Hosgri Fault Zone is subparallel to the San Andreas Fault and is a component of the Pacific Plate/North American Plate margin (Atwater, 1989). It is on a general structural trend with the San Simeon, Sur, and San Gregorio Fault Zones to the north (fig. 1), which form a well-documented, active coastal fault system (Graham and Dickinson, 1978; Sedlock and Hamilton, 1991). It is one of the fault zones believed to accommodate part of the "San Andreas discrepancy", defined as the component of relative motion between the Pacific and North American Plates that cannot be attributed to the San Andreas Fault (Argus and Gordon, 1991; Lettis and others, 2004). It is seismically active as evidenced by instrumental seismicity (McLaren and Savage, 2001). Thus, characterization of the Hosgri Fault Zone is very important to the understanding and development of regional tectonic and seismogenic models for coastal California.

Objectives and Scope of this Investigation

This investigation of the Hosgri Fault Zone began in 1983 with the objectives of (1) characterizing the fault zone along its entire 110 km length, (2) determining its Miocene to late Quaternary geologic history, and (3) identifying the tectonic regime responsible for its development. Accomplishing these objectives required the synergistic utilization of an extensive suite of geophysical and geological data to define the map traces and downdip geometry of the entire Hosgri Fault Zone and adjacent structures.

The initial phase of the study used existing seismic reflection data collected by both government agencies and exploration companies during the period between 1972 and 1984. As the study progressed, the need for additional data was recognized, and several seismic surveys were commissioned specifically for this project. In addition, post-1985 data sets were purchased from geophysical exploration contractors working in the offshore Santa Maria Basin. The seismic reflection data includes surveys collected with multi-channel common-depth-point (CDP) seismic reflection systems and single-channel, high-resolution analog seismic systems. The depths of investigation of the seismic reflection data range from deep crustal soundings of over 5 km to high-resolution images of the upper few meters of sediment obtained from 3.5-kHz subbottom profilers. Associated geological and geophysical investigations were undertaken to identify the stratigraphy of the offshore Santa Maria Basin and to establish its relation to the onshore geology. The supplemental investigations included onshore geological mapping, analyses of offshore well data, collection of seafloor sediment and rock samples, observations by diver-geologists, and analyses of gravity and magnetic data.

The scope of the investigation is divided into six elements that are the subjects of the main headings of this chapter:

- A review of the exploration history and previous characterizations of the Hosgri Fault Zone

- The acquisition and description of an extensive suite of geophysical and geological data that, at the time of the study, were not in the public domain

- Identification and descriptions of the lithology, ages, and seismic expressions of the geologic units and unit boundaries of the central offshore Santa Maria Basin

- Documentation of the methods used for the integration of geological and geophysical data and mapping of structural trends and unconformities

- Interpretation and presentation of the seismic data along the entire length of the fault zone to identify the complexities of its along-strike and downdip geometry

- Characterization of the Hosgri Fault Zone and adjacent structures with regard to their regional framework, structural features, basin-wide unconformities, tectonic history, and recency of activity

Presentations of the Data and Interpretations

The area of our study encompasses a 150-km-long section of the central California coastline and the adjacent eastern offshore Santa Maria Basin. It extends from Point Arguello in the south to north of Point Piedras Blancas. The study utilized over 10,000 km of CDP seismic reflection data including several hundred lines that crossed the Hosgri Fault Zone.

Two location maps (CDP seismic tracklines and offshore geological data points) and four interpretive maps (structural trends and structure contours on three unconformities) on plates accompany this chapter as separate PDF files. The maps are 1:200,000 scale and require a plotter capable of producing a 36-inch-wide plot. All of the maps on the plates, except the CDP survey shiptrack lines, are also included as figures within the text. These reduced figures serve as easy references while reading the paper, and the oversized plates are available for those who wish to have more detailed and accurate reference to the data and interpretations.

Examples of 18 seismic profiles are included in this report. Fourteen of the profiles cross the Hosgri Fault Zone. The illustrated seismic profiles were specifically selected to show the seismic stratigraphy of the offshore Santa Maria Basin, the northern termination of the Hosgri Fault Zone, and the diverse characteristics of the fault zone along its entire length. The seismic profiles also provide examples of data from several different surveys that used different energy sources and receiver configurations. The figures within the report are annotated with our interpretations of the Hosgri Fault Zone and the three basin-wide unconformities that we mapped. We attempted to annotate the figures so that our interpretations are clearly evident from the underlying data. Nevertheless, we realize that alternative interpretations of seismic data are often possible and that some readers would prefer to view both uninterpreted and interpreted seismic sections, where the conclusions are based on analysis of the seismic images. To limit the number of illustrations within the paper, we include the uninterpreted seismic sections in appendix B.

Many of the illustrated seismic sections are not in the public domain, and some extend into California State waters where current regulations prohibit the collection of similar types of seismic reflection data. Under permitting requirements, some of the seismic records from federal waters were deposited with the Minerals Management Service (MMS). The MMS releases seismic data in its files 25 years after collection. Most of the illustrated records are post-1980. Permission to use these illustrations in this paper has been granted by the data owners and licensees and does not automatically extend to their use in other publications.

Exploration History and Previous Characterizations of the Hosgri Fault Zone

Because it lies offshore along its entire reach, the principal source of physical evidence of the Hosgri Fault Zone is the analysis of seismic reflection images of the fault zone and associated geologic structures. The historical characterization of the fault is closely tied to the development of seismic exploration tools and data processing techniques, their utilization in the offshore Santa Maria Basin, and the development of plate tectonic models to explain Neogene to Quaternary deformation of coastal California.

Exploration of the offshore Santa Maria Basin began in the 1960s with regional seismic surveys, marine gravity surveys, and aeromagnetic surveys designed to identify the limits of the basin and the major structural features. In 1971, geologists from the Shell Oil Company published a paper in which they were the first authors to identify a major fault zone offshore south-central California (Hoskins and Griffiths, 1971). Their interpretation of the fault was based on analyses of widely spaced CDP seismic reflection data. Figure 2 in their report is a small-scale map that shows a continuous offshore fault trace extending from south of Point Sal approximately 140 km to the north end of the Piedras Blancas Structure. They do not characterize the nature of the fault nor provide any indication of the recency of activity. On two cross sections in

figure 3 of their paper, it appears as a high-angle fault at the eastern edge of the basin.

In the early 1970s, Pacific Gas and Electric Company (PG&E) was in the process of constructing and licensing the Diablo Canyon Power Plant (DCPP). The existence of the fault, approximately 4 km offshore from the site, resulted in several new surveys of the offshore central California coastal region conducted by the U.S. Geological Survey (USGS) and contractors for PG&E. S.C. Wolf and H.C. Wagner (written commun., 1970) reported on analog subbottom acoustic profiles collected by the USGS. In 1972, the USGS sponsored an extensive survey of the central California continental shelf under the direction of Eli Silver using the R/V *Bartlett*. The USGS also conducted a 1973 survey under the direction of H.C. Wagner on the R/V *Kelez*. Tracklines for these two surveys are shown in McCulloch and others (1980). Based on these data, and the work of Hoskins and Griffiths (1971), Wagner (1974) suggested that recent lateral displacement had taken place along the fault. He also suggested the name, Hosgri, for the fault, an acronym for the names of the authors who first publicly identified the fault.

In 1973, PG&E commissioned a survey conducted by the Geomarine Services Division of Bolt, Beranek, and Newman, Inc. (BBN). The survey collected 595 km of high-resolution, closely spaced data in the area of the DCPP and Estero Bay. In 1974, PG&E retained Aquatronics to collect 772 km of seismic data in the coastal area between Point Arguello and San Simeon (PG&E, 1974). The Aquatronics contract also provided for the collection of bottom samples and cores. Specifications for the Aquatronics survey and many of the later surveys are given in table 1.

During the same time period, the 1970s, academic researchers were assessing the role of the Hosgri Fault Zone in the tectonic evolution of coastal central California, its relation to other coastal California faults, and the deformational history of the San Andreas Fault. Seismic reflection data available to these researchers consisted primarily of single-channel records from sparker, boomer, and other shallow-penetration systems. The seismic images from these systems have significant vertical exaggeration and were interpreted to show large vertical displacements across nearly vertical faults. This vertical exaggeration also made it difficult to distinguish between small-scale folding and fault-generated diffractions that were prevalent on the single-channel data. As a result, the character of the fault zone was sufficiently nondescript so that it could be used to encompass a variety of tectonic models, including a coastal California fault zone having major lateral displacement. In these studies, the Hosgri Fault Zone was typically associated with the San Simeon-Sur-San Gregorio Fault System of lateral-slip faults that extended north of the Hosgri Fault Zone along the central California coast from San Simeon Point to north of San Francisco. These other faults are onshore or have onshore sections, where their characteristics are easier to assess than those of the submarine Hosgri Fault Zone. Silver and Normark (1978) summarized estimates of right-lateral displacement for the San Gregorio-San Simeon-

Table 1. Geophysical survey parameters for the common-depth-point (CDP) seismic survey data sets used for this study. The listed parameters are from the seismic record title blocks. The general survey areas are shown on figures 2 and 3, and individual ship track lines from selected surveys are shown on plate 1. Energy source sizes, when listed in the table, are in kilojoules (kj) for sparker surveys and cubic inches (in³) for surveys using air gun or water gun sources. The total length of all surveys is 11,929 kilometers (km).

Acquisition contractor[1]	Survey date	Energy source	CDP fold	Record length (sec)	Survey length (km)	General survey area
Aquatronics for PG&E	1974	Sparker	6	1.3	479	Point Arguello to San Simeon, within 10 km of coastline
Consolidated Geotechnical	1976	Sparker (30 kj)	12	2	1,340	Santa Maria Basin, Point Conception to Cape San Martin
Comap Alaska for PG&E	1986	Water guns (160 in³)	24	2	500	San Luis Obispo Bay to Cape San Martin, within 6 km of coastline
Digicon Geophysical for CSLC	1986	Air guns (3,520 in³)	60	4	592	Point Arguello to San Luis Obispo Bay, within 7 km of coastline
Digicon Geophysical for PG&E & EDGE	1986	Air guns (6,000 in³)	45	16	590	Santa Maria Basin, San Luis Obispo Bay to San Simeon Point, four lines across Santa Maria Basin and two tie lines
Fairfield Industries for MMS	1979	Sleeve exploder	12	1	4,720	Santa Maria Basin, Point Conception to Point Estero
Geophysical Services, Inc.	1980	Air guns	48	5	1,296	Santa Maria Basin, Point Pedernales to Point Estero
JEBCO Seismic, Inc.	1988	Air guns (3,360 in³)	60	4	58	Northeastern Santa Maria Basin, Point San Luis to Point Piedras Blancas
Nekton	1983	Water guns (400 in³)	36	3.5	154	East-central Santa Maria Basin
Nekton for CSLC	1986	Water guns (60 in³)	24	3	1,338	Point Arguello to San Luis Obispo Bay, within 7 km of coastline
Seiscom Delta	1977	Air guns	48	6	42	Southwest of San Luis Obispo Bay
U.S. Geological Survey	1979	Air guns	24	8	250	Santa Maria Basin, regional lines
Western Geophysical, Inc.	1974 to 1982	Air guns	46 & 60	6	570	Eastern Santa Maria Basin, Point Arguello to Cape San Martin

[1]The survey data sets are either in the public domain or owned in part or exclusively by PG&E. Some surveys were run for specific clients such as PG&E, California State Lands Commission (CSLC), and the Minerals Management Service (MMS), and others were speculative surveys conducted and owned by geophysical contractors and made available to interested parties on a licensed basis.

Hosgri Fault System. The estimates ranged from 20 km (Hamilton and Willingham, 1977) to 80 to 90 km (Silver, 1974; Hall, 1975) to 115 km (Graham and Dickinson, 1978). In a later synthesis, Sedlock and Hamilton (1991) estimate that the San Gregorio-San Simeon-Hosgri Fault System has accommodated less than 5 km of late Cenozoic dextral slip.

By the mid-1970s, several geophysical exploration companies (table 1) and the USGS had collected a large quantity of shallow- and moderate-penetration analog subbottom profiler and side-scan sonar data across the fault zone between Cape San Martin and Point Sal. Their data collection efforts focused on mapping offshore structures and evaluating the location and structural character of the Hosgri Fault Zone.

In preparation for Oil and Gas Lease Sale 53, the USGS conducted surveys of the continental shelf and Santa Maria Basin aboard the R/V *Sea Sounder* and R/V *Lee* (McCulloch and others, 1980). These two surveys were of a regional nature with a nominal line spacing of 4 to 6 km and included the area of the basin south of San Simeon Point. The USGS also contracted with Fairfield Industries for a high-resolution survey of the proposed blocks in the offshore Santa Maria

Basin and other basins along the California coast (Richmond and others, 1981). In the offshore Santa Maria Basin, the survey was concentrated in the area between Point Arguello and Point Sal with 35 to 40 km of multisystem data collected over each lease block.

Leslie (1981) utilized the USGS survey data from the 1970s and PG&E data from the 1973 and 1974 surveys to study the northern termination of the Hosgri Fault Zone in the nearshore area north of Estero Bay. He interpreted the data to demonstrate a connection between the offshore Hosgri Fault and the onshore San Simeon Fault. He also indicated that seafloor features and sedimentation patterns demonstrated Holocene activity on the near-coastal faults in this area. This interpretation of the northern termination has been adopted in some of the fault maps published by the California Division of Mines and Geology (Kennedy and others, 1987; Greene and Kennedy, 1989; Jennings, 1994) and in an AAPG publication by a USGS author (McCulloch, 1987). However, an earlier publication by the USGS (Buchanan-Banks and others, 1978) shows the Hosgri Fault Zone passing to the west of the Piedras Blancas Antiform rather than trending into San Simeon Point.

Beginning in the middle 1970s and continuing through the late 1980s, numerous multichannel CDP seismic reflection surveys were conducted in connection with intensifying petroleum exploration of the offshore Santa Maria Basin (table 1). Many of these data sets extended across the Hosgri Fault Zone. However, the data sets were the property of the exploration companies and not, at that time, publicly released.

In 1983, PG&E began the Long-Term Seismic Program (LTSP), a five-year effort to evaluate the earthquake potential of the central California coastal region and its impact on the DCPP. As part of this study, PG&E undertook an evaluation of the seismogenic potential of the Hosgri Fault Zone. This evaluation included the purchase of proprietary seismic data sets and the collection of new data (table 1). The data sets owned by PG&E were reviewed and interpreted by the authors and other consultants to PG&E and released to the USGS and academic researchers.

With the advent of the release of extensive multi-channel seismic imaging of the Hosgri Fault Zone, its linearity, continuity, and downdip character become sufficiently well documented so that these characteristics could become elements of primary evidence in determining the nature of the tectonic regime that developed coastal California. Continuing improvements in seismic data acquisition and processing, especially the advent of computer-based migration, resulted in significant enhancements to the seismic images of the fault zone, compared with the earlier, single-channel data from the 1970s. The improvements in image quality are most apparent at reflection times of 1 s and longer, which correspond to reflection depths of 1 km and greater. These improved images revealed multiple fault branches having dips ranging from vertical to steeply east dipping and further elucidated the complexity of the folding within and adjacent to the Hosgri Fault Zone.

West of the Hosgri Fault Zone, the post-1975 CDP seismic reflection records show several sets of shallow eastward-dipping reflectors that appeared to increase in dip with depth. On these records, images of some strands of the Hosgri Fault Zone appeared to become listric and decrease in dip with increasing depth. Fold geometries associated with the east-dipping reflectors are similar to fold/fault relations derived from quantitative analyses of compressional folding styles (Suppe, 1983; Suppe and Medwedeff, 1984; Crouch and Suppe, 1993). Crouch and others (1984) used CDP seismic lines selected from the Point Sal area and interpreted these reflectors as subhorizontal detachments, thrust faults, and reverse faults. Based on their analysis of the data from this area, they characterized the Hosgri Fault Zone as part of a system of low-angle detachments. They estimated 30 to 70 km of shortening related to thrust faulting across the offshore Santa Maria Basin and the Hosgri Fault Zone in the last 5.5 m.y. They also proposed that an aseismic crustal detachment exists at approximately 12 km depth and that the Hosgri Fault soles into the detachment (Crouch and others, 1984, fig. 13). Snyder (1987) offers an alternative explanation for the apparent low-angle faults shown by Crouch and others (1984). He compares the low-angle reflections to features observed in onshore outcrops of the Monterey Formation and characterizes them as local ramp

structures in which a rigid layer breaks and is overthrust while the overlying layers fold.

McCulloch (1987) used USGS data and characterized the Hosgri Fault Zone as transtensional with a compressional overprint that began in the Pliocene or later. D.S. McCulloch (oral commun., 1989) interpreted some of the PG&E data sets and argued that the Hosgri Fault Zone becomes listric at depth and that the Holocene displacements on the fault are primarily thrust or reverse faulting.

Namson and Davis (1988) used fault/fold modeling techniques to suggest that the Hosgri Fault Zone was a former basin-margin normal fault responsible for the thick Miocene to Pliocene section in the basin to the west and subsequently was rotated and reactivated as a reverse fault. In their cross section (Namson and Davis, 1988, fig. 12), thrust displacement on the Hosgri Fault is depicted as being responsible for the uplift of the Coast Ranges to the east of the fault. However, in a later paper (Namson and Davis, 1990), they minimize the role of the Hosgri Fault in the coastal tectonics and depict the Hosgri Fault Zone as a normal fault that has been tilted to the east at depth and reactivated as a reverse fault by the growth of anticlinal structures to the east. In their regional cross section (Namson and Davis, 1990, fig. 7), the Hosgri Fault Zone does not sole into a regional detachment at depth.

CDP seismic reflection, wide-angle reflection, and refraction data were collected in 1986 for the PG&E/EDGE central California deep-crustal seismic experiment (Ewing and Talwani, 1991). Data were recorded to a two-way travel time of 16 s on some of the lines. Interpretations of the deep penetration seismic records have been published in a number of papers, including Meltzer and Levander (1991), McIntosh and others (1991), Trehu (1991), Miller and others (1992), Nicholson and others (1992), Howie and others (1993), Miller and Meltzer (1999), and Sorlien and others (1999b). The onshore/offshore wide-angle refraction data are detailed in Trehu (1991) and Howie and others (1993).

Images of both low-angle (thrusts) and high-angle faults are observed within the eastern offshore Santa Maria Basin on these records. However, even with the long recording time, the interactions of the two sets of faults at depths below 3 km were not clearly imaged in these data. Several researchers used research-level processing techniques to improve the images along the Hosgri Fault Zone (Worden, 1992; Lafond and Levander, 1993; Pullammanappallil and Louie, 1994). Whereas details of the interpretation of the Hosgri Fault Zone differ amongst those who have studied these lines, a general consensus is that the Hosgri Fault was originally a vertical or west-dipping transtensional feature that has subsequently been rotated to east dipping and reactivated with varying estimates of the relative amounts of strike-slip and vertical (reverse) movement.

In 1986, the California State Lands Commission (CSLC) contracted for two seismic reflection surveys (table 1) offshore between Point Arguello and the Santa Maria River for the purposes of assessing potential geologic hazards in the 3-mi-wide zone of California State waters (Leighton and Associates, 1987). The analyses of these data by Cummings and Johnson

(1994) indicate that, south of Purisima Point, the Hosgri Fault Zone decreases in both vertical and right-slip displacement, turns east, and splays toward the Santa Ynez River Fault Zone (fig. 1). They interpret this area as the southern termination of the Hosgri Fault Zone. Steritz (1986) and Steritz and Luyendyk (1994), using different sets of seismic reflection data from the same general area, conclude that the fault zone extends farther south, but that significant changes occur in the style of faulting south of Purisima Point. North of Point Arguello, they indicate that the Hosgri Fault Zone appears to dip at a high angle in the upper 2,000 m of section and is distinguishable from the thrust and reverse faults mapped to the west. However, to the south between Point Arguello and Point Conception, they map the Hosgri Fault as a northeast-dipping thrust fault. Sorlien and others (1999a) propose a block rotation model for the southern termination, where the right-lateral slip on the Hosgri Fault Zone is "absorbed by folding, thrust overlap, and clockwise vertical axis rotation of elongate blocks between strands of the fault".

Further explorations of the Hosgri Fault Zone and the offshore Santa Maria Basin continued until 1988 when lease sales were discontinued and California State waters were closed to further exploration with large-energy seismic reflection systems. PG&E contracted with Comap Alaska (Comap) for a high-resolution multichannel CDP survey of the north end of the Hosgri Fault Zone north of San Luis Obispo Bay and augmented parts of the Comap survey data with deeper penetration CDP imaging purchased from the JEBCO Seismic, Inc. (JEBCO) 1988 survey. In the period from 1985 through 1990, PG&E consultants reviewed all of the data sets discussed above in conjunction with a license requirement for the DCPP. They concluded that the Hosgri Fault Zone north of Point Sal is active and characterized by predominantly right strike slip of 1 to 3 mm/yr with the amount of slip decreasing to the south. The evidence for current activity included both seafloor offsets and seismicity data (PG&E, 1988, 1990). Their investigation did not indicate any evidence of late Quaternary activity on the low-angle thrust faults adjacent to the Hosgri Fault Zone

McLaren and Savage (2001) analyzed instrumental macroseismicity and microseismicity of south-central coastal California. They concluded that the locations and focal mechanisms of microearthquakes document the strike-slip nature of the Hosgri Fault Zone.

Although all who have worked on the Hosgri Fault Zone since it was first studied over 40 years ago appear to agree that it is an active fault, there is no consensus on such specific elements of characterization as downdip geometry, sense and rate of slip, history of deformation, northern and southern terminations, and implications for seismic hazards. In the following sections of this chapter, we present our data sources, technical approaches to fault characterization, and the maps and seismic sections used to support our conclusion that the present Hosgri Fault Zone is an active, 110-km long, convergent right-slip (transpressional) fault with identified northern and southern terminations.

Geophysical and Geological Data

The data used in this investigation consists of both public and proprietary marine geophysical survey data; offshore geologic information from wells, cores, and nearshore observations by diver-geologists; and onshore geologic mapping. The onshore geologic mapping and data are discussed in Hanson and others (2004) and Lettis and others (2004). Key elements of the offshore data are shown on two maps (pls. 1, 2). The horizontal datum for all maps in this paper is the 1983 North American Datum (NAD 83). Map coordinates are given in latitudes and longitudes and UTM zone 10, in meters. The large maps, included as PDF files, are referred to as plates in this text. If plotted at full size at a scale of 1:200,000, they will require 36-in-wide (91-cm-wide) paper. Page-sized copies of the maps, except plates 1 and 3, are included as figures within the text with minor modifications for clarity at the reduced scale.

Geophysical Survey Data

During the course of this study, geophysical data sets were acquired over a 5,000-km^2 area of the offshore Santa Maria Basin. The data sets included high-resolution analog survey records, both high-resolution and deep-penetration CDP seismic reflection data, marine gravity and magnetic data, and aeromagnetic survey data. The data were acquired from various sources, including the USGS, CSLC, geophysical contracting companies, and petroleum companies. Several seismic reflection surveys were contracted specifically for this project. Selected seismic-reflection CDP survey data sets collected and processed prior to 1985 were reprocessed using more advanced techniques.

High-Resolution Surveys

Approximately 10,000 km of shallow-penetration, high-resolution analog and high-resolution CDP data were analyzed to assess shallow geologic hazards. The high-resolution data provide images of the shallow sediment, bedrock outcrop, near-surface fault traces, and seafloor features. The depth of investigation of the various seismic systems varies from a few meters in bedrock areas to over 1 km in thick sediment sections. The data were used to map bathymetry, latest Pleistocene and Holocene sediment distribution and thickness, and bedrock outcrop areas (pl. 2); to assess surface location and recency of activity along the various fault traces; and to correlate onshore geologic data with the CDP data east of the Hosgri Fault Zone.

During the high-resolution surveys, data were commonly collected simultaneously along closely spaced track lines using three to six data acquisition systems. Echo sounders, side-scan sonars, 3.5 kHz or boomer-type subbottom profilers, single-channel reflection systems using a spark array source, and marine magnetometers were the more common systems used in the early surveys. Beginning in the mid-1970s, the single-channel reflection systems were replaced with multichannel (6 to 24 channels) reflection systems using spark arrays, sleeve exploders, small air guns, or water guns as energy sources.

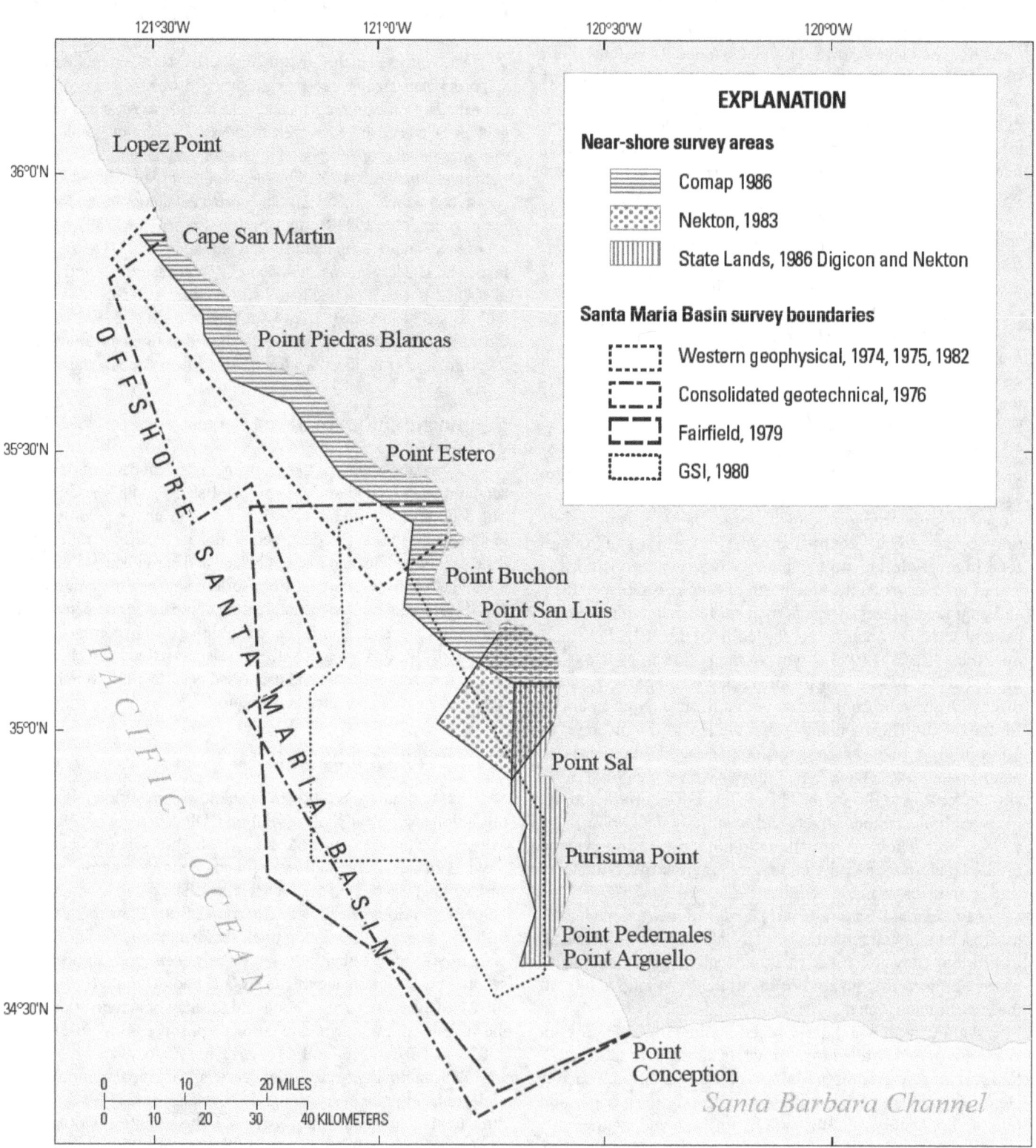

Figure 2.   Map of the offshore Santa Maria Basin indicating the general areas of major marine CDP seismic data used in this report. Individual surveys are designated with the name of the geophysical survey contractor that collected the data and the years in which the data were collected. Principal facts for the surveys are listed in table 1. Shiptrack lines for selected surveys are shown in detail on plate 1.

High-resolution data sets used in this investigation included surveys commissioned by PG&E, USGS, and CSLC. Surveys that included high-resolution CDP systems are listed in table 1, and figure 2 shows outlines of post-1976 survey areas. Approximately 6,500 km of these data were collected in conjunction with the Comap, Aquatronics, Fairfield Industries, and CSLC Nekton surveys (table 1, fig. 2). The other data were from pre-1980 public data collected by or for the USGS. Approximately 50 percent of the high-resolution data were in the shallow-water areas within the 3-mi state lands limit. Except for the Comap survey, shiptrack lines for the high-resolution surveys are not shown on plate 1 to avoid overcrowding the display in the nearshore areas.

The PG&E surveys included the 1973–1974 nearshore survey between Point San Luis and southern Estero Bay, the 1974 survey by Aquatronics between Point Arguello and San Simeon (table 1), and the 1986 survey by Comap between San Luis Obispo Bay and Cape San Martin (table 1, fig. 2). Survey shiptrack lines for the two earlier surveys are in PG&E (1974) and for the Comap survey are on plate 1.

USGS high-resolution survey data used in this investigation included data collected aboard the R/V *Bartlett* in 1972, the R/V *Kelez* in 1973, the R/V *Sea Sounder* in 1979, and the R/V *Lee* in 1975 and 1979. The *Bartlett*, *Sea Sounder*, and *Lee* 1979 surveys were of a regional nature with nominal 4- to 6-km line spacing and covered the offshore Santa Maria Basin from Point Conception to north of Cape San Martin. The *Kelez* and *Lee* 1975 survey lines were within 2 to 15 km of the coastline from Point Sal to north of Cape San Martin. The combined line spacing for the latter surveys was 1 to 2 km (McCulloch and others, 1980). The USGS also commissioned a survey by Fairfield Industries in 1979 for a geologic hazard evaluation for Oil and Gas Lease Sale 53. Principal facts for this survey are in table 1, and the general area of the survey is shown on figure 2. Survey details and shiptrack lines for the Fairfield survey are in Richmond and others (1981). In 1986, the CSLC commissioned a high-resolution survey of the California State waters from Point Arguello to southern San Luis Obispo Bay (table 1, fig. 2). Survey details and shiptrack lines for the CSLC survey are in Leighton and Associates (1987).

CDP Seismic Reflection Surveys

Moderate- to deep-penetration CDP seismic reflection data (generally 1.0 s or more two-way travel time of signal penetration) are the primary source of information on the characteristics of the Hosgri Fault Zone and adjacent structures. More than 10,000 km of CDP data were analyzed in this investigation. The areas of the primary CDP seismic surveys used in this investigation are shown on figure 2, and shiptrack lines and shotpoints for some of the CDP survey data are displayed on plate 1. Some proprietary lines were not included on this map and, in some areas, only representative lines are shown to improve the legibility of the map. Principal facts for the individual surveys are included in table 1 and also on plate 1.

Seismic reflection data were acquired from a variety of sources. Nearshore reflection data along the reach of the Hosgri Fault Zone south of San Luis Obispo Bay were acquired from the CSLC's 1986 Digicon Geophysical (Digicon) and Nekton surveys (Leighton and Associates, 1987). In addition, purchases were made of several sets and subsets of proprietary exploration seismic data from the eastern offshore Santa Maria Basin, including the Geophysical Services, Inc. (GSI)/Ogle Petroleum, Nekton 200 Series, Western Geophysical, Inc., JEBCO, and Seisdata Services (onshore) survey lines. Shiptrack lines from these later surveys are on plate 1.

Two CDP reflection surveys were commissioned by PG&E. A high-resolution survey was conducted in 1986 for PG&E by Comap along the Hosgri Fault Zone and adjacent structures from San Luis Obispo Bay to north of Point Piedras Blancas (table 1, fig. 2). Another CDP data-collection effort was designed by PG&E and collected as part of an EDGE cooperative data acquisition effort in 1986 with Rice University, the Houston Area Research Council, and the USGS (table 1, fig. 3). The PG&E/EDGE survey consisted of offshore deep-crustal reflection lines and onshore/offshore refraction data. Shiptrack lines for the PG&E and EDGE lines used in this study are shown on figure 3.

CDP Seismic Processing

Seismic data processing has been one of the most rapidly advancing areas in applied geophysics. Driven by the continuous and prodigious improvement in the computational speed of modern computers, more and more refined algorithms are being applied to the analysis of existing data sets. This refinement allows significant improvements in seismic imaging simply by reprocessing the data.

Reprocessing projects and tests were undertaken in 1986 and again in the early 1990s to take advantage of advances in processing technology. Improvements were sought in imaging the vertical extent and dip of the Hosgri Fault Zone and in defining stratigraphic units and unconformities important to evaluating the age of structural events. In 1986, 400 km of existing proprietary CDP seismic data from the GSI data set (table 1) were reprocessed. An advisory group, composed of both industry and academic experts in processing technology, was assembled to review the original data and the reprocessing methods selected and to help in the selection of a processing contractor.

Trial data were provided to eight United States processing companies. Each contractor was requested to provide a processing flow that would accomplish the following objectives:

- Suppress water bottom and interbed multiple energy

- Improve the coherency of the seismic reflection horizons and suppress random noise

- Improve the imaging and accuracy of event location in complexly folded regions

- Improve the definition and location of faulting

- Improve the imaging, dip, and location accuracy of "deep" events—those occurring between about 3.0 and 5.0 s two-way travel time.

These processing flows were then applied to the test line provided to each contractor, and the advisory group reviewed the results for all of the contractors. As a result of this selection process, the contract for this work and subsequent reprocessing was awarded to the contractor considered to have produced the best seismic imaging. Table 2 shows the typical processing flow used for the 1986 reprocessing of the 400 km of proprietary GSI data. Descriptions of the individual processing procedures listed in the table can be found in Sheriff (2002) and Yilmaz (1987, 2001).

Marine seismic imaging quality is very sensitive to the degree of success achieved in suppression of multiple reflections and to the accuracy of velocity analysis. For these reasons, an iterative loop was established in the processing flow to take advantage of the fact that suppression of multiples improves velocity results, which in turn improves suppression of the multiple reflections.

To optimize processing results, key lines were reprocessed under the direct supervision of the authors, who assisted the processing contractor in distinguishing

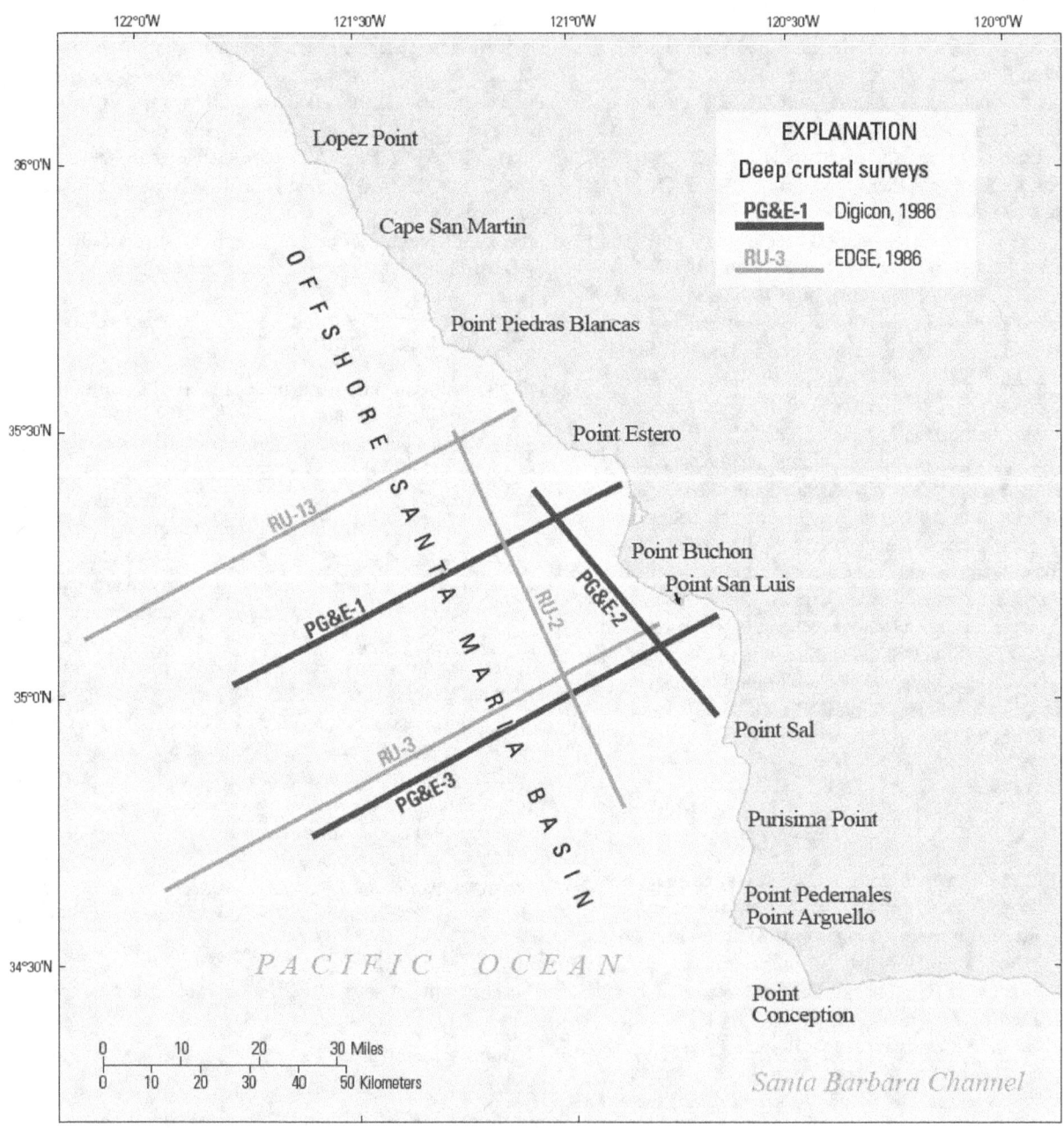

Figure 3. Map showing the approximate locations of CDP seismic reflection lines from the 1986 PG&E/EDGE deep crustal reflection survey that were used in this study. The reflection data were collected with a 6,000 in³ air-gun array. Nominal recording parameters were 45 fold with a 16 s record length.

Table 2. Sequence of basic procedures applied in CDP post-stack migration seismic data processing. These were applied to the common-depth-point (CDP) seismic reflection data sets (Comap and PG&E/EDGE) collected for PG&E in 1986. Data from several of the surveys conducted prior to 1986 (table 1), including Western Geophysical, (1974 to 1982), Geophysical Service Inc. (GSI, 1980), and Nekton (1983), were reprocessed using these procedures. Descriptions of the processing procedures can be found in Sheriff (2002) and Yilmaz (1987).

1. Demultiplex

2. Gain recovery

3. Deconvolution—Spiking or predictive with time variant gates

4. Bandwidth filter

5. Sort CDP gathers and apply statics

6. Pre-stack water bottom and long-period multiple attenuation

7. Velocity analysis every 0.8 km or less, based on geological structural complexity

8. Normal moveout

9. Trace muting

10. Common-depth-point stack

11. Time variant filter

12. Automatic gain control 250 to 500 ms gate, depending on data type

13. Residual statistics correction and noise rejection filter (NRF)

14. Remove statics applied in step 5

15. Wave equation migration

16. Displays of steps 12, 13, and 15, stacked, noise rejection filtered, and migrated sections, respectively

---

between seismic artifacts and seismic reflections from key geologic horizons. These decisions were based on previous interpretations of the data. The multidisciplinary feedback placed constraints on the range of acceptable seismic processing parameters and on what could be considered geologically relevant seismic images. Though not common in 1986, this multidisciplinary approach is now generally considered within the petroleum industry to be an essential component to achieve optimum processing results.

In an additional attempt to improve velocity determinations, the advanced method (at that time) of dip moveout (DMO) was applied to a test line. This process compensates for velocity variations resulting from steeply dipping beds or sudden reversals in dip angle and generally provides a substantially improved velocity determination for the stacking step in processing. The application of DMO did not significantly improve the final imaging and, in some areas, caused degradation of image quality. Two-dimensional DMO does not work well in the coastal regions of the offshore Santa Maria Basin, apparently because of its inability to adequately handle coherent out-of-plane energy that is commonly observed as conflicting dip directions in seismic records from the region. This energy results from abrupt, along-strike variation of structures in the Hosgri Fault Zone that negates the structural assumptions that two-dimensional DMO algorithms are based upon.

Three lines were selected from the GSI data set for another reprocessing effort in 1991. The purpose of the test was to compare the 1986 conventional poststack migration-processing results used on these data against the new techniques of prestack depth migration being introduced in the early 1990s. This technique, which was state-of-the-art at that time, produced minor improvements compared with the migration methods used for the 1986 processing. A comparison of the 1986 and 1991 processing results is shown in figure 4.

The EDGE survey line RU-3 (fig. 3) was subjected to processing experiments by a number of researchers in the early 1990s (Worden, 1992; Lafond and Levander, 1993; Pullammanappallil and Louie, 1994; Shih and Levander, 1994). Line RU-3 had acquisition parameters identical to those of the 1986 PG&E series lines; it images the same reach of the Hosgri Fault Zone as line PG&E-3. Shih and Levander (1994) used a prestack depth migration method, similar to that used in our 1991 reprocessing effort, and obtained seismic images of the Hosgri Fault Zone qualitatively similar to those obtained from the 1991 reprocessing. The Shih and Levander work imaged the main trace of the Hosgri Fault Zone, displayed on line RU-3 as a steeply east dipping feature extending to a depth of over 2 s. Their results are similar to those obtained from nearby line PG&E-3 (profile H-H', pl. 4) using conventional post-stack migration methods and a processing flow similar to that presented in table 2.

Figure 4. Seismic sections showing examples of two CDP seismic reflection migration techniques applied to the same seismic section. The primary CDP seismic reflection data sets used in this study were processed or reprocessed in the period between 1986 and 1988, using the processing steps listed in table 2. The wave equation migration technique was the advanced industry standard at that time for use in areas of known lateral velocity variations such as those encountered across the Hosgri Fault Zone, which is located between shotpoints 1220 to 1260. Pre-stack depth migration was tested on several lines in an effort to improve the positional accuracy of reflections. The lower processing example is a pre-stack depth migration product recompressed to time for comparative purposes. It shows some improvements in coherency on the left side of the fold present in the central portion of the section, a reduction in diffraction patterns within the fault zone, and minor improvement in imaging to the right of the fault zone. Minor improvement also is apparent in the coherency of the strong event at 2.25 s on the left side of the diagram. Although the use of pre-stack depth migration is more common today than in the early 1990s, it is still considered one of the more advanced processing techniques.

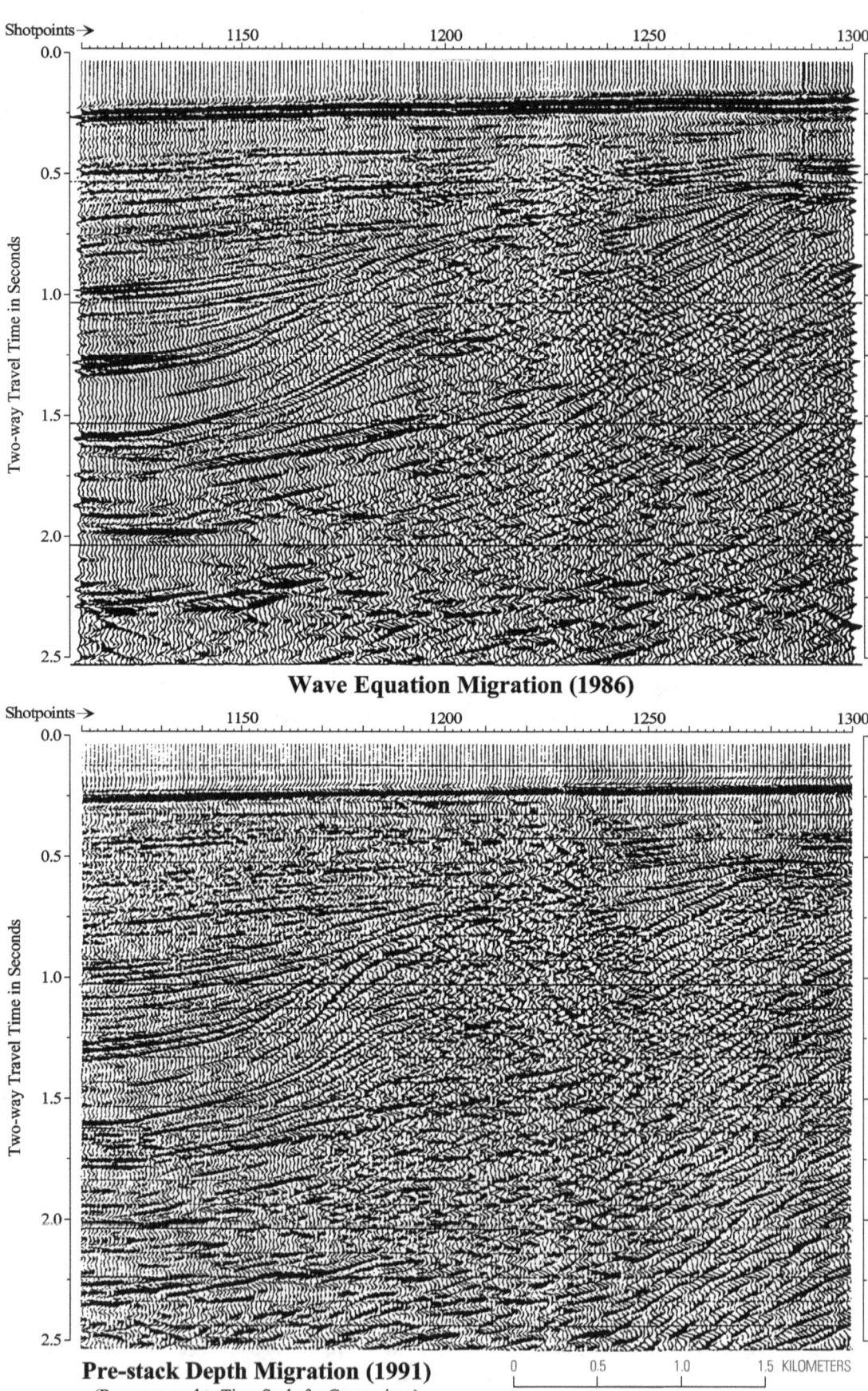

Wave Equation Migration (1986)

Pre-stack Depth Migration (1991)
(Recompressed to Time Scale for Comparison)

Horizontal scale
Vertical exaggeration = 2.0 at Sea Floor

Gravity and Magnetic Data

Publicly available gravity and magnetic data were used to confirm basement topography interpretations and continuity of fault traces. McCulloch and Chapman (1977) compiled aeromagnetic maps with coverage of part of the offshore Santa Maria Basin. Rietman and Beyer (1982) compiled a Bouguer gravity contour map of the southern half of the offshore basin and adjacent coastal area. Sauer and Mariano (1990) provide large-scale maps of both isostatic residual gravity and aeromagnetic data.

Geological Data

Geological data incorporated into the seismic interpretations include onshore geologic mapping, seafloor samples and cores, diver-geologist observations, and offshore well data. The first three types of data were used to establish continuity with onshore stratigraphic and structural relations and to aid in the identification of lithologic units on nearshore seismic lines. The well data were used to establish the offshore stratigraphy and as input to the velocity model used for depth conversion.

Table 3. List of well logs from 29 wells that are used in this study. The logs were used to establish the offshore stratigraphy and identify the depths of the three mapped unconformities. The types of logs and other information available from the individual wells are tabulated below. Descriptions of the logs are given at the end of the table. Selected logs are shown in figure 10 and plate 3. The well locations are shown in figure 5 and plate 2. Microfossil data are in appendix A. Analyses of the data are summarized in table 6.

Well P-#	Mud	E-log	Sonic	Density	NGL	NML	Dip	Dir.	Other Data
0060-1	X	X	X	X			X		
0395-1	X	X	X	X			X	X	Velocity
0396-1	X	X	X	X		X	X	X	Velocity
0397-1	X	X	X	X	X		X		Velocity
0397-2	X	X	X	X	X		X		
0402-1	X	X	X	X	X		X		Velocity
0406-1	X	X	X	X	X		X	X	
0409-3	X	X	X	X	X		X		
0409-4	X	X	X	X	X		X		
0411-1	X	X	X	X			X	X	
0413-1	X	X	X	X	X		X		Velocity
0415-1	X	X	X	X	X	X	X		Microfossils and velocity
0415-2	X	X	X	X	X		X		Microfossils
0416-1	X	X	X	X	X	X	X		Microfossils
0422-1	X	X	X	X			X	X	Microfossils and velocity
0424-1	X	X	X	X	X	X	X	X	Microfossils
0425-1	X	X	X	X	X		X		
0425-2	X	X	X	X	X		X	X	
0426-1	X	X	X	X	X		X	X	
0427-1	X	X	X	X	X	X	X		
0430-1	X	X	X	X	X		X	X	Microfossils
0434-1	X	X	X	X	X		X	X	
0435-1	X	X	X	X	X		X		Microfossils and velocity
0440-1	X	X	X	X	X		X	X	
0440-2	X	X	X	X	X	X	X	X	
0443-1	X	X	X	X	X		X		
0443-2	X	X	X	X	X	X	X		
0444-1	X	X	X	X	X				
0496-1	X	X	X	X	X				

Log Descriptions:

Mud—Provides lithologic descriptions of drill cuttings
E-log—Measures electrical properties of the rocks
Sonic—Measures acoustic properties of the rocks
Density—Measures density of the rocks
NGL—Natural gamma log measures natural radioactivity in the rocks
NML—Nuclear magnetism log measures and identifies types of pore fluids
Dip—Measures orientation of rock discontinuities
Dir.—Measures directional orientation of borehole
Velocity—Vertical seismic profile (VSP) or checkshot data
Microfossils—Paleontological data presented in appendix A

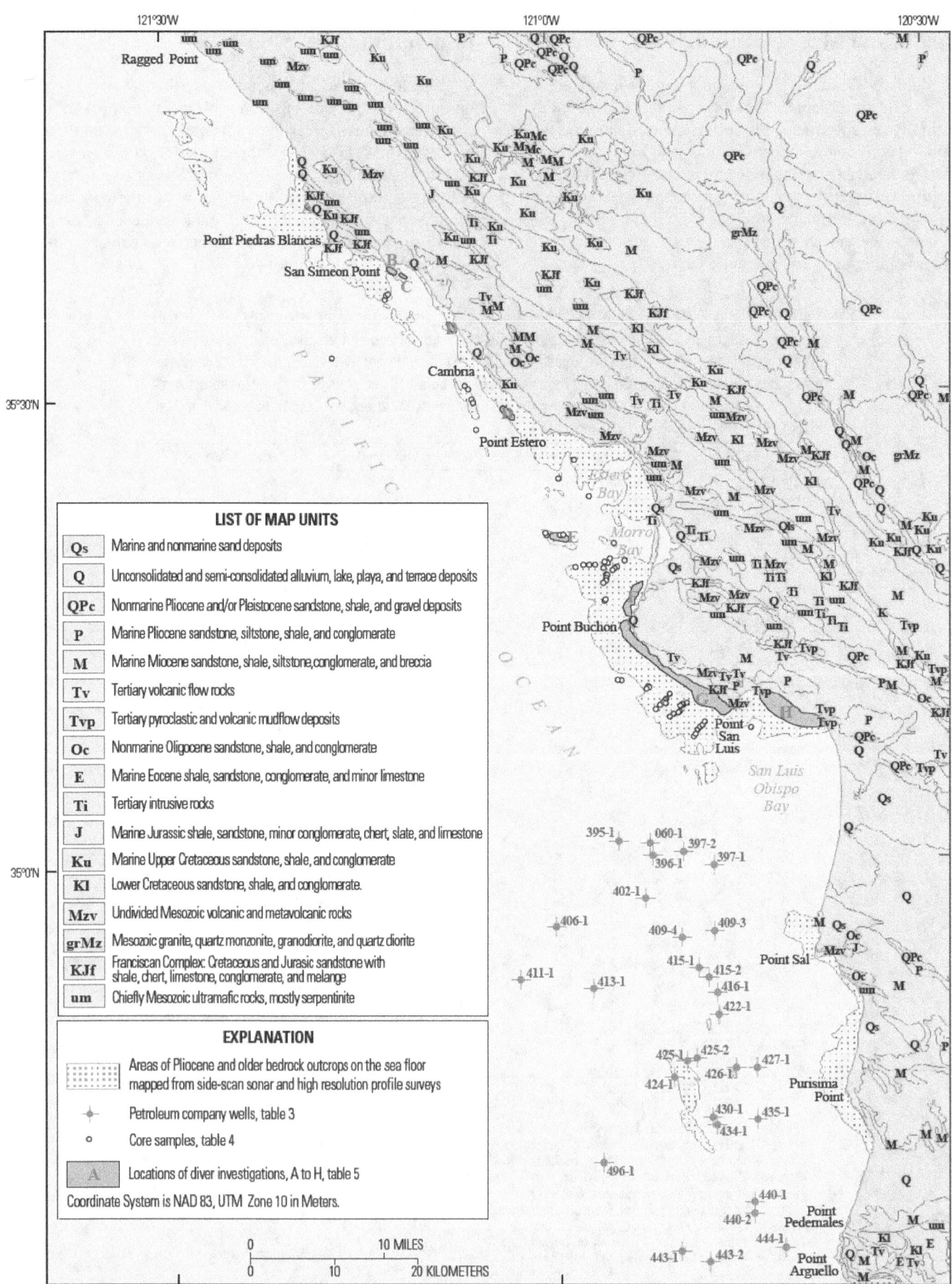

LIST OF MAP UNITS

Qs	Marine and nonmarine sand deposits
Q	Unconsolidated and semi-consolidated alluvium, lake, playa, and terrace deposits
QPc	Nonmarine Pliocene and/or Pleistocene sandstone, shale, and gravel deposits
P	Marine Pliocene sandstone, siltstone, shale, and conglomerate
M	Marine Miocene sandstone, shale, siltstone, conglomerate, and breccia
Tv	Tertiary volcanic flow rocks
Tvp	Tertiary pyroclastic and volcanic mudflow deposits
Oc	Nonmarine Oligocene sandstone, shale, and conglomerate
E	Marine Eocene shale, sandstone, conglomerate, and minor limestone
Ti	Tertiary intrusive rocks
J	Marine Jurassic shale, sandstone, minor conglomerate, chert, slate, and limestone
Ku	Marine Upper Cretaceous sandstone, shale, and conglomerate
Kl	Lower Cretaceous sandstone, shale, and conglomerate.
Mzv	Undivided Mesozoic volcanic and metavolcanic rocks
grMz	Mesozoic granite, quartz monzonite, granodiorite, and quartz diorite
KJf	Franciscan Complex: Cretaceous and Jurasic sandstone with shale, chert, limestone, conglomerate, and melange
um	Chiefly Mesozoic ultramafic rocks, mostly serpentinite

EXPLANATION

Areas of Pliocene and older bedrock outcrops on the sea floor mapped from side-scan sonar and high resolution profile surveys

Petroleum company wells, table 3

Core samples, table 4

Locations of diver investigations, A to H, table 5

Coordinate System is NAD 83, UTM Zone 10 in Meters.

0   10 MILES
0   10   20 KILOMETERS

Offshore Well Data

More than 50 wells have been drilled in the offshore Santa Maria Basin since 1980. Many of these wells were made public during the late 1980s and early 1990s. Twenty-nine wells are used as primary data sources for correlation with the seismic sections or in the establishment of the chronostratigraphy. Wells were selected for use based on availability of detailed velocity data, their location, and the degree of confidence in horizon picks derived from the well logs. Locations of the 29 wells are plotted on plate 2 and figure 5. The types of data available for the wells used in this investigation are summarized in table 3.

Offshore Cores

Aquatronics collected shallow cores for PG&E's investigation in 1974 in the nearshore area between Point Estero and San Luis Obispo Bay. The USGS collected seafloor cores in 1975 between San Simeon Point and Point San Luis. Core locations are shown on figure 5 and plotted and labeled on plate 2. Analyses of both sets of cores are presented in McCulloch and others (1985) and summarized in table 4. This information has been incorporated into the analysis of the seismic records to augment the geologic mapping of nearshore rock units and structural trends and to identify the age of the bedrock outcrops mapped by the high-resolution geophysical systems.

Seafloor Samples and Diver Observations

Diver-geologists under contract to PG&E collected seafloor geologic data in shallow-water areas between Point San Simeon and San Luis Obispo Bay. Seventy-three dives were made in September 1986; the divers made numerous observations and collected 116 rock samples. In late October and early November 1989, an additional 79 sites were sampled during 40 more dives. The general locations of diver observations and sampling are shown on figure 5 and plate 2.

The divers described seafloor topography and recorded and videotaped geologic and structural information from seafloor rock outcrops. The rock samples were described and identified by comparing the lithologies of the submarine samples to samples collected from onshore outcrops. In

Figure 5.   Map of surface and subsurface geological data used in this study. The map shows wells drilled by petroleum exploration companies and nearshore areas where cores and diver samples were collected. The well data that were used are summarized in table 3, and the core data and diver samples and observations are listed in tables 4 and 5. The onshore geology and offshore data points are presented in color and at a larger scale on plate 2; the onshore geology is modified from Saucedo and others (2000).

addition, three dredge samples were collected in mid-1988 at a seafloor ridge northwest of Point Buchon. These data are summarized in table 5. Additional references to selected samples may be found in PG&E (1988, 1990) and Hall and others (1994).

Both the seafloor samples and diver-geologist observations were used to confirm the locations of pre-Tertiary and Tertiary seafloor outcrops shown on plate 2 and figure 5. They also were used to interpret geologic formation boundaries on seismic sections in areas of shallow water.

Onshore Geologic Studies

Geologic maps and reports were used, along with nearshore data (cores, diver samples and observations, and high-resolution geophysical data) to establish onshore-offshore stratigraphic correlations that correspond with the moderate- to deep-penetration CDP seismic data and offshore wells.

Numerous geologic studies have been conducted in the onshore areas adjacent to the offshore Santa Maria Basin. A generalized map of the onshore geologic units is on plate 2 and figure 5. These figures are for general reference only and are reproduced from Saucedo and others (2000); the geologic units are generalized from more detailed mapping by academic researchers, the California Division of Mines and Geology, and the USGS, including Clark (1990), Dibblee (1950), Dunham and Blake (1987), Hall (1973a,b, 1981, 1982, 1991), and Hall and others (1979). Consultants for PG&E also conducted detailed mapping of the coastal areas of south-central California. Their studies are described in PG&E (1974, 1988, 1990), Lettis and Hall (1990, 1994), Lettis and Hanson (1992), Lettis and others (1990, 1994, 2004), Hanson and Lettis (1994), and Hanson and others (1987, 1992, 1994, 2004). Onshore-offshore correlations are based on the maps contained in the reports referenced above.

Seismic Expression of Geologic Units and Unit Boundaries in the Central Offshore Santa Maria Basin

Seismic-Stratigraphic Correlation Procedures

Background

Hoskins and Griffiths (1971) published the first description of the stratigraphy of the offshore Santa Maria Basin. They described the basin as floored by Paleogene and older metamorphic and granitic rocks overlain by highly deformed remnants of Eocene to early Miocene nonmarine clastic and volcanic material and

Table 4.   Summary of geologic data from core samples from the eastern offshore Santa Maria Basin, California. Sample source and collection year: A, Aquatronics for PG&E in 1974; N, U.S. Geological Survey in 1975. Sample locations are labeled on plate 2 and general locations are on figure 5. Formation and age designations are based on lithologic descriptions and (or) nannofossils and are summarized from McCulloch and others (1985).

Sample No.	Sample area	Abbreviated lithology	Formation or age
A-4	SE of Point Estero	Graywacke	Cretaceous
A-24	SW of Morro Bay	Argillite	Not determined
A-34	W of Pt. San Luis	Argillaceous carbonate	Probably Monterey Formation
A-101	Estero Bay	Ultramafic rock	Mesozoic
A-103	W of Morro Bay	Silty argillite	Probably Monterey Formation
A-104	W of Morro Bay	Silty argillite	Not determined
A-108	W of Morro Bay	Argillite	Not determined
A-110	W of Morro Bay	Argillite	Not determined
A-111	W of Morro Bay	Silty argillite	Not determined
A-113	SW of Morro Bay	Argillite	Probably Monterey Formation
A-115	SW of Morro Bay	Argillite	Not determined
A-118	San Luis Obispo Bay	Graywacke	Not determined
N-1G	SW of Pt. San Luis	Siltstone	Not determined
N-1I	SW of Pt. San Luis	Sandstone	Not determined
N-1K	SW of Pt. San Luis	Sandstone	Not determined
N-1L	SW of Pt. San Luis	Sandstone	Not determined
N-1M	SW of Pt. San Luis	Sandstone	Not determined
N-1Q	SW of Pt. San Luis	Sandstone	Not determined
N-2A	W of Pt. San Luis	Sandstone/siltstone	early to middle Miocene
N-2B	W of Pt. San Luis	Sandstone/shale	middle Miocene
N-2C	W of Pt. San Luis	Sandstone/siltstone	early to middle Miocene
N-2D	W of Pt. San Luis	Siltstone/shale	early to middle Miocene
N-2H	W of Pt. San Luis	Sandstone/mudstone	middle(?) Miocene
N-2K	W of Pt. San Luis	Mud over shale	Not determined
N-2M	W of Pt. San Luis	Siltstone or shale	Not determined
N-2O	W of Pt. San Luis	Sand over shale	Not determined
N-2Q	W of Pt. San Luis	Clay/siltstone/limestone	Monterey Formation type lithology
N-3A	W of Pt. San Luis	Siltstone/tuff	Miocene(?)
N-3E	W of Pt. San Luis	Shale	Not determined
N-3I	W of Pt. San Luis	Siliceous shale	Not determined
N-3J	W of Pt. San Luis	Siltstone	Not determined
N-3K	W of Pt. San Luis	Siltstone or shale	Not determined
N-3L	W of Pt. San Luis	Siltstone/chert	Miocene type lithology
N-3N	W of Pt. San Luis	Siltstone	Miocene type lithology
N-4O	W of Pt. San Luis	Mudstone/siltstone/chert	middle or late Miocene
N-4P	W of Pt. San Luis	Mud over mudstone	Not determined
N-5A	W of Pt. San Luis	Mud/sandstone	Not determined
N-5D	W of Pt. San Luis	Siltstone	Not determined
N-8C	W of Morro Bay	Mudstone/siltstone/shale	Not determined
N-8G	W of Morro Bay	Clay/silt	Miocene(?)
N-8H	SW of Morro Bay	Mudstone	Not determined
N-8I	SW of Morro Bay	Shale	Miocene type lithology
N-8O	SW of Morro Bay	Clay over shale	Not determined
N-8Q	SW of Morro Bay	Mudstone/chert	Middle(?) Miocene
N-8S	SW of Morro Bay	Mudstone	Not determined
N-8T	SW of Morro Bay	Mudstone	Not determined
N-9B	W of Morro Bay	Mudstone	Not determined
N-9C	W of Morro Bay	Clay over mudstone	Not determined
N-9I	W of Morro Bay	Clay over shale/siltstone	middle to late Miocene
N-9K	W of Morro Bay	Sand over mudstone	Not determined
N-9N	W of Morro Bay	Sand over mudstone	Not determined
N-9P	W of Morro Bay	Siltstone	Not determined
N-10B	W of Morro Bay	Shale or siltstone	Not determined
N-10E	W of Morro Bay	Clay over siltstone	Quaternary coccoliths
N-12F	S of Pt. Estero	Sand over clay	Quaternary coccoliths
N-17C	W of Pt. Estero	Siltstone	late Miocene or early Pliocene
N-18A	NW of Pt. Estero	Sand over shale	Not determined
N-18E	NW of Pt. Estero	Sand over sandstone	Not determined
N-18F	NW of Pt. Estero	Sandstone and shale	Not determined
N-18G	NW of Pt. Estero	Shale or sandstone	Not determined
N-23A	W of Cambria	Clay	late Miocene or early Pliocene
N-25A	S of San Simeon Pt.	Siltstone	middle Miocene, Relizian(?) benthic foraminiferal zone (bfz)
N-25E	S of San Simeon Pt.	Siltstone	middle Miocene, Relizian(?) (bfz)
N-25F	S of San Simeon Pt.	Siltstone in clay matrix	middle Miocene, Luisian (bfz)

Table 5. Summary of bottom samples and diver observations conducted for PG&E. Areas of investigations are outlined and labeled on figure 5 and plate 2.

Area	General location of investigation	Diver observations and samples
A	La Cruz rock area between Ragged Point and Point Piedras Blancas	Eight samples with Franciscan Complex type lithology
B	Southwestern side of San Simeon Point	Thirty-three observations from western side of San Simeon Fault, probable Monterey Formation lithology
C	Southeastern side of San Simeon Point	Nine samples, probably from eastern side of San Simeon Fault, probable Franciscan Complex lithology
D	Two areas of seafloor outcrops between Cambria and Point Estero	Outcrops of sedimentary rocks appear similar to lithology of onshore Cretaceous rocks
E	"59-Meter Ridge", 11 km west of Morro Bay	Three dredge samples collected from ridge near intersection of Los Osos and Hosgri Faults. Siltstone, possible Monterey Formation type lithology
F	Along coastline between Point Buchon and south end of Morro Bay	Thirty-six samples and observations of Miocene (Monterey Formation?) type lithology
G	Along coastline between Point Buchon and Point San Luis	One hundred-ten samples and observations along coastal zone. Predominately Miocene type lithology overlain by patches of Holocene sediment
H	Northeastern side of San Luis Obispo Bay	Fifty-five samples and observations along coastal zone offshore Shell Beach. Tertiary volcanic and sedimentary rocks

overlain by 2,000 to 3,000 m of mildly deformed Neogene sediments. Their depiction of basin stratigraphy was based on integration of onshore geology, a few offshore petroleum company wells south of the basin, and seismic reflection data tied to the wells. In their pioneering work, they established the first seismic-stratigraphic correlations in the basin and presented them in the form of structural cross sections that projected stratigraphic units away from geologic tie points, using the seismic data as a guide. Most of the seismic reflectors that they mapped are coincident with major unconformities in the basin.

PG&E (1974) and Wagner (1974) used seismic reflection data as the basis for constructing contour maps of geologic horizons in the offshore Santa Maria Basin. These works also used seismic signatures associated with unconformities as boundaries between major lithologic units. Both of these publications relied heavily on the one available well in the basin, the Oceano well (P-060-1, pl. 2), to establish seismic-stratigraphic correlations.

The increase in petroleum exploration in the offshore Santa Maria Basin between 1977 and 1984 resulted in an abundance of high-quality CDP seismic data and in the drilling of more than 50 wells between Point Conception and 15 km north of Point Sal (fig. 5, pl. 2). North of Point San Luis, however, there still is a lack of borehole information for establishing precise seismic-stratigraphic correlations. Heck and Mannon (1988) published form-line contours on the "Near top of the Monterey Formation" based on an integration of well and seismic data. However, the seismically defined unconformities, used by the early workers in the basin and their refined counterparts presented in this paper, remain the primary tool for defining offshore rock units in the north half of the offshore Santa Maria Basin.

General Procedures

We use seismic reflection data to correlate and map key geologic units and unconformities that occur throughout the offshore Santa Maria Basin. The seismic horizons established in this manner are assigned ages based upon correlation with geologic and paleontological information derived from boreholes in the region. These seismic-stratigraphic horizons, of known age or age range, are then mapped and used in the analysis of the deformational history of the Hosgri Fault Zone.

Our method for defining seismic-stratigraphic horizons consists of the following steps:

1. Use correlations based upon descriptions of onshore formations and well-log character to identify offshore lithologies, formations, and unconformities in the wells.

2. Establish qualitative relations between stratigraphic units, based on the relative position and thickness of the rock units in offshore wells, and the seismic stratigraphy as determined from the seismic reflection records.

3. Use synthetic seismograms to quantitatively associate seismic reflection horizons with specific lithologic boundaries and rock units (pl. 3).

4. Use age assignments established in the literature for onshore and offshore rock units and unconformities, and use paleontological data (appendix A) from offshore wells to further refine ages for key horizons in offshore wells.

Several papers published since 1984 have utilized data from exploratory and Ocean Drilling Program (ODP) wells in the offshore Santa Maria Basin. These papers include Bishop and Davis (1984), Clark and others (1991), Crain and others

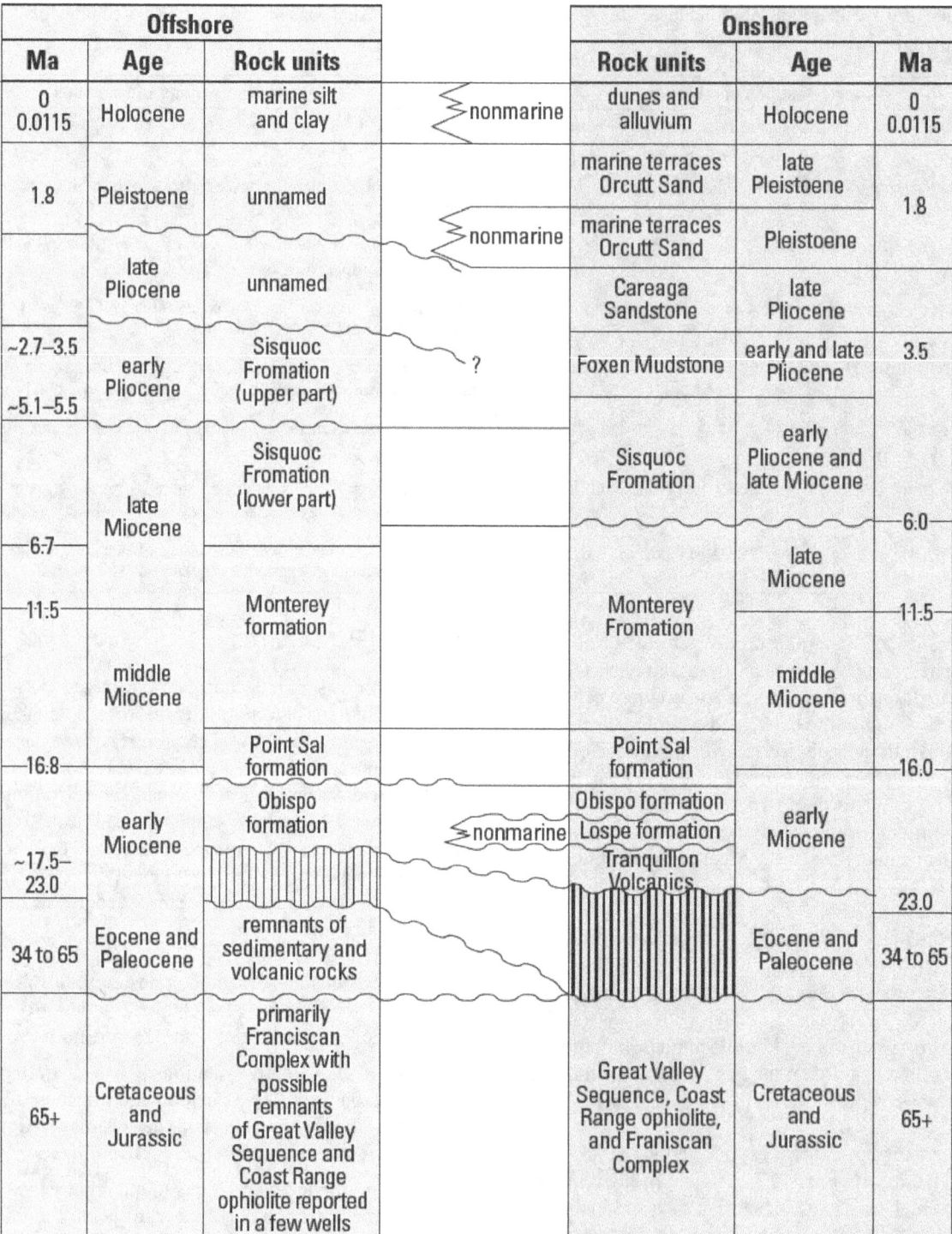

Figure 6.   Generalized stratigraphic correlation chart between the onshore Santa Maria Basin and the central offshore Santa Maria Basin. The chart shows major unconformities (wavy lines) and the approximate age and geologic unit relations. The age and geologic unit relations between the onshore Santa Maria Basin and the central offshore Santa Maria Basin. The age scales (Ma) are not linear. The onshore section is after Woodring and Bramlette (1950) and Tennyson and Isaacs (2001). The presence of the Tranquillon Volcanics onshore is after Dunham and Blake (1987). The offshore section is modified from Clark and others (1991) based on seismic reflection and well data (lithological and paleontological) presented in this report. The ages (Ma) for the epochs and subepochs are from McDougall (2008) and follow recent revisions of the time scale (Gradstein and others, 2004; USGS, 2007). Ages and age ranges for unconformities and unit boundaries are discussed in the section "Geologic Units and Unit Boundaries."

(1985, 1987), Heck and Mannon (1988), McCrory and others (1995), McCulloch (1987), Miller and Meltzer (1999), Sorlien and others (1999a), Maruyama (2000), Tennyson and Isaacs (2001), and Barron and Isaacs (2001). These papers have greatly increased our knowledge of the offshore stratigraphy and provide the basis for correlating offshore rock units with similar onshore strata.

On figure 6, we synthesize the data from the available literature, well logs, and seismic records to produce an updated stratigraphy for the central offshore Santa Maria Basin and present a correlation of this stratigraphy with a generalized representation of onshore units from approximately the same latitude. (Supporting paleontological data for the offshore stratigraphic column are presented in appendix A.) Specific references for the lithology and ages of the units and unit boundaries are provided in the discussions of the individual units.

Importance and Age of Basin-Wide Unconformities

One of the basic tenets of seismic stratigraphy is that seismic reflectors image time-stratigraphic horizons (Sheriff, 2002). Lithostratigraphic changes are detected through alterations of phase and amplitude laterally along these horizons. Because of the relatively long time hiatuses during formation of the unconformities in the offshore Santa Maria Basin, rocks with significantly different acoustic properties are placed in contact across the unconformities. Thus, the unconformities provide easily identified seismic reflectors, and their identification is further enhanced by the angular discordance of these reflections at the unconformities. We have mapped these boundaries throughout the basin and use them to form the basis for seismic-stratigraphic correlations presented in this paper. In addition, we have established age ranges for the major unconformities.

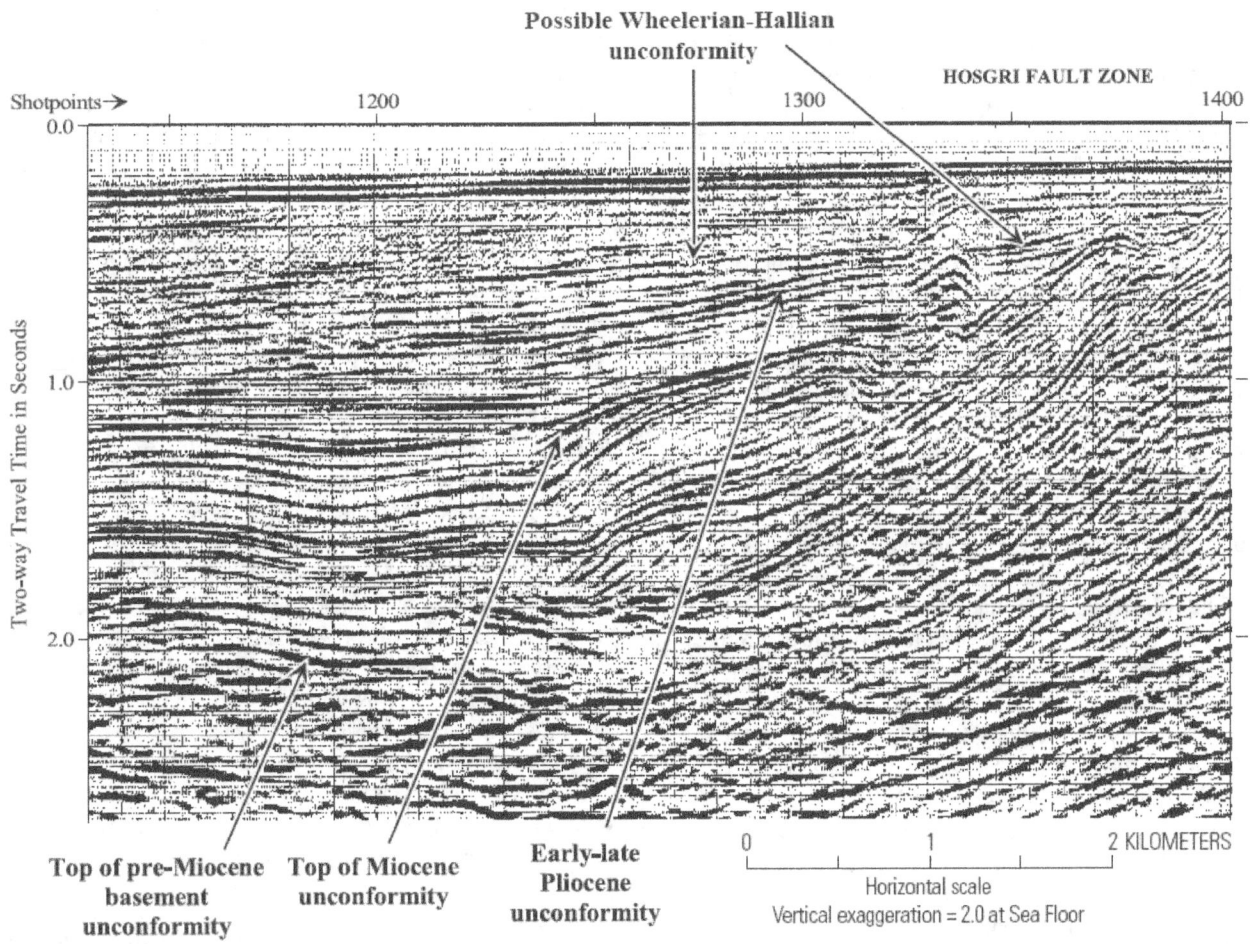

Figure 7.   Migrated seismic reflection record showing the three major unconformities that are mapped in this study: the top of pre-Miocene basement unconformity, the top of Miocene unconformity, and the early–late Pliocene unconformity. The data are from a reflection line that crosses the Hosgri Fault Zone in the west-central part of San Luis Obispo Bay (line GSI-97, pl. 1). Note the change in seismic character across the top of pre-Miocene basement unconformity, the truncation of the fold by the top of Miocene unconformity, and the onlap of younger sediments onto the early–late Pliocene unconformity. The 200-ms-thick swath of reflections at shotpoint 1200 immediately above the top of pre-Miocene basement unconformity may represent acoustic signatures of Paleogene and early Miocene formations.

Only three seismic reflection horizons, each representing an unconformity, can be reliably mapped over the entire offshore Santa Maria Basin. We named these horizons top of pre-Miocene basement, top of Miocene, and early–late Pliocene unconformities. Figure 7 shows the character of these unconformities on a seismic reflection line crossing the Hosgri Fault Zone. (This illustration is from the northeast end of line GSI-97 [pl. 1] and transects the west-central part of San Luis Obispo Bay in a southwest to northeast direction.) Locally, in areas of the offshore Santa Maria Basin with dense offshore well control and dense seismic coverage, additional seismic-stratigraphic correlations can be made in the rock units between the unconformities.

The seismic sections on plate 3 and those illustrated throughout this paper demonstrate the line-to-line consistency and the distinct seismic character of the rock units bounded by the three major unconformities. In contrast, lithostratigraphic boundaries generally do not have regionally consistent seismic signatures. For example, the boundary between the Monterey Formation and the Sisquoc Formation (lower part) is not readily detected seismically, as shown by the synthetic seismogram to seismic data ties displayed on plate 3. Comparison of the indistinct seismic character of this boundary with the seismic signature of the three basin-wide unconformities illustrates the value of the unconformities in establishing correlations between seismic records and offshore geologic units of the basin.

Angular unconformities represent a discontinuity or hiatus in rock sequence across which bedding dip is discordant (Sheriff, 2002). To use angular unconformities to estimate rates of deformation, the maximum and minimum ages of the hiatus must be constrained using the ages of deposits overlying and underlying the unconformity. When these age limits have been established, the unconformity can be used as a time range to constrain the approximate age of geologic events. In the offshore Santa Maria Basin, the rock units bounding the hiatuses are commonly time-transgressive (fig. 6, Dumont and Barron, 1995; McCrory and others, 1995). The following age bounds for the three basin-wide unconformities that we mapped are based on the age ranges of the oldest rock units directly overlying the unconformity and the youngest rock units beneath the unconformity. These age bounds are shown on figure 6 and figure A1 of appendix A. Data used to develop these age bounds are presented in discussions of the individual unconformities.

- Top of pre-Miocene basement unconformity, 23 to 17.5 Ma,

- Top of Miocene unconformity, 5.5 to 5.1 Ma,

- Early–late Pliocene unconformity, 3.5 to 2.7 Ma.

Additional age considerations in the use of unconformities as time markers arise when one unconformity truncates another. The geometries formed by basin-margin unconformities and onlaps may not clearly establish age relations, such as the re-cutting of existing surfaces by a younger unconformity. These conditions are evident in the sections from the northern part of the Hosgri Fault Zone between Cambria and Estero Bay.

Integration of Offshore and Onshore Data

Three conditions combine to make the correlation of onshore and offshore geologic units a difficult process in the Santa Maria Basin. First, the geography and atmospheric conditions of the central California coast, high sea cliffs, windswept coastline, and treacherous surf make onshore to offshore (nearshore) transition-zone seismic surveys difficult and, in some places, nearly impossible to conduct. Second, the rocks between the Hosgri Fault Zone and the coastline commonly are highly folded and faulted bedrock units that, in some areas, are of limited horizontal extent. These bedrock units severely limit seismic-signal penetration and result in poor data quality for all types of seismic reflection systems. Third, most of the east boundary of the offshore Santa Maria Basin cannot be tied directly to onshore or nearshore geology, because of vertical and horizontal slip and associated deformation along the Hosgri Fault Zone.

There is a nominal 3- to 5-km-wide area between the end of the moderate-to-deep seismic exploration reflection data and the coastline (pl. 1). High-resolution CDP surveys use shorter cables than the moderate-to-deep penetration surveys and generally approach to within 1 to 2 km of the coastline (Comap lines, pl. 1). Currently available single-channel analog surveys using a short receiver cable sometimes approach within 0.5 to 1 km of the coastline. However, both high-resolution CDP and analog surveys are generally limited in their depth of investigation to less than 1 km in this nearshore area due to surf noise, the complex geology, and the relatively low energy output of their seismic sources.

Figure 8 is a schematic depicting the structural and stratigraphic relations typical of the central part of the Hosgri Fault Zone. Sediments on the west, which are less deformed, are juxtaposed across the fault zone against strongly deformed sedimentary rocks and basement rock on the east, which are uplifted relative to the basin. The figure is a composite drawing of moderate- to deep-penetration exploration CDP seismic reflection data, short-cable high-resolution CDP seismic data, and analog geophysical survey data used to minimize the gap between onshore and offshore structural and stratigraphic data. By using both conventional and high-resolution system surveys that overlap, the composite interpretation displays both deep and shallow structure. Cores and diver-geologist investigations provide additional geologic data on the rocks in the shallow-water areas. Geologic mapping by Hall and others (1979) is the basis for the onshore geologic interpretation.

Correlation of Seismic Reflectors and Offshore Well Data

Driller's logs, well logs (fig. 9, pl. 3), and paleontological data (appendix A) were used to identify lithologic units and unit boundaries in the offshore wells. To establish the seismic signatures of major unconformities and rock units, synthetic seismograms were computed for ten wells within the basin.

Synthetics for four of these wells are presented on plate 3, along with resistivity, gamma ray, and velocity logs. The data shown on this plate span a 35-km reach of the offshore Santa Maria Basin, extending from a location 15 km north of Point Sal to Purisima Point. These data demonstrate the seismic characteristics discussed in detail in the following sections. The horizon picks annotated on the synthetic seismograms are those of the authors and are based on our interpretations of seismic, geologic, and borehole data.

The synthetic seismograms were constructed from borehole-compensated sonic logs corrected for velocity drift using vertical seismic profiles. Density values were derived directly from bulk density logs that were manually edited to correct for anomalous response associated with variation in borehole diameter and rugosity. In wells where bulk density logs were not available, the Gardner equation (Gardner and others, 1974) was used to synthesize density values from the sonic logs. Bandpass filter limits were determined empirically for each synthetic seismogram and adjusted to provide the best fit between synthetic and seismic data. All synthetics were generated using petroleum-industry standard commercial software, using a 1-ms sample rate. Multiple and ghost reflections that appear on the seismic reflection records are not present in the sonic log data and are not present in the synthetics. The synthetic seismograms shown in plate 3 have been automatic-gain compensated to match the character of nearby seismic lines.

Geologic Units and Unit Boundaries

Despite the many advances that have been made in establishing an onshore/offshore chronostratigraphy, there are still many uncertainties in the geographic distribution of rock units and the ages and definition of formations. In the offshore Santa Maria Basin, this is true with regard to pre-Monterey Formation rocks and the Pliocene Foxen Mudstone. Figure 6

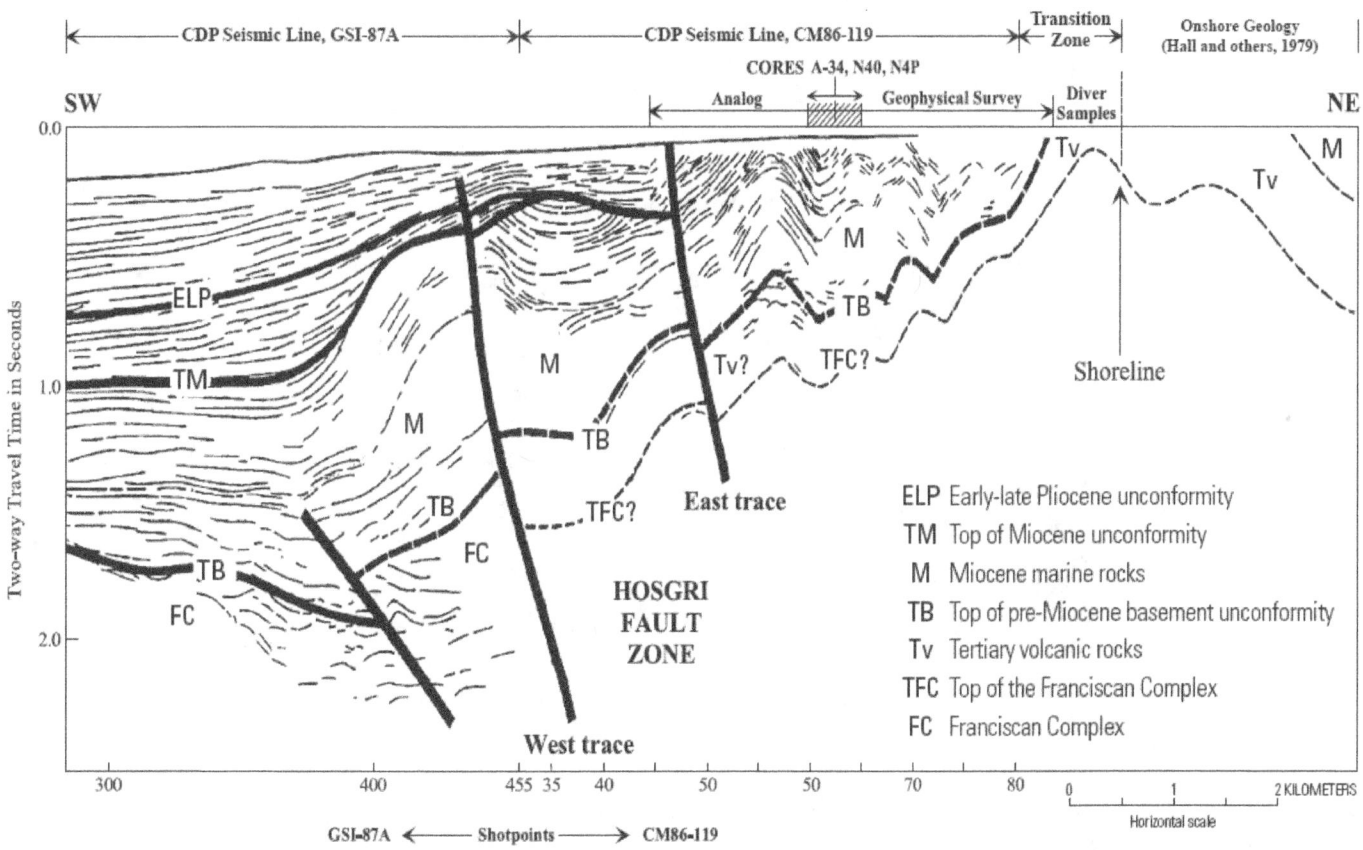

Figure 8. Composite offshore to onshore geologic cross section. The section trends from offshore, across the Hosgri Fault Zone, to onshore midway between Point Buchon and Point San Luis. This figure illustrates the integration of various data sets to establish a geologic correlation between onshore and offshore units. The figure is a composite of conventional (GSI-87) and high-resolution (CM-119) CDP seismic reflection data, high-resolution analog data (side-scan sonar and subbottom profilers), core data, diver observations, and onshore mapping. Complex folding and faulting often make extrapolation of structure and stratigraphy trends across the transition zone difficult without the ground truth and high-resolution analog data that can be collected near shore. As indicated in this section, the top of pre-Miocene basement unconformity is generally interpreted to be the top of the Franciscan Complex. However, as shown on the northeast side of the figure, volcanic rocks also can locally act as acoustic basement.

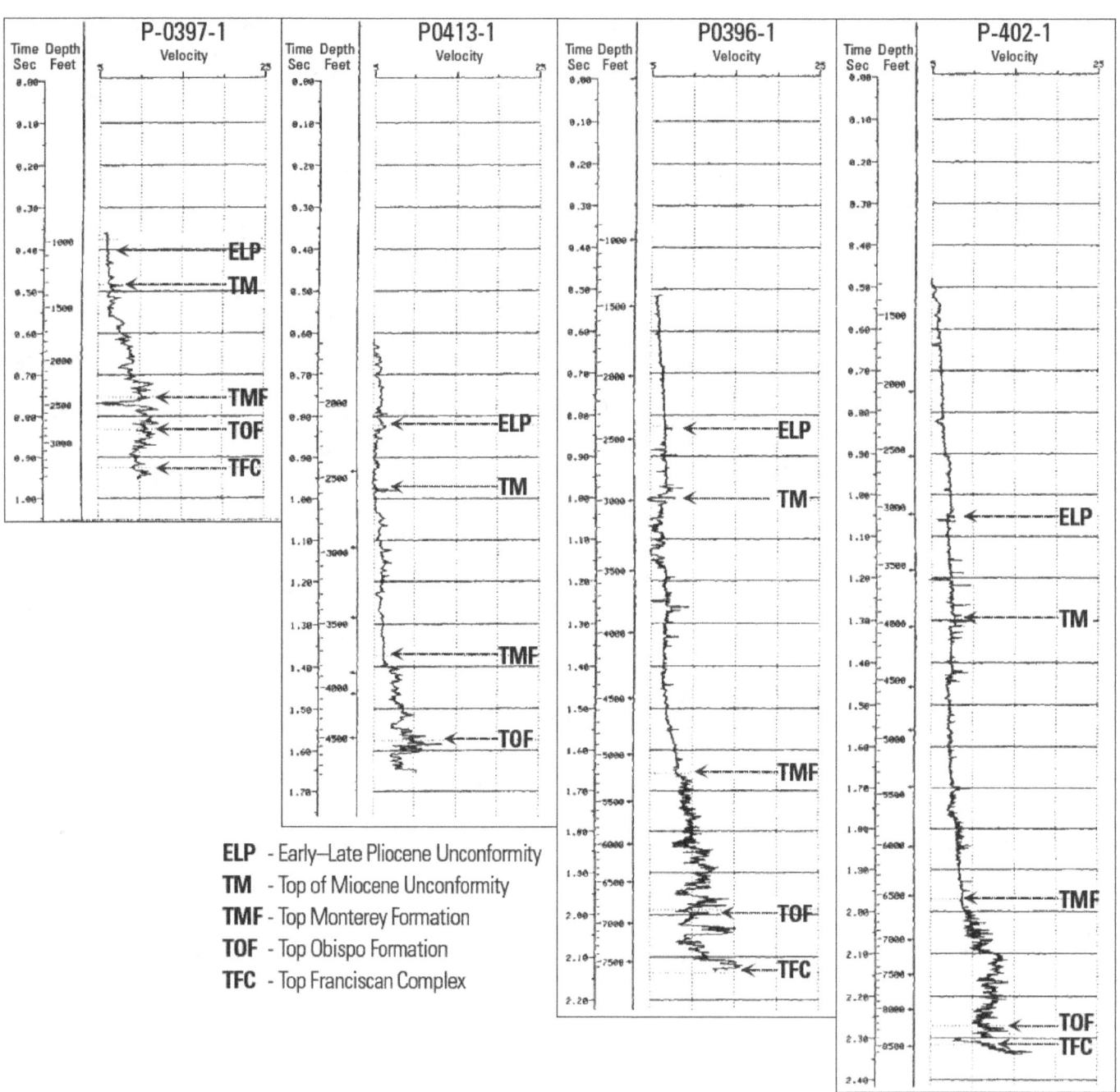

ELP - Early–Late Pliocene Unconformity
TM - Top of Miocene Unconformity
TMF - Top Monterey Formation
TOF - Top Obispo Formation
TFC - Top Franciscan Complex

Figure 9.   Velocity logs from four wells offshore Point Sal. The logs show typical time-depth and velocity-depth relations encountered in the offshore Santa Maria Basin (see well locations on fig. 5 and pl. 2). Well-velocity data were used in conjunction with seismic stacking velocities to develop the 3-D velocity model used to produce the structure contour maps of the unconformities (pls. 5–7). There is little velocity contrast across the early–late Pliocene unconformity, and generally the increase in velocity begins at the top of Miocene unconformity. Larger velocity increases usually occur within the Miocene section at the opal-CT-to-quartz diagenetic transformation boundary (see annotations, pl. 3) and below the top of the Monterey Formation. Additional velocity logs, at a larger scale and with additional annotations, are shown on plate 3. The scales of the velocity logs are in feet and feet/second, the units commonly used for petroleum exploration well logs in the United States.

includes a generalized stratigraphic chart for the offshore Santa Maria Basin showing the geologic units, major unconformities, unit ages, and relations to units in the onshore Santa Maria Basin. Figure 7 is a part of a seismic profile that depicts the major geologic units and bounding unconformities. Figure 8 illustrates the integration of various data sets to establish geologic correlation between onshore and offshore units. In the following sections we discuss the basis for the age assignments and stratigraphic correlations presented on figure 6, as well as the descriptions of the lithology of the units, the sources of age data, and the seismic expression of the units and unconformities.

Basement Rocks

In the central offshore Santa Maria Basin, the geologic basement is composed predominantly of rocks of the Franciscan Complex. This interpretation is based on lithologic data from onshore and nearshore outcrops, offshore exploratory wells, and regional tectonic models for the coastal provinces of California. Several offshore wells shown on plate 3 (P-0397-1, P-0415-1, P-0422-1, P-0424-1, P-0435-1) encountered graywacke and serpentinite, interpreted as the Franciscan Complex. Logs and synthetic seismograms for these wells are presented on plate 3. High resistivity, gamma-ray response, high velocity, and mud-log data form the basis for our picks of the top of Franciscan Complex on the logs on plate 3. Sorlien and others (1999b) list additional wells interpreted to bottom in the Franciscan Complex. A few wells have bottomed in different pre-Miocene basement lithologies. These units have been variously described as possible Cretaceous to Eocene sedimentary rocks, Great Valley sequence, Coast Range ophiolite, and remnants of pre-Miocene volcanic rocks (appendix A; Sorlien and others, 1999b; Miller and Meltzer, 1999). These older units may image, on a local basis, as acoustic basement on the seismic reflection records.

Throughout most of the central offshore Santa Maria Basin, Miocene sedimentary and volcanic rocks of the Monterey, Point Sal, and Obispo Formations unconformably overlie the Franciscan Complex basement rocks. No radiometric ages are available for rocks of the Franciscan Complex in the offshore; however, in the onshore Santa Maria Basin, the age of the Franciscan Complex is placed at 140 to 155 Ma or older by Bishop and Davis (1984).

The typical seismic signature of the Franciscan Complex basement is a series of discontinuous, subhorizontal, low frequency events (fig. 7). These intrabasement seismic reflection events commonly have the appearance of horizontal continuity on a single record, but usually they cannot be correlated between more than two adjacent seismic lines. These reflectors may have diverse origins, some geologic in nature, such as relict bedding, relict structures, active or inactive detachments, and others attributable to acoustic artifacts, such as multiple reverberations, out-of-plane seismic reflections, or seismic processing artifacts. Typical intrabasement seismic-reflection events are illustrated on several of the seismic profiles presented later in this report.

In localized areas of the central and southern offshore Santa Maria Basin, seismic images suggest that deformed sedimentary rocks are present directly above the Franciscan Complex. By analogy with the sedimentary sequences mapped onshore near Point Arguello (Berkland and others, 1972) and also known in the offshore near Point Arguello (Crain and others, 1985, 1987), these may be Cretaceous or Paleogene sedimentary rocks. Bishop and Davis (1984) place the top of the Cretaceous rocks of the Espada and Jalama Formations (Dibblee, 1950), which crop out in the Santa Ynez Mountains to the east, at the Albian/Cenomanian (~100 Ma) and Maastrichtian/Danian (~65.5 Ma) stage boundaries, respectively. The boundary ages are from Gradstein and others (2004).

Top of Pre-Miocene Basement Unconformity

The top of pre-Miocene basement unconformity (pl. 5) is related to a period of major tectonism inferred to be associated with the collision of the Pacific-Farallon spreading-ridge system with North America and with a contemporaneous low-sea-level stand (Nilsen, 1984). The unconformity truncates the Franciscan Complex and, locally, remnants of overlying Cretaceous and Paleogene strata. On the CDP seismic records, it is the boundary between low-frequency "acoustic" basement reflectors and overlying reflectors of relatively high continuity and amplitude (fig. 7). In limited areas between Point Buchon and Point Sal, the seismic signature of the pre-Monterey volcanic sequences may not be distinguishable from that of the top of the Franciscan Complex rocks, and parts of the Paleogene or early Miocene volcanic units may have been included within the basement complex in our seismic mapping.

Seismic reflectors overlying the top of pre-Miocene basement unconformity are interpreted to be Miocene volcanic rocks and Miocene and younger sedimentary rocks. These reflectors generally are parallel or subparallel to the unconformity west of the Hosgri Fault Zone and onlap the unconformity, where the basement complex is structurally uplifted within the fault zone and on the flanks of the major anticlinal structures.

Because of the inferred presence of Oligocene rocks beneath the unconformity (Crain and others, 1985, 1987; Hoskins and Griffiths, 1971) and the ages of Neogene sedimentary rocks above the unconformity, the maximum age of the unconformity is placed at about 23 Ma, using the age for the top of the Oligocene given by Gradstein and others (2004) and USGS (2007). McCrory and others (1995) estimated the oldest age of sedimentary rocks above the unconformity to be approximately 24.5 Ma from data obtained from the Texaco Nautilus well (P-0496-1) west of Point Pedernales (fig. 5, pl. 2). Their age of 24.5 Ma was based on the age of the Saucesian-Zemorrian benthic foraminiferal zones (bfz) boundary. That boundary age was revised to 23 Ma in Gradstein and others (2004) and is the value now used by the USGS (2007).

The rocks deposited on top of the unconformity vary widely in age and type. In the more northerly onshore and offshore regions of the Santa Maria Basin, the Miocene volcanic Obispo Formation/Tranquillon Volcanics, Lospe Formation, and Monterey

Formation are in contact with the unconformity. Ages provided by McCrory and others (1995) from onshore exposures at the latitude of Point Sal place the base of the Lospe and Point Sal Formations at 17.7 Ma and 17.0 Ma, respectively, and the base of the lower Monterey Formation at 15.5 Ma. The 17.7 Ma date is constrained by an ^{40}Ar/^{39}Ar date. The 17.0 Ma date was based on the Relizian/Saucesian bfz boundary, which is now placed at 17.5 Ma (McDougall, 2008). The volcanic units are also present in the Nautilus well (P-0496-1) where McCrory and others (1995) show the Monterey Formation overlying volcanic and volcaniclastic rocks as young as 17.5 Ma.

Farther south in the COST well, which is offshore from Point Conception, just south of the plate 2 map boundary, an unnamed unit of interbedded sandstone and conglomerate overlies the unconformity and marks the initial subsidence from neritic to middle bathyal depths at about 18 Ma (McCrory and others, 1995). In the COST well, these unnamed rocks have been assigned an age of 18.0 Ma.

Paleogene and Early Miocene Formations

Throughout most of the central and southern offshore Santa Maria Basin, the Franciscan Complex is directly overlain by Miocene sedimentary or volcanic rock formations, as shown by the logs on plate 3. However, biostratigraphic analysis of well samples and lithologic logs from cuttings indicate local remnants of Paleogene formations are occasionally present (pl. 3; appendix A, tables A1, A2, and A4 for wells P-0415-1, P-0-415-2, and P-0422-1, respectively).

The offshore Miocene volcanic rocks are inferred to be correlative with the early Miocene (Saucesian bfz) Tranquillon Volcanics described by Crain and others (1987) in the offshore Point Arguello and Point Conception area. Similarly, in the central part of the basin, Miller and Meltzer (1999) associate these rocks with the Point Sal Formation and the Obispo Formation described by Hall (1981) in the onshore Santa Maria Basin. In the southern part of the basin, they relate the rocks to the Tranquillon Volcanics and Point Sal Formation. Miller and Meltzer (1999) also provide an example of well penetration and coincident seismic imaging of these pre-Monterey formations in a sequence associated with the Oceano well (P-060-1, pl. 2) and seismic line PG&E-2. Data presented in McCrory and others (1995) for the Lospe and Point Sal Formations and by Turner (1970) for the Tranquillon Volcanics assign age ranges to these rocks of 16.0 to 17.7 Ma. Turner (1970) provides potassium-argon ages for the onshore Obispo Formation that range from 16.5 to 15.3 Ma. Cole and Stanley (1998) later modified these ages to range from 16.9 to 15.7 Ma.

Onshore, the Point Sal Formation lies either conformably on the Lospe Formation (Stanley and others, 1995) or, as is indicated in maps by Hall (1973a,b), overlies the Obispo Formation. Hall's mapping may be interpreted to suggest the possibility of interfingering relations between the Monterey, Point Sal, and Obispo Formations. We generalize these complex local relations and show part of the Obispo and the Lospe Formations as contemporaneous and overlying the Tranquillon Volcanics where the latter are present (fig. 6).

The resolution of the seismic data is not sufficient to differentiate between the pre-Monterey Formation rock units. However, groups of pre-Monterey Formation rock units can be distinguished seismically by a combination of stratigraphic position, high-amplitude reflections at the base and top of their seismic signature package, and poor coherence of intrapackage events. Seismic signature packages interpreted to represent pre-Monterey Formation rock units lie above the pre-Miocene basement unconformity on figure 7 (shotpoints 1125 to 1225, 1.8 to 2.0 s) and also are marked on the electric logs accompanying the sections on plate 3 (above the TB).

Monterey Formation

During middle and late Miocene time, the Monterey Formation was deposited over most of the California coastal margin and is present throughout the offshore Santa Maria Basin (Pisciotto and Garrison, 1983; Heck and Mannon, 1988; McCrory and others, 1995). In the offshore Santa Maria Basin, the thickness of the Monterey Formation varies greatly, ranging from 180 m over paleotopographic highs, to 900 m in paleotopographic basins (Heck and Mannon, 1988). The Monterey Formation in this region can generally be divided into three lithofacies based on composition: a lower calcareous/dolomitic basal section of interbedded dolostone, shale, and chert; a middle member of phosphatic, calcareous, and organic-rich shale; and an upper siliceous section of siliceous shale, porcelanite, and chert (Pisciotto and Garrison, 1983; Heck and Mannon, 1988).

The base of the Monterey Formation is time-transgressive and has been assigned an age of 15.7 Ma by Obradovich and Naeser (1981). This age is similar to the 15.5 Ma age determined for the top of the lowest member of the formation in the COST well by McCrory and others (1995). They indicate an age of 17.5 Ma for the tops of the units underlying the Monterey Formation in both the COST and P-0496-1 wells. Barron (1986) places the age of the base of the Monterey Formation in the Santa Barbara coastal area at about 18 Ma. The seismic signature of the lowermost member consists of relatively high frequency, high-amplitude, coherent parallel to subparallel reflection patterns as shown at 1.8 to 2.0 s beneath shotpoints 1150 to 1200 in figure 7.

In the onshore Santa Maria Basin, the Monterey Formation/Sisquoc Formation contact is locally an unconformity dated at about 5 Ma by Barron (1986) and Dumont (1989). However, in many areas of the onshore Santa Maria Basin and also in the offshore, the contact between the Monterey and Sisquoc Formations is time-transgressive and lithologically gradational and can be distinguished only through detailed lithologic and petrophysical analysis.

Obradovich and Naeser (1981) assign an age of 8 Ma to the top of the Monterey Formation at the type locality in Monterey Canyon. Ages assigned to the uppermost occurrences of the Monterey Formation in the COST and the Texaco Nautilus wells are 7.2 Ma and 6.5 Ma, respectively (McCrory and others, 1995). Clark and others (1991) assigned an age of 6.5 Ma to the "Top Monterey" in their chronostratigraphy of the offshore Santa Maria Basin, and Dumont and Barron (1995) assigned an age of 6.0 Ma for the Monterey Formation/Sisquoc Formation boundary from observations in the onshore Santa Maria Basin near the latitude of Point Arguello. Barron and Ramirez (1992) place the top of the Monterey Formation at 6.7 Ma. These ages may eventually need to be revised downward as the age of the top of the Mohnian bfz has been revised from 6.5 Ma to a range of 8.6 to 7.3 Ma (McDougall, 2008). Based on these determinations, we assign a minimum age of 6.7 Ma for the top of the Monterey Formation in the offshore Santa Maria Basin (fig. 6). This age corresponds to the top of Subzone a of the *Nitzschia reinholdii* Zone (Barron and Isaacs, 2001), which Barron currently places at 6.7 Ma. (J.A. Barron, personal commun., 2008).

In the offshore Santa Maria Basin, the top of the Monterey Formation is conformable with the base of the Sisquoc Formation. This observation is based on comparison of seismic images with synthetic seismograms developed from offshore well-log data (pl. 3) and the examination of the contact zone on seismic sections. In fact, one of the significant problems confronting early petroleum exploration in the offshore Santa Maria Basin was the development of criteria to identify this contact, because no distinct change in the character of the well-log data was observed at the contact in any of the standard log suites (Heck and Mannon, 1988) and diagnostic fauna are nonexistent. To assist in identifying the top of the Monterey Formation, seven wells were selected (P-0424-1, P-0430-1, P-0435-1, P-0427-1, P-0416-1, P-0415-1, P-0415-2) and the cuttings were microscopically reviewed to determine sedimentary characteristics and lamination patterns. Differences between the two formations in rock fabric, such as laminations and color, proved to be consistent; for example, a massive (46–134 m, average 99 m), lighter colored Sisquoc Formation section overlies the darker, microlaminated Monterey Formation siliceous shales in all of the wells. This contact is located approximately 60 m above the first Monterey Formation resistivity marker in the electric logs (J.D. Kronen, personal commun., 1985).

Sisquoc Formation and the Top of Miocene Unconformity

The Sisquoc Formation consists of a series of siltstones, clays and clay shales, and diatomaceous or siliceous mudstone with rare limestone or dolostone beds. The age of the Sisquoc Formation in the central offshore Santa Maria Basin is late Miocene and early Pliocene (appendix A). An unconformity marks the contact between the upper Miocene and lower Pliocene rocks of the Sisquoc Formation (fig. 6, pl. 3). We refer to this late Miocene/early Pliocene unconformity as the top of Miocene unconformity (p. 6).

Analyses of mud logs and cores from offshore wells show that upper Miocene siltstone, siliceous mudstone, and claystone underlie the unconformity (pl. 3). These well data also show that lower Pliocene rocks directly overlying the unconformity have similar lithology. This unconformity can be traced confidently on seismic data over most of the offshore Santa Maria Basin (fig. 7). According to Clark and others (1991), in the central offshore Santa Maria Basin, the top of Miocene unconformity separates the upper

and lower parts of the Sisquoc Formation. The upper part is early Pliocene and has been called the "Foxen Mudstone" in McCrory and others (1995). However, the well data available to the authors do not reveal a distinct seismic-stratigraphic unit, which can be identified in the offshore Santa Maria Basin, that is equivalent to the onshore Foxen Mudstone. Upper Pliocene sediments are shown as unnamed on figures 6 and A1 of appendix A. Further discussion of the Foxen Mudstone may be found under the heading "Foxen Mudstone and Unnamed Sedimentary Rocks".

Dumont (1989) correlates diatom zonations in the onshore Santa Maria Basin to paleomagnetic chronostratigraphy of the southern California continental borderland. Based on these correlations, the age of the Miocene/Pliocene boundary in the basin is 5.35 Ma. This date conforms to Bishop and Davis (1984), Barron and Isaacs (2001), and McDougall (2008). Dumont and Barron (1995) recognize that a younger estimate of the Miocene/Pliocene boundary age (4.83 Ma) at Capo Rossello, Italy, based on correlation of magnetostratigraphic data and biostratigraphic events by Zijderveld and others (1986), is receiving increasing support from biostratigraphers and may be correct. Channel and others (1988), working farther south at Capo Spartivento, Italy, also used magnetostratigraphic-biostratigraphic correlations to place the age of the boundary at 4.93 Ma. The diatom zonations of Dumont and Barron (1995) in the onshore Santa Maria Basin are significant to the offshore area. As a general rule, there is a paucity of benthic foraminifera in the offshore samples, but the *Thalassiosira oestrupii* diatom zone is identified in many of the wells associated with the late Miocene/early Pliocene unconformity. The base of the *T. oestrupii* zone was previously dated as 5.1 Ma by Dumont and Barron (1995), however, Maruyama (2000) and Barron and Isaacs (2001) generally agree on an age for the base of the zone as 5.49 and 5.5 Ma, respectively (late Miocene). In the P-0435-1 well, the first occurrence of *T. oestrupii* is in sample 8 that came from the depth immediately above the unconformity mapped by seismic data. Sample 9, from below the unconformity, contains *T. miocenica* and should be older than 6.0 Ma (appendix A, table A7). Therefore, based on the first occurrence of *T. oestrupii* occurring above the unconformity, the top of Miocene unconformity can be as old as 5.5 Ma or as young as 5.1 Ma. On the generalized stratigraphic section (fig. 6), we give the range suggested above.

The top of Miocene unconformity is well expressed on the seismic records throughout most of the offshore Santa Maria Basin. A single coherent and continuous reflector of slightly higher amplitude than surrounding events distinguishes the unconformity (fig. 7). It is most readily identified on the basis of its truncation of underlying reflections on the crests of folds and the truncation of overlying reflections to form buttress or onlap relations along the margins of folds. The unconformity is annotated on many of the accompanying seismic reflection records. The seismic reflection signatures of rocks beneath the unconformity are similar to those above the unconformity, except where the former generally has a slightly greater degree of coherency and continuity (fig. 7).

Seismic imaging shows there are several additional minor unconformities present in the sedimentary column near the top of the Miocene unconformity. These unconformities are particularly well developed south of Purisima Point along the flanks of the

Purisima structure west of the Hosgri Fault Zone. In this area, it is difficult to differentiate the top of Miocene unconformity from these minor breaks in deposition.

Early–Late Pliocene Unconformity

A prominent unconformity, the early–late Pliocene unconformity (pl. 7), is present within the Pliocene section throughout the offshore Santa Maria Basin. This unconformity is a well-defined reflector on seismic data (fig. 7) and is annotated on most of the seismic profiles illustrated in this report. Crain and others (1985, 1987) observed this unconformity on seismic data near the Point Arguello and Point Conception areas, where it is placed within the Pico Formation, near the base of the upper Pliocene section. In the southern offshore Santa Maria Basin, Crain and others (1987) correlate the Sisquoc Formation below the early–late Pliocene unconformity with the upper part of the Sisquoc Formation at Point Arguello and with rocks containing the early Pliocene diatom zones of Dumont (1989) in the onshore Santa Maria Basin. In the central and northern parts of the offshore Santa Maria Basin, the unconformity separates the upper part of the Sisquoc Formation from a poorly consolidated sequence of upper Pliocene through Holocene sediments. We refer to the overlying Pliocene sediments as an unnamed rock stratigraphic unit on figure 6.

We estimate an age range of 3.5 to 2.7 Ma for the early–late Pliocene unconformity in the central offshore Santa Maria Basin. This range is based on microfossil data from wells P-0424-1 and P-0435-1 west of Purisima Point. Well locations are shown on figure 5 and plate 2 and the microfossil data are in appendix A. Depths in wells are in meters (m) below mean lower low water (MLLW), the vertical datum used in this chapter. The ages of the North Pacific Diatom zones (NPDZ) are from Maruyama (2000) and are shown in figure A1.

The siliceous microfossil data in well P-0424-1 (appendix A) place the early–late Pliocene unconformity at a depth between 408 and 417 m below MLLW. The last occurrence of *N. koizumii* is in sample 4 at a depth of 356 to 362 m. This marks the boundary between NPDZ 10 and NPDZ 9 with an age of 2.0 Ma. The presence of *N. koizumii* without *N. kamtschatica* in samples 4 through 9 (depth range 356–408 m) indicates NPDZ 9 (age 2.68–2.61 to 2.0 Ma.) (appendix A). Neither *N. koizumii* nor *N. kamtschatica* are noted in sample 10 (depth range 408–417 m). Sample 11 (depth range 417–426 m) contains the last occurrence of *N. kamtschatica,* indicating the top of NPDZ 8 or NPDZ 7Bb, if NPDZ 8 was removed at the unconformity. The age range of NPDZ 8 is 2.68–2.61 to 3.59–3.53 Ma and the age range of NPDZ 7Bb is placed at 3.59–3.53 Ma (top) and 5.49 Ma (base) (fig. A1). Thus we interpret the early–late Pliocene unconformity in well P-0424-1 to occur in the depth range of sample 10 or between 408 and 417 m. The seismic data projected through the location of the P 0424-1 well indicates that the unconformity is at approximately 410 m (1,345 ft) (pl. 7). This depth is close to the depth of 407 m (1,335 ft) estimated from the drilling-rate and lithology data from the mud log (pl. 3).

We interpret the siliceous microfossil data in well P-0435-1 to place the early–late Pliocene unconformity at a depth of 297 m.

Sample 2, depth range 269 to 297 m, contains the first occurrence of *N. koizumii*, indicating the late Pliocene NPDZ 9 (age range 2.68–2.61 at the base to 2.0 Ma at the top) (Maruyama, 2000). The diatom zone in sample 3, at a depth range of 297 to 324 m, indicates an early Pliocene age, while the *N. kamtschatica* zone (NPDZ 7Bb) ranges in age from 5.49 Ma at the base to 3.59–3.53 Ma at the top (Maruyama, 2000). The seismic data projected to the P 0435-1 well indicates that the unconformity is at a depth of approximately 275 to 300 m (pl. 7).

Dumont and Barron (1995) and McCrory and others (1995) indicate rocks no younger than 3.5 to 3.4 Ma underlie the early–late Pliocene unconformity and rocks no older than 3.4 to 2.5 Ma onlap the unconformity. These ages are in agreement with the early Pliocene ages determined by Dumont and Barron (1995) for onshore sediments and bracket the youngest age estimate for the early–late Pliocene unconformity between 3.0 and 2.7 Ma, based on the Santa Maria Basin stratigraphic correlation charts of Bishop and Davis (1984) and the 3.0 Ma age provided by Behl and Ingle (1998) for the uppermost member of the Foxen Mudstone (see below). Maruyama (2000) places the early–late Pliocene boundary at approximately 3.5 Ma based on correlation of NPDZs offshore California with magnetostratigraphic time scales. McDougall (2008) also places the boundary at about 3.5 Ma.

Offshore, the early–late Pliocene unconformity is imaged seismically as a combination of truncated reflections and differences in seismic signature between the rocks of the upper part of the Sisquoc Formation and the overlying unnamed sedimentary units (fig. 7). The seismic signature of the overlying unnamed sediment is characterized by events with substantially less trace-to-trace coherency than is observed in the underlying Sisquoc Formation reflections. The reflections in the upper Pliocene unit are disrupted at some locations by diffractions interpreted to be associated with gas charging. These unnamed rocks also have regions of acoustic transparency that show few or no seismic reflections. This contrasts with the signature of the early Pliocene upper Sisquoc Formation rocks, which displays a relatively high degree of coherency and continuity.

The truncations of reflection events against the early–late Pliocene unconformity are most prominent against the flanks of the large folds (fig. 7). At some locations, the top of Miocene unconformity and early–late Pliocene unconformity intersect one another. This generally occurs across the crests of large folds, such as the Lompoc and Purisima folds, and structures directly west of the Hosgri Fault Zone near Point Sal. In such localities, it is assumed the younger unconformity truncated the older event, unless reflection geometries clearly indicate the termination of the younger event against the top of Miocene unconformity. Both unconformities are annotated on many of the examples of seismic reflection records from this paper.

Foxen Mudstone and Unnamed Sedimentary Rocks

The Foxen Mudstone is a formal stratigraphic name assigned to marine rocks described by Canfield (1939) from a type section in Foxen Canyon in the Santa Maria Valley. Behl and Ingle (1998) assign ages of 3.8 Ma to the base of this unit and about 3.0 Ma to the top. Dumont and Barron (1995) date the boundary between the Sisquoc Formation and the Foxen Mudstone at about 3.8 Ma at Harris Grade (approximately at the latitude of Purisima Point) but identify the boundary as being about 5.0 Ma in the Casmalia Hills near the latitude of Point Sal. These age assignments, from the diatom zonation work of Dumont and Barron (1995), suggest an approximate age range for the Foxen Mudstone that is mostly older than the lower age of 3.5 Ma that McCrory and others (1995) ascribe to the early–late Pliocene boundary and older than the age range (3.5–2.7 Ma) we assign to the unconformity. Clearly, many complexities exist with regard to time transgression and local environment of deposition in the region of Pliocene sediments.

Offshore stratigraphy in the upper Pliocene and Pleistocene appears less complicated than its onshore counterpart described above. Mud-log data and particularly drilling rates help determine the location of the early–late Pliocene unconformity in the offshore wells (pl. 3). Depths of the early–late Pliocene unconformity mapped from seismic reflection records (pl. 7) that are correlated with well-log data (pl. 3) provide depth estimates for the unconformity at the wells. Paleontological data from the wells (P-0415-1, P-0422-1, P-0424-1, P-0435-1, appendix A) provide a relatively consistent age of about 3.5 Ma for the uppermost strata below the unconformity. In the P-0424-1 and P-0435-1 wells, siliceous microfossil zones in the strata overlying the unconformity indicate that the unconformity formed there prior to approximately 2.68–2.61 Ma. These data suggest that the offshore sediments above the early–late Pliocene unconformity are younger than the onshore Foxen Mudstone. Therefore, we have referred to the offshore sediments above the unconformity as "unnamed".

The unnamed sediments overlie the generally better-sorted and stratified rocks of the upper part of the Sisquoc Formation. Analysis of lithology from offshore well cuttings show that the unnamed sediments consist of poorly consolidated clay, silt, sandstone, and thin limestone interbeds with fossil shell fragments. The lithology logs based on the cuttings from wells P-0424-1 and P-0397-1 (pl. 3) show that the upper Sisquoc Formation has a different lithology from the unnamed units above the early–late Pliocene unconformity. The upper Sisquoc Formation consists of approximately 50 percent siltstone and 50 percent claystone with occasional thin beds of limestone and dolomite. In both wells, changes in drilling rate occurred slightly above and within about 30 m of the lithologic changes. The mud log for well P-0397-1 shows drilling rates declining from 38 m/hr (125 ft/hr) to 30 m/hr (98 ft/hr) at a depth of about 328 m (1,075 ft) and shows lithology changes inferred to represent entry into the top of the Sisquoc Formation at about 317 m (1,040 ft). The combination of lithologic and drilling-rate changes marks, in our interpretation, the transition from the unnamed upper Pliocene and Pleistocene sediments into the lower Pliocene Sisquoc Formation. Further, we correlate

the drilling-rate change with the approximate stratigraphic location of the seismic reflection horizon associated with the early–late Pliocene unconformity, although at the location of the P-0424-1 and P-0435-1 wells the microfossil data indicate the unconformity is slightly higher in the stratigraphic section than the early–late Pliocene boundary interpreted from the other logs shown on pl. 3.

Figure 6 illustrates our generalized correlation of offshore units to nearshore and onshore formations for the central part of the Santa Maria Basin. These correlations indicate that the onshore Foxen Mudstone was deposited at the same time as the uppermost part of the offshore Sisquoc Formation or during the late Pliocene. Onshore, the Foxen Mudstone is overlain by the Careaga Sandstone and Paso Robles Formation that, based on the work of Crain and others (1987), are correlative in the offshore with our unnamed sedimentary units. Plate 3 shows a sand unit in the logs from well P-0397-1 (depth range <950 to 1,050 ft, <290 to 320 m) and well P-0424-1 (depth range <1,150–1,330 ft, <351–405 m) within the unnamed sequence above the early–late Pliocene unconformity. We interpret this unnamed sequence to be approximately contemporaneous with the Careaga Formation. This sand unit within the unnamed sequence contains siliceous microfossils from NPDZ 9 and 10, which implies an age of about 2.6 Ma or younger (appendix A, well P-0424-1, samples 1 to 7, and well P-0435-1, samples 1 and 2).

Pliocene-Pleistocene Contact and Pleistocene Sediments

Late Pliocene and Pleistocene sedimentary units are recognized in the onshore Santa Maria Basin (McCrory and others, 1995). However, their contacts typically are not identified in wells or on seismic data in the offshore area, because most drilling locations are on structurally elevated areas of the basin where this section is thin or absent (Clark and others, 1991). Some wells drilled on structures of low relief or on the flanks of structures (pl. 7), such as wells P-0424-1 and P-0397-1 discussed above and shown on plate 3, have penetrated shallow beds of unconsolidated sediments that probably are equivalent to the onshore, nonmarine, local Pleistocene Paso Robles Formation as defined by Woodring and Bramlette (1950). We correlate these rocks with the upper part of our unnamed sediment units (fig. 6).

The contact within the Pleistocene unnamed unit between Hallian bfz sediment and the underlying Wheelerian bfz is poorly defined in well data. However, the acoustic signature of the inferred Hallian bfz sediments is different from that of the underlying sediment (fig. 7). An unconformity at about 0.4 s at shotpoint 1350 (fig. 7) is interpreted as the Wheelerian-Hallian bfz unconformity. Large areas of acoustic transparency and diffracted energy typify the Hallian bfz strata. Also, the reflectors that are imaged generally display a lower frequency response than underlying reflection events and a lower degree of reflector coherency and continuity.

Post-Late Wisconsin Sediments

The shallow eastern shelf of the offshore Santa Maria Basin was subjected to late Pleistocene and Holocene erosion as a result of the regression and subsequent transgression of the shoreline associated with the onset and end of the late Wisconsin glacial period. This erosional surface is called the late Wisconsin unconformity (PG&E, 1988). Seafloor exposures of the Franciscan Complex, Monterey Formation, and unnamed Pliocene rocks are common within and to the east of the Hosgri Fault Zone. Locally, these units are covered with a thin veneer of post-late Wisconsin sediment. These sediments also occur in small pockets 8 to 10 m thick that fill small depressions and pull-apart basins within the Hosgri Fault Zone. They are as much as 40 m thick off the mouths of the major rivers. The surficial, unconsolidated, post-late Wisconsin deposits generally are too thin to be observed on the CDP records illustrated in this report but were imaged by the high-resolution analog systems (fig. 10).

Interpretation Methods and Products

Our interpretations of the Hosgri Fault Zone and adjacent structures are presented as a series of annotated seismic profiles and four maps. The maps include a structural trend map (pl. 4) of the eastern offshore Santa Maria Basin and structural contour maps (pls. 5–7) of the three basin-wide unconformities: top of pre-Miocene basement unconformity, top of Miocene unconformity, and early–late Pliocene unconformity. In the following paragraphs we describe the data and interpretational criteria used to (1) identify and annotate the structures on the seismic profiles, (2) assess the timing of structural activity, and (3) construct the structural trend and structure contour maps.

Structural Identification and Annotation Criteria

High-Angle Faults

On our maps, we define high-angle faults as those with apparent dips in excess of 45° in the upper 1 to 2 km of section. We further classify them as normal, reverse, strike slip, or oblique slip depending on the relative sense of displacement of the rocks across the fault zone. The strike-slip component of displacement generally cannot be determined from two-dimensional (2–D) seismic records; therefore, we have not indicated the relative sense of displacement on the individual seismic sections. High-angle faults can be difficult to image directly with the 2–D seismic data collection techniques used in this investigation, particularly if dip angles exceed 60° (Yilmaz, 1987). This is especially true if the faults occur in areas of complex structure and (or) regions of reflections with low coherence. Therefore, our identification and mapping

of steeply dipping fault planes are based on a set of indirect criteria. The following observations on seismic records are considered indicators of steeply dipping fault planes:

- Abrupt termination of reflection events

- Vertical offset of reflector packages, such as regularly bedded strata or unconformity surfaces

- Vertical or subvertical arrays of hyperbolic diffraction patterns on nonmigrated displays

- Vertical or subvertical arrays of chaotic reflection patterns or zones devoid of internal reflections

- Sudden changes in reflector dips across a vertical or subvertical zone of anomalous reflectivity

- Vertical or subvertical aligned zones displaying localized bending of horizons that produced geometries congruent with drag folding or other fault-related geometries

- Changes in seismic character across boundaries that juxtapose images interpreted to indicate different structural styles

Any one of these features can result from causes other than faulting. However, a high probability of faulting is indicated by a combination of observations and the continuity of a sequence of events from line to line. Fault planes have been interpreted on the seismic sections only if two or more of these criteria are observed. We adopted this approach to add consistency to our definition of faulting as applied to a dataset with a wide variety of seismic data types and vertical and horizontal resolutions, as well as complex and different structural styles.

Adherence to the criteria also allows more consistent projection of faults into the deeper, lower resolution parts of the seismic data, where discontinuity of seismic reflection horizons within basement rocks may preclude direct recognition of either steeply dipping or listric fault planes. On our interpreted sections, many steeply dipping fault planes are shown extending downward as dashed lines to reflect the uncertainties in interpreting such events in the basement rock. In addition, some fault traces are extended upward to the seafloor on time sections, where there is little direct evidence on the CDP records for shallow displacements. This is done where nearby, or coincident, high-resolution data indicate the presence of near-surface deformation (for example, displaced beds, deformation of the post-late Wisconsin unconformity, and seafloor scarps). On the east side of the Hosgri Fault Zone, the evidence for faulting on the CDP records is augmented by analysis of individual high-resolution CDP and sparker lines (for example, the Aquatronics and Comap surveys in table 1).

Low-Angle Faults

Low-angle-fault planes (dips <45°) may be imaged directly by seismic data. However, as their dip approaches that of the local bedding planes, detection becomes more difficult. In the case of bedding-parallel horizontal detachments, the fault may be imaged, but it is for practical purposes indistin-

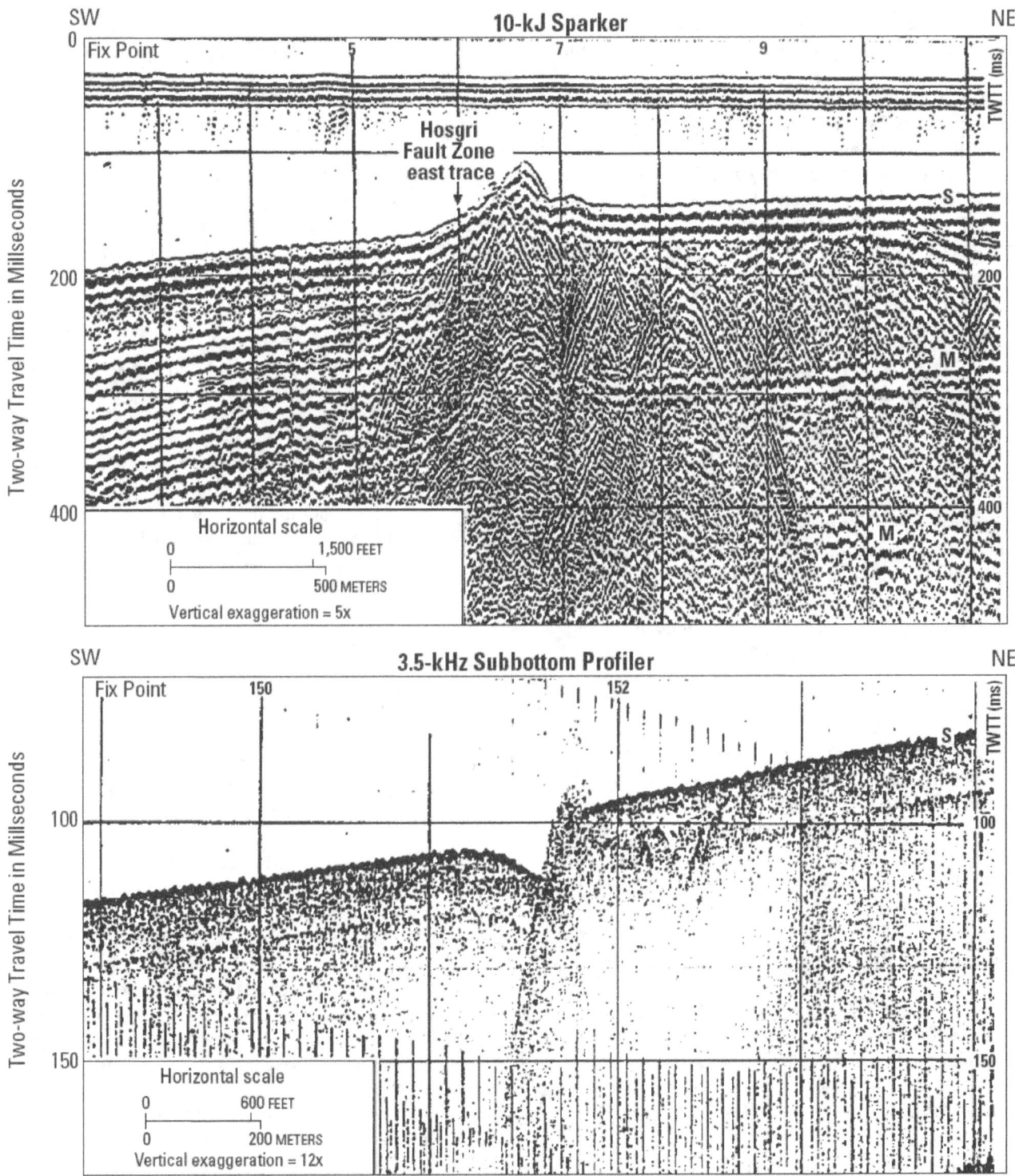

Figure 10. Seismic profiles showing two examples of near-surface structural features imaged by the high-resolution analog seismic systems along the central reaches of the Hosgri Fault Zone. Records showing seafloor displacements are one line of evidence indicating Holocene activity along some traces of the fault. The top image is from a sparker record collected in the 1970s. It shows a seafloor feature interpreted as a pressure ridge near the junction of the Hosgri and the Los Osos Fault Zones northwest of Point Buchon. There is an increase in seafloor slope to the southwest across the Hosgri Fault Zone. In the immediate vicinity of the fault zone, the seafloor slope increases east of fix point 5 and is uplifted about 25 m between fix points 5 and 7. The top of the ridge is approximately 25 m above the seafloor. The bottom image is a subbottom profile record from south of Point Buchon that shows post-late Wisconsin sediments overlying late Tertiary deposits. The seafloor is vertically displaced about 4 m across the fault trace, and the slope is slightly greater on the northeast side of the fault. On both images the seafloor reflector is labeled "S" and the seafloor multiple reflection is labeled "M".

guishable from bedding. Where low-angle faults are not bedding parallel, many of the seismic criteria listed for recognizing high-angle faults also apply.

Structural analysis and modeling of fold geometry provide another means for identifying low-angle faults. Two basic types of fault/fold relations were recognized in our analysis of the folds associated with the Hosgri Fault Zone: fault-propagation folds (Suppe and Medwedeff, 1984) and fault-bend folds (Suppe, 1983). Faults forming fault-propagation folds usually terminate in the interior of the fold, and the fault planes commonly are recognized on seismic records. Generally, there is little uncertainty associated with identifying and mapping the upper part of the fault plane, but the downdip extension of the fault may terminate in a bedding-parallel detachment that is not recognizable on the seismic records. In such cases, the downdip extension of the fault has been dashed.

Folds also form above bends or ramps of a thrust fault. The fault-ramp shape can be modeled from analysis of the fold geometry, but both the upper and lower levels of the detachment continue an unknown distance as subhorizontal detachments. Dashed lines also are used to indicate such possible extensions of the discontinuity. If the fault ramp is not apparent on the seismic record, its vertical location is generally uncertain, because modeling of the ramp position based on the fold shape usually allows a great deal of latitude in defining the vertical position of the associated discontinuity.

Folds

Folds axes are interpreted from the CDP seismic exploration data sets. Folds associated with major structural trends like the Purisima and Lompoc structures are labeled on the seismic profiles and the maps. Imbricate fault planes within these anticlinal structures are evident from repeat sections in some wells and are also evident and marked on some of the seismic profiles (see pl. 3).

Assessment of the Timing of Structural Activity

Where permitted by the seismic data, we estimate the relative ages of the most recent deformation that has occurred on both faults and folds. The relative age estimates are depicted by the use of different patterns for the fault traces and fold axes on the structural trend map (pl. 4).

Late Quaternary Activity on High-Angle Faults

The evidence for late Quaternary activity on the high-angle faults comes from two sources: (1) the analyses of the high-resolution geophysical data and (2) historical seismicity (McLaren and Savage, 2001).

Figure 10 is an example of the high-resolution analog data that are used to indicate the recency of activity for fault traces that are at, or near, the seafloor. The large vertical exaggeration and the higher frequency of the energy sources used for the analog records depict sediment and near-surface

structural features that are not typically resolved on exploration CDP data. The two records in figure 10 show seafloor features and slope changes that are interpreted to be images of late Quaternary deformation along the Hosgri Fault Zone.

Deposits of the surficial, unconsolidated, post-late Wisconsin sediments occur off the mouths of the major rivers as a thin veneer over nearshore bedrock outcrops and in small pockets that have formed within the Hosgri Fault Zone. These deposits are usually too thin to be resolved on the CDP exploration seismic reflection data but were mapped using the high-resolution analog and CDP seismic data (PG&E, 1988).

Post-Late Pliocene Fold and Thrust Fault Activity

The timing of latest deformation associated with folds and their underlying detachments is not as apparent as for the high-angle faults. Unless the fold deformation also involves the seafloor, the features may not be visible on the shallow-penetration, high-resolution data. Even where a seafloor slope indicates a fold, the detachment associated with the folding most likely remains buried. The youngest reflector that can be recognized over most of the offshore Santa Maria Basin is the early–late Pliocene unconformity. We have indicated on the maps where fold axes deform that unconformity and where the unconformity is not involved in the folding. The former case may be indicating structures that are active into the late Quaternary.

Relative Deformation Indicated by the Diagenetic Transformation Zone Reflections

The lower part of the Sisquoc Formation and the upper part of the Monterey Formation are composed of highly siliceous rocks that undergo substantial changes in physical properties due to silica-phase transformations. Silica in the form of Opal-A transforms to opal-CT, and opal-CT transforms to quartz. These transformations occur at relatively low temperatures and pressures as a result of burial diagenesis (Pisciotto, 1981; Isaacs, 1981; Murata and Larson, 1975). The factors that govern these transformations are generally considered to be temperature related to depth of burial and mineralogical composition. In both diagenetic transformations, rock volume decreases and rock density increases. This causes significant differences in the pre-transformation versus post-transformation acoustic properties of the sediments, including a large increase in P-wave velocity in the transformed rocks. As illustrated on figure 11, these changes in rock properties create changes in acoustic response that can be observed on seismic records. The temperature of phase transformation depends upon the amount of silica relative to terrigenous detritus (Isaacs, 1982). This dependency on lithologic composition of the rocks most likely is the reason that the seismic manifestation of the diagenetic transformation zone is not observed uniformly throughout the basin.

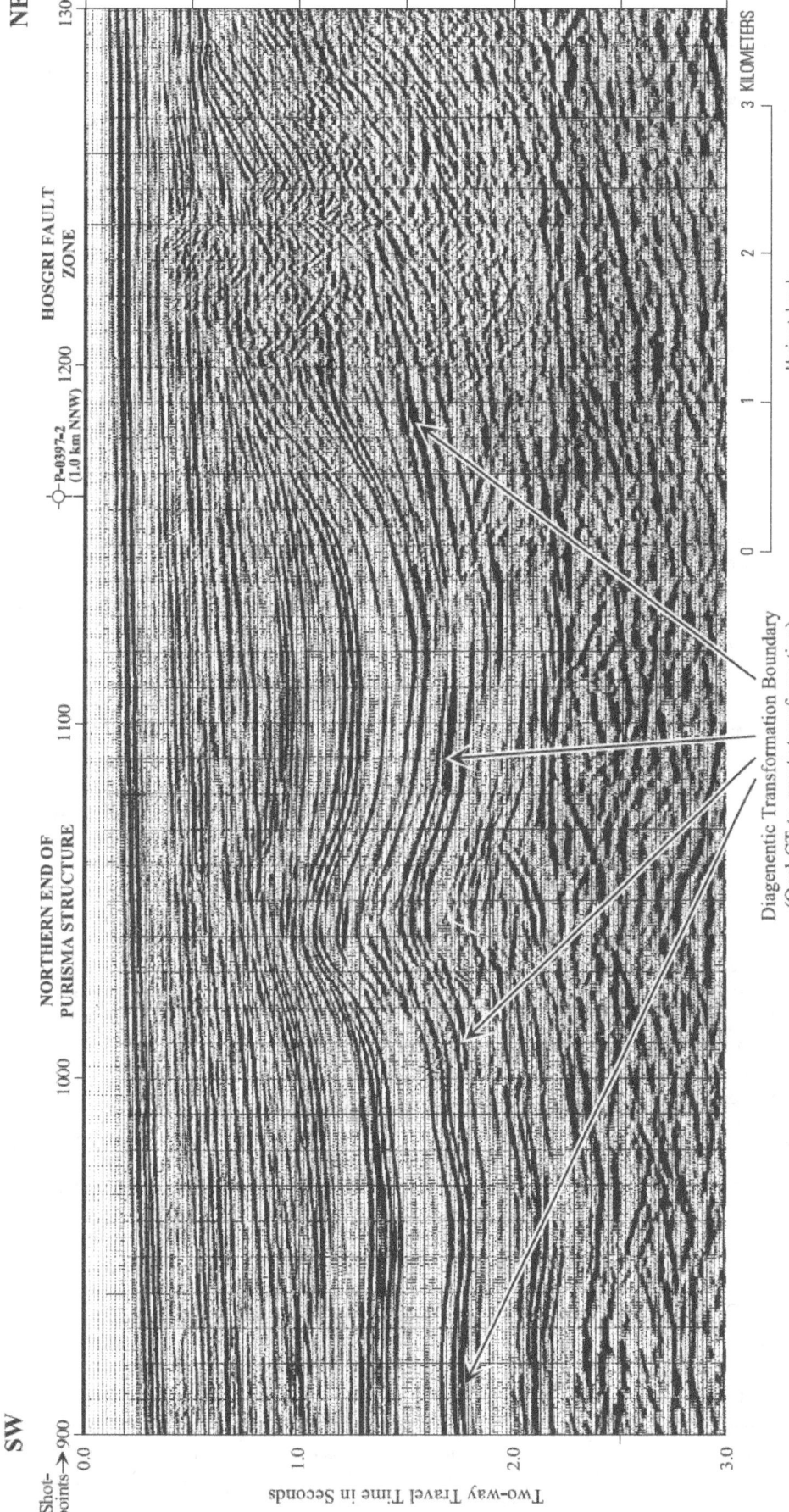

Figure 11. Seismic image showing a diagenetic transformation boundary attributed to the opal-CT-to-quartz transformation. The record is from line GSI-100, north of Point Sal (pl. 1), between the Hosgri Fault Zone and the north end of the Purisima structure. Between shotpoints 1150 and 1200, on the west side of the Hosgri Fault Zone, the diagenetic transformation boundary reflection is uplifted to the east but cuts across folded strata. This relation implies that folding began prior to formation of the transformation boundary. Between shotpoints 1000 and 1100, the diagenetic transformation boundary reflection is folded at the north end of the Purisima structure, suggesting that the fold formed after the formation of the transformation boundary. A common effect of the diagenetic transformation boundary seen on the seismic records is that the bedding images of the lower Sisquoc or Monterey Formations are suppressed beneath the boundary reflection. This effect is evident between shotpoints 900 and 1100.

The acoustic signatures of the two silica-phase transformations in the offshore Santa Maria Basin have the following characteristics:

- The opal-A to opal-CT boundary seldom is observed on seismic sections where the frequency response ranges are those typical for petroleum exploration (15 Hz to 60 Hz.).

- The opal-CT to quartz transformation produces a low-frequency seismic reflection on typical petroleum exploration CDP data (fig. 11).

- The opal-A to opal-CT and the opal-CT to quartz transformations are not observed on high-resolution seismic data.

- Both transformations suppress reflection amplitude and the variation in reflection amplitude within the transformed rocks. Therefore, the manner and extent of automatic gain compensation used in processing is a major factor in the extent to which these transformations can be observed on seismic data.

The extent of amplitude reduction associated with the opal-CT to quartz transformation is sufficient on many seismic lines in the basin to render parts of the lower Sisquoc and upper Monterey Formations acoustically transparent (fig. 11, pl. 3). Moderate- and high-amplitude reflection events associated with unaltered middle and upper members of the Monterey Formation abruptly terminate where they encounter the less steeply dipping diagenetic front (fig. 11), causing seismic images related to the diagenetic front to cut across structure. In limited areas of the offshore Santa Maria Basin, the opal-CT to quartz transformation may be correlated between seismic lines.

Structural deformation can be dated relative to the time of formation of the opal-CT to quartz phase transformation. Because this transformation is a mineral-phase boundary related to temperature and pressure, it forms synchronously over areas of the basin that have similar sedimentary composition and depth of burial. Therefore, it can be used as a marker horizon initially established at approximately the same depth below the seafloor. It will crosscut existing geologic structures and will be deformed by geologic movements subsequent to its formation. The section on figure 11 (line GSI-100, west of San Luis Obispo Bay and approximately halfway between Point San Luis and Point Sal on plate 1) shows the involvement of the opal-CT to quartz transformation boundary in the folding of the northern part of the Purisima structure and only a gentle upwarp of the transformation signature west of the Hosgri Fault Zone. There is no involvement of the opal-CT to quartz transformation in the complex folding directly west of the Hosgri Fault Zone at this location. These observations suggest the Purisima structure postdates the folding west of the Hosgri Fault Zone.

Structural Trend Map

A map of the structural trends of the Hosgri Fault Zone and adjacent offshore structures is presented on plate 4 at a scale of 1:200,000. A simplified version of the map is presented at a reduced scale on figure 12.

Both the high-resolution and CDP exploration seismic-reflection data were used to map the continuity and locations of individual high-angle-fault traces. In many locations, the use of a dense data grid gave a more complex picture of the Hosgri Fault Zone than would be expected from examination of widely spaced CDP lines. The Hosgri Fault Zone typically consists of two or more traces embedded within a complex zone of faulting and folding. Heavier lines denote the primary traces of the fault zone. The criteria used to identify the primary traces include (1) evidence of late Quaternary activity associated with apparent progressive displacements over a long period of geologic time; (2) lateral and downdip continuity; and (3) position of the trace as a major boundary, either at the margin of a sedimentary basin or between different structural trends. At locations where one trace is dying out and displacement is apparently being transferred to another trace, both traces may be designated as primary. Fault traces are dashed on the structural trends map (pl. 4, fig. 12), where lateral continuity is not definitively established but is strongly suggested by the form and relations of the associated structures. This most commonly occurs where either the fault trends are dying out into the limbs of folds or the data are not spaced closely enough to allow a one-to-one correlation of fault traces.

Low-angle faults are also indicated as primary or secondary on the structural trend maps (pls. 4–7). Those with a length of 10 km or greater are designated as primary and shown in a bold line. These faults normally do not reach the seafloor, and their traces have been mapped where the vertical projection of the upper fault tip, or ramp for fault-bend folds, would intersect the seafloor. Low-angle faults that cut the early–late Pliocene unconformity, or whose associated folds deform that surface, are considered potentially active and are shown as solid or dashed lines. Also, low-angle faults are classified as potentially active if there are no marker horizons (unconformities or diagenetic zone reflections) on which to base recency of activity. Low-angle faults and associated folds that do not deform the early–late Pliocene unconformity were considered inactive and denoted by dotted lines.

Fold axes are mapped using both analog high-resolution and CDP reflection data. The former are useful on the east side of the Hosgri Fault Zone where CDP data commonly do not have the resolution to image the tight, near-surface folds. In the area of the Purisima and Lompoc structures south of Point Sal, (pl. 4, fig. 12), there are many overlapping folds that have plunging axes. In general, these major structures are composed of a series of closely spaced parallel to subparallel plunging folds. This is also true of the Piedras Blancas anticlinorium at the north end of the map (pl. 4, fig. 12). Basement topographic trends are not mapped as structural trends unless they are associated with deformation that penetrates into the shallower part of the sedimentary column or have some evidence of involvement in Neogene deformation. Unless there were other data to the contrary, folds that show Neogene deformation and also affect the

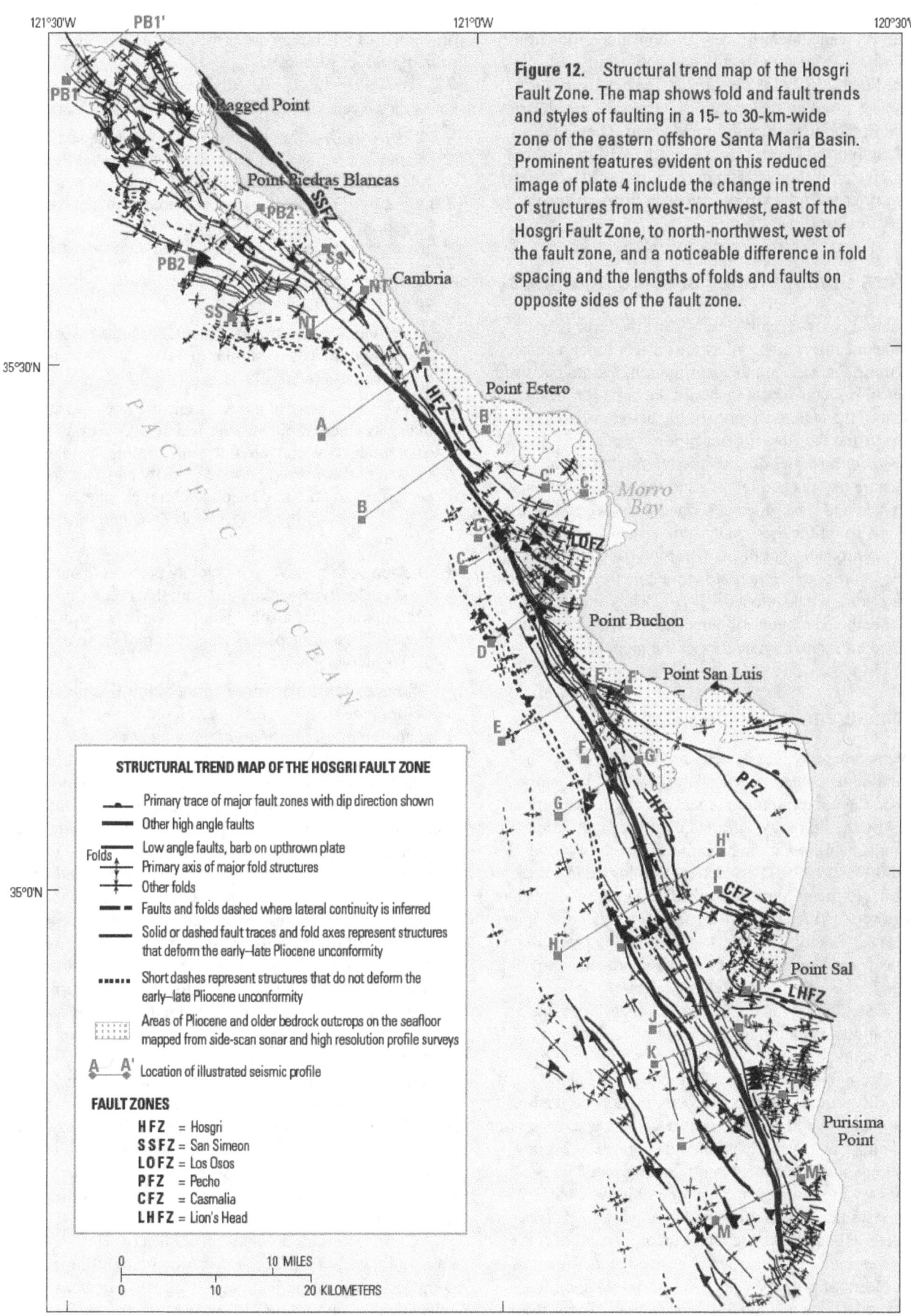

Figure 12. Structural trend map of the Hosgri Fault Zone. The map shows fold and fault trends and styles of faulting in a 15- to 30-km-wide zone of the eastern offshore Santa Maria Basin. Prominent features evident on this reduced image of plate 4 include the change in trend of structures from west-northwest, east of the Hosgri Fault Zone, to north-northwest, west of the fault zone, and a noticeable difference in fold spacing and the lengths of folds and faults on opposite sides of the fault zone.

STRUCTURAL TREND MAP OF THE HOSGRI FAULT ZONE

Primary trace of major fault zones with dip direction shown

Other high angle faults

Low angle faults, barb on upthrown plate

Folds — Primary axis of major fold structures

Other folds

Faults and folds dashed where lateral continuity is inferred

Solid or dashed fault traces and fold axes represent structures that deform the early–late Pliocene unconformity

Short dashes represent structures that do not deform the early–late Pliocene unconformity

Areas of Pliocene and older bedrock outcrops on the seafloor mapped from side-scan sonar and high resolution profile surveys

A — A'   Location of illustrated seismic profile

FAULT ZONES

HFZ = Hosgri
SSFZ = San Simeon
LOFZ = Los Osos
PFZ = Pecho
CFZ = Casmalia
LHFZ = Lion's Head

early–late Pliocene unconformity are considered potentially active. Folds that do not affect that unconformity are considered inactive. Folds also are designated as primary or secondary based on their size. Primary folds are shown by a thick line on the structural trends map. They have an overall length of 10 km or more, a width of 1 km or more, and a relative amplitude of 500 m or more. Although these are arbitrary criteria, they provide easily distinguishable characteristics for illustration.

Structure Contour Maps of Unconformities

Structure contour maps (pls. 5–7) of the three major basin-wide unconformities reflect the current topographic relief of these surfaces and the deformation that has occurred since their formation. These maps are the basis for the discussion of the tectonic history of the eastern offshore Santa Maria Basin and the Hosgri Fault zone.

The unconformities are initially interpreted on the time-based seismic records and loop-tied to form a 3–D grid of points in x, y, and time for each surface. However, when the vertical axis is in time, horizontal and vertical variations in velocity can produce significant distortions of true subsurface geometry. In order to produce structure contour maps without such distortions, we developed a 3–D velocity model that provides depth conversions of points anywhere within the vertical and horizontal boundaries of the model.

The Velocity Model

To construct the 3–D velocity model, we use the "layer-cake" method described by Marsden (1989). This method is based on the assumption that rock velocity is determined primarily by the lithology, age, and degree of induration of rock units achieved at their maximum depth of burial (Grant and West, 1965). Two factors, lithology and degree of induration, are the primary controls of the bulk modulus and density of rock, which, in turn, are the elements governing rock P-wave velocity. The effect of overburden pressure on velocity is considered secondary in this approach and is not addressed in this velocity-modeling scenario.

Because lithology is the primary element in defining rock formations, velocity layers commonly coincide with formation boundaries. Also, because velocity is linked to age, velocity boundaries also frequently correspond to unconformity surfaces. Hence, velocity models derived using the layer-cake method assign constant velocities to rock units bounded either by distinctive lithologies or unconformities. This assignment of velocities to lithostratigraphic units that may vary in thickness and geometry allows us to accommodate lateral variations in the velocity field. The layer-cake method allows the direct incorporation of borehole velocity data, seismically derived velocities, and any other form of primary velocity control into a unified regional model. The method also places geologic constraints on velocities when they are projected into areas of sparse primary velocity control.

The following steps describe the procedure that we used to construct the velocity model for the offshore Santa Maria Basin:

- Velocity values were obtained from borehole sonic logs, seismic refraction data, seismic stacking velocities, and velocity information obtained from pre-stack depth migration. These data were compared with geologic formation boundaries and unconformities. In this manner, geologic boundaries were associated with velocity units.

- Velocity units were assigned values based on the primary velocity information.

- Velocity units were mapped in a loop-tied network throughout the basin (similar to a two-dimensional seismic interpretation).

- At every kilometer along each seismic line, and at shorter intervals where rapid structural changes occur, the layer-cake model was converted to pairs of time/average-velocity values. In this sense, iterative velocity analyses were performed to take into account lateral changes in velocity in the vicinity of the Hosgri Fault Zone and other structures within the basin.

- The suite of time/average-velocity pairs were input into a 3–D velocity-modeling program that creates a suite of isotime maps that display velocity variation within the time planes. These time planes extend from 0.0 s to 3.0 s, in 0.33-s increments.

Sources for the offshore Santa Maria Basin velocity model include seismic stacking velocities, seismic refraction data, and velocity information from eight of the offshore wells (table 3). The model is primarily dependent on information derived from seismic data. More than 1,500 average velocity columns were computed from root-mean-square stacking velocities along CDP seismic lines distributed throughout the area of interest. The velocity volume derived from these data was compared and calibrated against offshore wells for which check-shot data and (or) vertical seismic profiles were available. The velocity profiles from seven of these wells are shown on either figure 9 or plate 3. The annotations on the velocity profiles illustrate the relation of velocity to both unconformities and formation boundaries. There is little or no velocity increase associated with the early–late Pliocene unconformity. The top of Miocene unconformity typically is marked by no velocity increase or a small velocity inversion followed by a gradual increase in velocity. The top of the Monterey Formation is distinguished by a distinct velocity increase. However, because of the difficulty of recognizing and mapping this horizon using the seismic profiles, it was necessary to select other horizons that could be mapped throughout the basin for use as boundaries in the velocity model.

Construction of a velocity volume covering more than 5,000 km^2 of surface area to a depth of 3 km is a computationally significant task, especially in areas of low seismic data density and well control. To facilitate this

Table 6. The 3–D velocity model key components. The 3–D velocity model is derived from the integration of available well velocity logs and seismic stacking velocity data. Average interval velocity values are assigned to the rock horizons bounded by the unconformities. In the model, major changes in velocity occur at the sea floor, top of Miocene unconformity, and top of pre-Miocene basement unconformity. There is little or no velocity change across the early-late Pliocene unconformity. Figure 13 shows a vertical slice through the 3–D velocity model.

Geologic age	Rock units and stratigraphic boundaries	Velocities (m/sec)
Holocene	Sea water	1,500
Sea floor		
Holocene to late Pliocene	Unnamed sedimentary rocks and sediments	1,770
Early–late Pliocene unconformity		
Early Pliocene	Sisquoc Formation (upper part)	1,770
Top of Miocene unconformity		
Early to late Miocene	Sisquoc Formation (lower part), Monterey, Point Sal, and Obispo Formations	2,638
Local unconformity		
Eocene and older	Paleogene sedimentary formations	2,638
Top of pre-Miocene basement unconformity		
Primarily Cretaceous and older rocks	Seismic basement rocks consisting primarily of Franciscan Complex but locally including remnants of Paleogene volcanic rocks, Great Valley Sequence, and Coast Range Ophiolite	3,800

effort, the model uses the major unconformities that can be mapped throughout the offshore Santa Maria Basin to define its lithostratigraphic units. The velocity values assigned to these units are listed in table 6. Figure 13 is a schematic two-dimensional slice through the 3–D velocity model. In this model the velocity boundaries are placed at the seafloor, top of Miocene unconformity, and top of pre-Miocene basement unconformity.

The lower part of the Sisquoc Formation, the upper part of the Monterey Formation, and the early Miocene formations are merged with an assigned velocity of 2,638 m/s. The velocity profiles (fig. 9, pl. 3) would suggest nominal velocities in the range of 1,900 to 2,200 m/s for the lower part of the Sisquoc Formation, 2,700 to 3,500 m/s for the Monterey Formation, and 3,000 to 3,800 m/s for the early Miocene Obispo Formation. The relatively large thickness of the lower Sisquoc Formation compared to the two other units results in the average velocity being at the lower end of the Monterey Formation velocity range. Similarly, remnants of Paleogene rock units were merged with the basement, which was assigned a velocity of 3,800 m/s even though measured velocities are in the range of 3,000 to 4,500 m/s.

Downward-continuation-based, pre-stack depth-migration processing performed on selected lines in 1990 (fig. 4) produced vertical velocity structures similar to those used in the velocity model. In addition, the velocities were compared with published information (Hatton and others, 1981; Howie and others, 1993; Shih and Levander, 1994). These studies compare well with our model, with the exception of Shih and Levander (1994). Their model shows good correspondence in the shallower part of the sedimentary section, but their deep-sediment velocities are about 25 percent slower than ours.

Figure 13. Figure showing a representative cross section through the 3–D velocity model. The model was developed to convert the three unconformity horizons identified in the seismic time sections to structural contour maps in elevation below mean lower low water (MLLW). The seafloor early–late Pliocene unconformity layer and the early–late Pliocene unconformity/top of Miocene unconformity layer represent different rock units but are assigned the same velocity. They are separated in the model for consistency in annotation because either one, or both, of the layers are occasionally absent in parts of the basin.

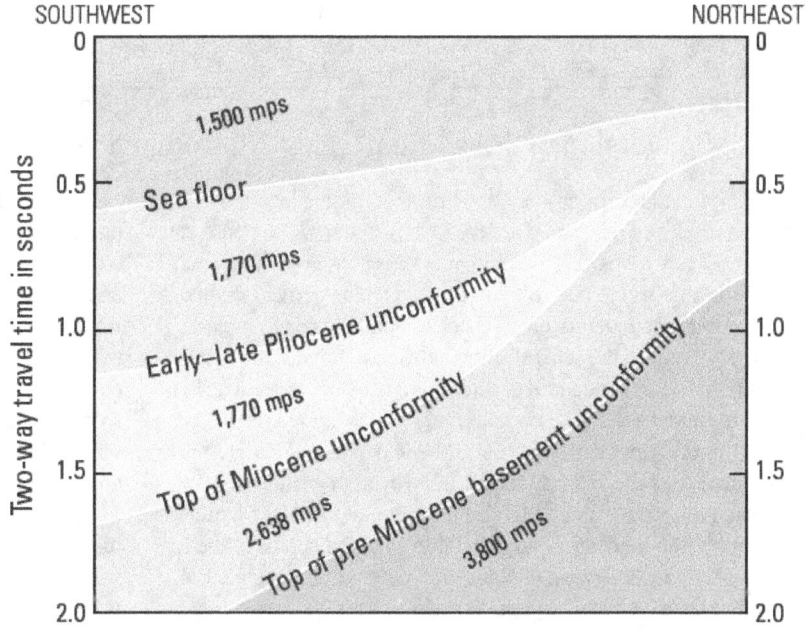

Table 7. List of interpreted horizon depths from 29 wells used in this study. These data are used as primary tie points in the interpretation of the seismic records and in the construction of the structure contour maps of the three major unconformities. The types of data available from the individual wells are summarized in table 2. The values in this table represent our interpretations of the depths below mean lower low water (MLLW) to the sea floor, top, and base of the Monterey Formation, and the three mapped unconformities (early–late Pliocene, top of Miocene, and top of pre-Miocene basement). The depths are based on our analyses of the well logs and paleontological data. NP, mapped unconformity is not present in the well; NR, pre-Miocene basement unconformity was not reached by the well. *, Sorlien and others (1999b) interpreted horizons in five of the listed wells. Minor differences between our interpreted horizon depths and those of Sorlien and others (1999b) are less than 10 percent of the listed values.

Well No. P-#	Sea floor	Early–Late Pliocene	Top of Miocene	Top Monterey Formation	Base Monterey Formation	Top pre-Miocene basement	Bottom of well
				Depth below mean lower low water (m)			
0060-1*	168	701	1,032	1,662	2,019	NR	2,434
0395-1	236	841	1,084	1,542	1,895	NR	2,355
0396-1	169	732	914	1,582	2,087	2,345	2,351
0397-1	97	320	403	736	852	1,006	1,092
0397-2	125	503	911	1,766	2,176	2,405	2,426
0402-1	198	927	1,210	1,995	2,512	2,588	2,622
0406-1	413	737	928	1,248	1,601	NR	1,728
0409-3	109	582	1,052	1,764	2,646	NR	2,899
0409-4	153	594	1,024	1,817	2,163	NR	2,234
0411-1	365	NP	NP	761	1,389	1,537	1,605
0413-1*	310	658	780	1,143	1,391	NR	1,489
0415-1	128	365	412	1,382	2,058	2,898	3,000
0415-2	116	NP	466	1,057	1,627	1,752	1,951
0416-1	134	NP	298	727	1,252	1,307	1,807
0422-1	105	NP	579	1,585	2,390	2,499	2,508
0424-1*	156	405	610	911	1,024	1,076	1,201
0425-1	122	NP	NP	672	888	NR	1,099
0425-2	123	400	1,162	1,337	1,578	1,627	1,731
0426-1	91	NP	406	1,472	2,174	2,390	2,433
0427-1	80	NP	NP	658	1,225	NR	1,848
0430-1	99	NP	496	1,091	1,539	1,593	1,740
0434-1	95	NP	NP	1,085	1,502	NR	1,772
0435-1	75	297	461	1,360	1,903	1,903	2,074
0440-1	81	503	811	1,184	1,380	1,403	1,680
0440-2	93	580	1,150	1,432	1,537	1,537	1,768
0443-1*	271	722	1,103	1,344	1,489	2,082	2,119
0443-2	227	904	1,162	1,442	1,585	1,595	1,746
0444-1	66	NP	549	1,560	2,209	2,434	2,451
0496-1*	366	564	786	1,016	1,155	1,383	1,845

Depth Conversion and Well Ties

Depth values for any x-y and time-coordinate location within the boundaries of the model are created by extrapolation between the isovelocity maps. The velocity model is then applied to each unconformity grid to convert it to depth. Depths derived in this manner are subsequently cross-checked and adjusted to match depth estimates to the unconformity surfaces derived from 29 wells (table 7) in the central and southern offshore Santa Maria Basin to produce the final contour maps.

A formal error analysis has not been conducted to determine the accuracy of the velocity model. However, in most cases, the depths predicted by the model tied to within 6 percent or better with our borehole determinations (table 7) of the depths to the top of pre-Miocene basement unconformity and within 1 percent to 3 percent for the two overlying unconformities.

Structure Contour Map Parameters

The structure contour maps of the three unconformities are presented at a scale of 1:200,000 on plates 5, 6, and 7 and at reduced scales as figures 14, 15, and 16. Well control is shown on the plates and depths are listed in table 7. Faults that displace the unconformities are shown on the respective maps. The contour intervals of the three maps reflect our estimates of the accuracies (±0.5 of the contour interval) of the depth estimates from the seismic reflection records and the application of the velocity model. The contour interval for the structure contour map of the top of pre-Miocene basement unconformity (pl. 5, fig. 14) is 250 m with an estimated accuracy of ±125 m. The contour interval for the top of Miocene unconformity map (pl. 6, fig. 15) is 100 m with an estimated accuracy of ±50 m, and the contour interval for the early–late Pliocene unconformity map (pl. 7, fig. 16) is 50 m with an estimated accuracy of ±25 m.

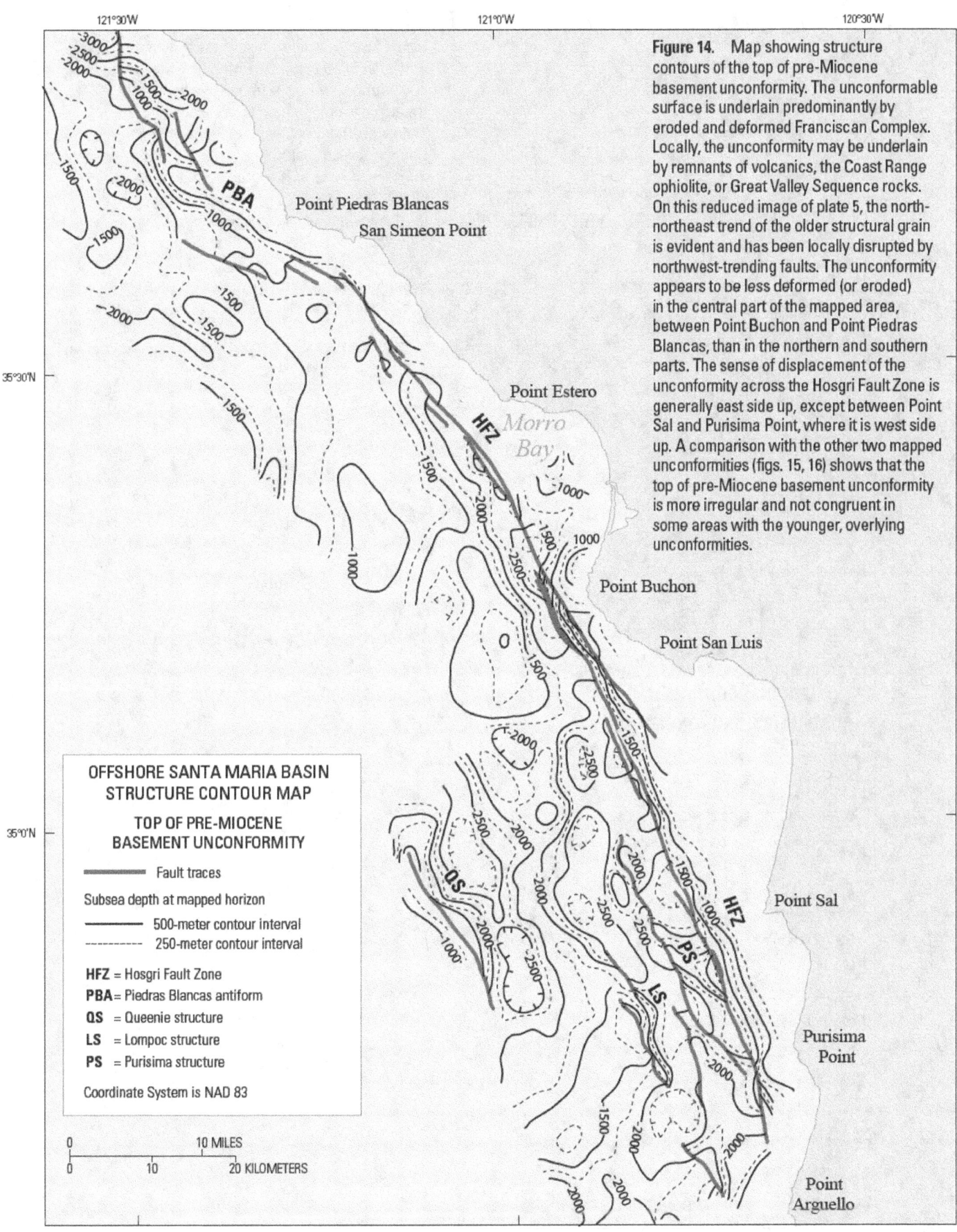

Figure 14. Map showing structure contours of the top of pre-Miocene basement unconformity. The unconformable surface is underlain predominantly by eroded and deformed Franciscan Complex. Locally, the unconformity may be underlain by remnants of volcanics, the Coast Range ophiolite, or Great Valley Sequence rocks. On this reduced image of plate 5, the north-northeast trend of the older structural grain is evident and has been locally disrupted by northwest-trending faults. The unconformity appears to be less deformed (or eroded) in the central part of the mapped area, between Point Buchon and Point Piedras Blancas, than in the northern and southern parts. The sense of displacement of the unconformity across the Hosgri Fault Zone is generally east side up, except between Point Sal and Purisima Point, where it is west side up. A comparison with the other two mapped unconformities (figs. 15, 16) shows that the top of pre-Miocene basement unconformity is more irregular and not congruent in some areas with the younger, overlying unconformities.

OFFSHORE SANTA MARIA BASIN
STRUCTURE CONTOUR MAP

TOP OF PRE-MIOCENE
BASEMENT UNCONFORMITY

Fault traces

Subsea depth at mapped horizon

500-meter contour interval

250-meter contour interval

HFZ = Hosgri Fault Zone
PBA = Piedras Blancas antiform
QS = Queenie structure
LS = Lompoc structure
PS = Purisima structure

Coordinate System is NAD 83

0   10 MILES

0   10   20 KILOMETERS

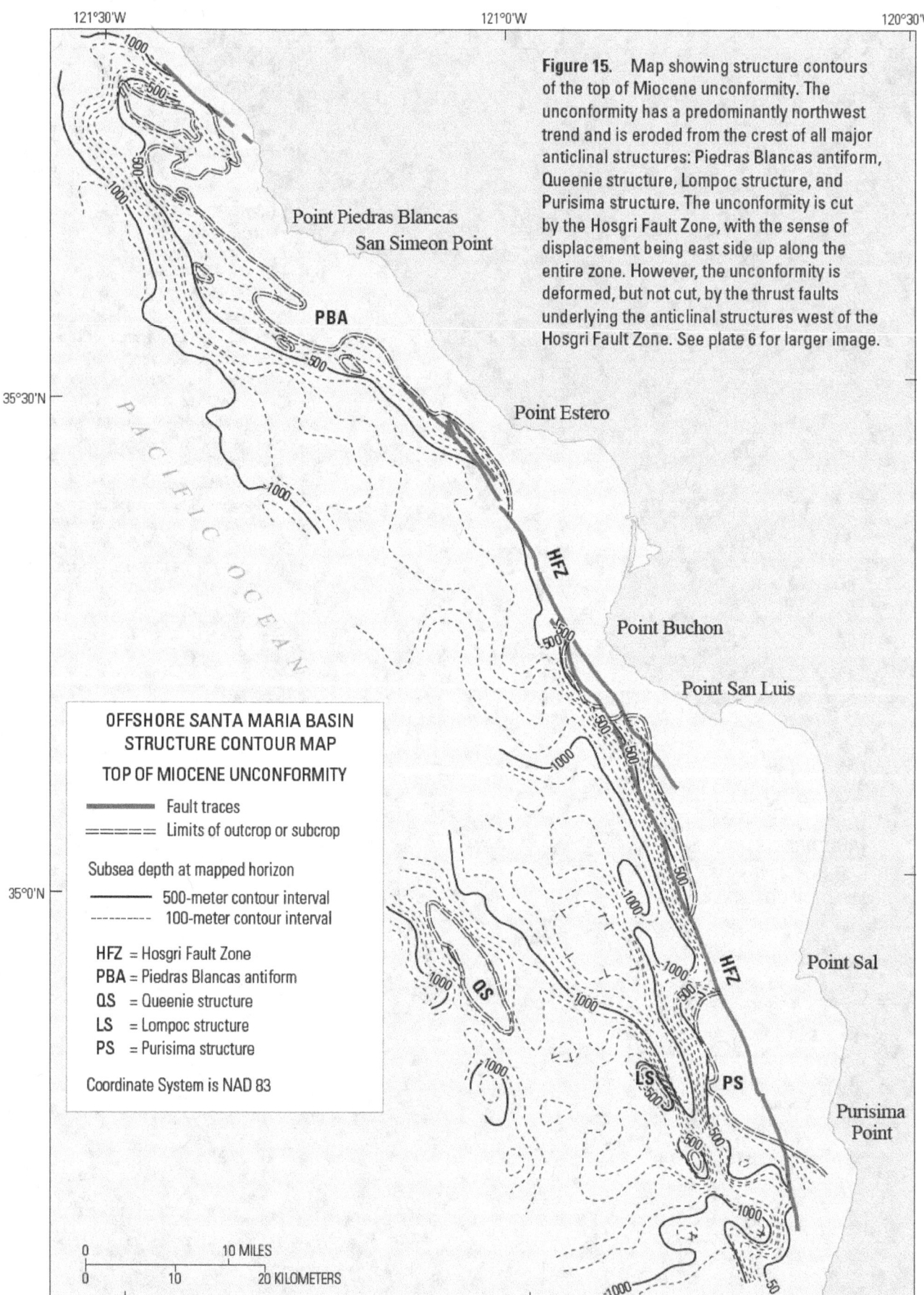

Figure 15.   Map showing structure contours of the top of Miocene unconformity. The unconformity has a predominantly northwest trend and is eroded from the crest of all major anticlinal structures: Piedras Blancas antiform, Queenie structure, Lompoc structure, and Purisima structure. The unconformity is cut by the Hosgri Fault Zone, with the sense of displacement being east side up along the entire zone. However, the unconformity is deformed, but not cut, by the thrust faults underlying the anticlinal structures west of the Hosgri Fault Zone. See plate 6 for larger image.

OFFSHORE SANTA MARIA BASIN
STRUCTURE CONTOUR MAP

TOP OF MIOCENE UNCONFORMITY

Fault traces
Limits of outcrop or subcrop

Subsea depth at mapped horizon
500-meter contour interval
100-meter contour interval

HFZ = Hosgri Fault Zone
PBA = Piedras Blancas antiform
QS = Queenie structure
LS = Lompoc structure
PS = Purisima structure

Coordinate System is NAD 83

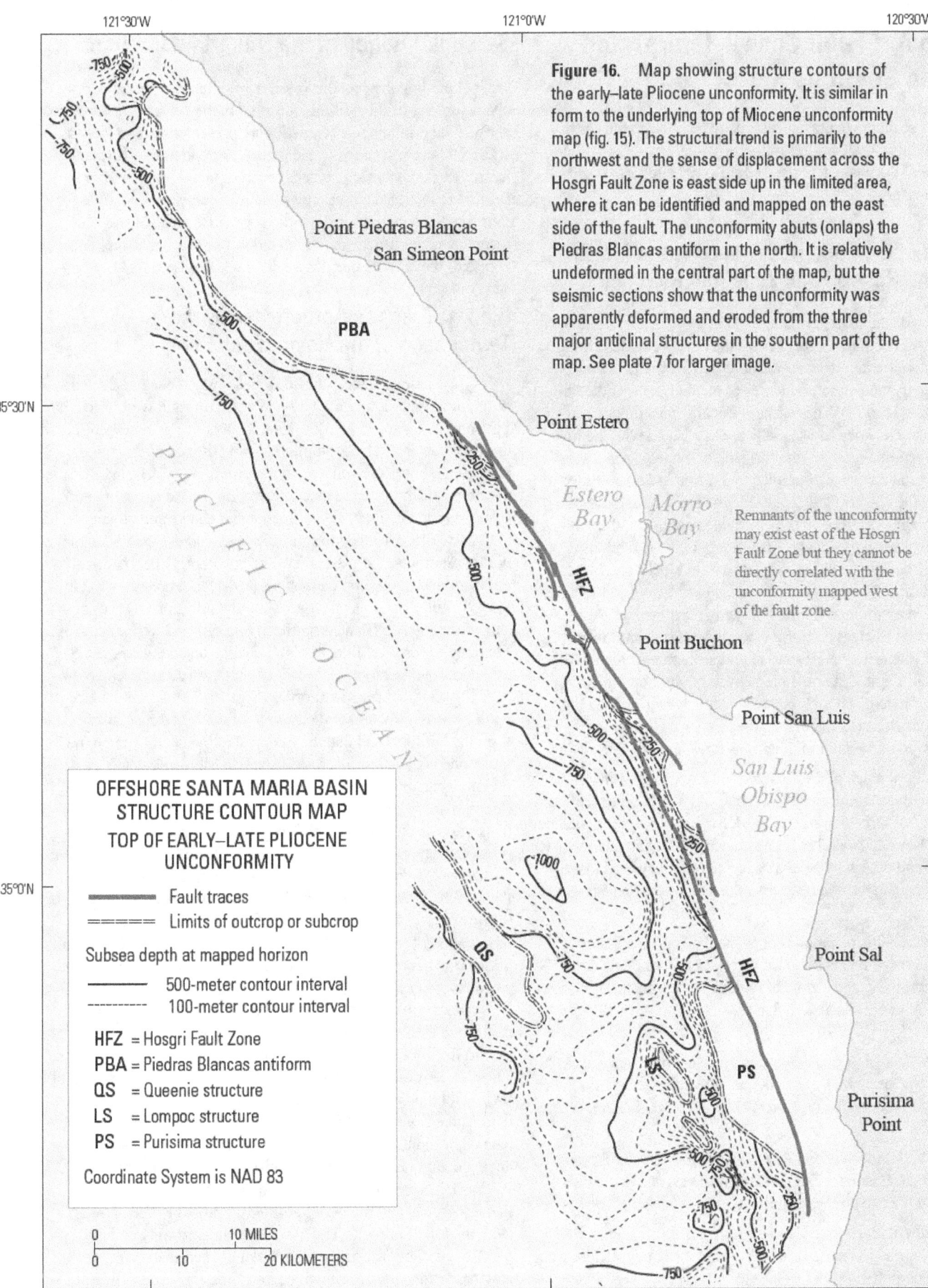

Figure 16. Map showing structure contours of the early–late Pliocene unconformity. It is similar in form to the underlying top of Miocene unconformity map (fig. 15). The structural trend is primarily to the northwest and the sense of displacement across the Hosgri Fault Zone is east side up in the limited area, where it can be identified and mapped on the east side of the fault. The unconformity abuts (onlaps) the Piedras Blancas antiform in the north. It is relatively undeformed in the central part of the map, but the seismic sections show that the unconformity was apparently deformed and eroded from the three major anticlinal structures in the southern part of the map. See plate 7 for larger image.

Remnants of the unconformity may exist east of the Hosgri Fault Zone but they cannot be directly correlated with the unconformity mapped west of the fault zone.

Point Piedras Blancas
San Simeon Point

PBA

Point Estero

Estero Bay   *Morro Bay*

HFZ

Point Buchon

Point San Luis

San Luis Obispo Bay

Point Sal

Purisima Point

PS

HFZ

PACIFIC OCEAN

QS

LS

121°30'W   121°0'W   120°30'W

35°30'N

35°0'N

OFFSHORE SANTA MARIA BASIN
STRUCTURE CONTOUR MAP
TOP OF EARLY–LATE PLIOCENE
UNCONFORMITY

—————— Fault traces
====== Limits of outcrop or subcrop

Subsea depth at mapped horizon

—————— 500-meter contour interval
------------ 100-meter contour interval

HFZ = Hosgri Fault Zone
PBA = Piedras Blancas antiform
QS = Queenie structure
LS = Lompoc structure
PS = Purisima structure

Coordinate System is NAD 83

0   10 MILES
0   10   20 KILOMETERS

The Hosgri Fault Zone—Interpreted Seismic Sections

In this section, we present a sequence of interpreted seismic profiles and large-scale figures of the structural trends along with discussions of the characteristics of the Hosgri Fault Zone and adjacent structures.

Division of the Eastern Offshore Santa Maria Basin and Hosgri Fault Zone into Reaches

We divide the eastern offshore Santa Maria Basin and the Hosgri Fault Zone into six reaches for the purpose of describing and illustrating variations in strike, downdip geometry, along-strike geometry, and structural trends of the fault zone and adjacent structures (fig. 17). The reaches typically have unique sets of physical characteristics and spatially are associated with the major onshore structural blocks on the east side of the fault zone. Most of the structural blocks are bounded by faults that trend oblique to the trend of the Hosgri Fault Zone, and the reach boundaries are placed at the intersections or projected intersections of these block-bounding faults and the Hosgri Fault Zone. Lettis and others (2004) provide a discussion of the onshore structural blocks and block-bounding faults. The structural trend maps and associated seismic illustrations are provided for the following reaches:

- The Piedras Blancas antiform extends southeastward from north of Point Piedras Blancas to the northern termination of the Hosgri Fault Zone offshore between Point San Simeon and Point Estero. Though not technically a reach of the Hosgri Fault Zone this area establishes the relation of the northern termination of the fault to other structures in the region.

- The northern reach of the Hosgri Fault Zone extends from the northern termination of the fault zone south to the intersection with the Los Osos Fault Zone in Morro Bay. This reach includes the San Simeon/Hosgri pull-apart basin (Lettis and others, 1990; Hanson and others, 2004) that is formed between the Hosgri Fault Zone and the southeastern extension of the San Simeon Fault Zone.

- The San Luis/Pismo reach is opposite the San Luis/Pismo structural block and is bounded by the Los Osos Fault Zone on the northwest and a zone of faulting, including the Pecho, Wilmar Avenue, Olson, and San Luis Bay Faults, on the southeast (fig. 17, pl. 4).

- The San Luis Obispo Bay reach is opposite the Santa Maria Valley structural block and is bounded by the intersection with the Pecho Fault on the northwest and the Casmalia Fault on the southeast.

- The Point Sal reach is opposite the Casmalia structural block between the Casmalia Fault on the northwest and the Lion's Head Fault Zone on the southeast.

- The southern reach extends south from the Point Sal reach to the southern termination of the Hosgri Fault Zone offshore from Point Pedernales north of Point Arguello.

Seismic Images of the Hosgri Fault Zone

The following sections discuss and illustrate the primary characteristics of the faulting observed in the six reaches described above. The primary characteristics are presented in map view as 1:200,000-scale sections of the structural trend map (pl. 4) and in profile (vertical) view as selected interpreted profiles from the seismic reflection data set. The seismic sections are chosen to illustrate the complexity, downdip geometry, sense of slip, and most recent behavior of faulting in the individual reaches. Noninterpreted copies of the seismic profiles are included in appendix B.

Piedras Blancas Antiform to Northern Termination of the Hosgri Fault Zone

The Piedras Blancas antiform lies north of the interpreted northern termination of the Hosgri Fault Zone and west of the San Simeon Fault Zone (figs. 12, 17; pl. 4). It is a large basement-cored uplift characterized by multiple folds and thrust faults formed in response to northeast-southwest compression (PG&E, 1988). Some previous illustrations and characterizations of the Hosgri Fault Zone (Hoskins and Griffiths, 1971; Buchannan-Banks and others, 1978; D.S. McCulloch, oral commun., 1989) extend the fault zone to the northwest around the west end of the antiform. Other maps and publications have followed Leslie's (1981) interpretation that the Hosgri Fault Zone joins the San Simeon Fault Zone on the south side of the Piedras Blancas antiform (Greene and Kennedy, 1989; Jennings, 1994; McCulloch, 1987; Dickinson and others, 2005).

Our interpretation, documented in the structural trend map (fig. 18, pl. 4) and seismic profiles (figs. 19–22), is that the Hosgri Fault Zone terminates southeast of the folds and thrust faults that form the antiform and that the majority of the lateral slip on the fault zone is transferred across to the San Simeon Fault Zone in a region displaying geometry similar to a right-releasing stepover (Hanson and others, 2004). Lettis and others (1990) interpret this region as the San Simeon/Hosgri pull-apart basin. It is also possible that a part of the lateral motion on the Hosgri Fault Zone is absorbed in the compressional deformation of the southwest flank of the Piedras Blancas antiform in a manner similar to that proposed by Sorlien and others (1999b) for the southern termination of the Hosgri Fault Zone. Worden (1992) notes similar dissipation of strike-slip motion into compressional folding at the terminations of strike-slip faults in other areas.

The complex fold and fault structures that form the offshore part of the Piedras Blancas antiform are shown on figure 18. They extend from south of Point San Simeon to north of Ragged Point. These structures were mapped from a relatively dense network of high-resolution and moderate-penetration CDP seismic reflection data with an average line spacing of 1.5 to 2 km (pl. 1). These data were supplemented with a similar network of high-resolution analog data. The four illustrated seismic profiles that cross the Piedras Blancas antiform show evidence of folding that began in the Miocene and regional uplift that is probably still active. Both the top of pre-Miocene basement unconformity and the top of Miocene unconformity have been eroded over parts of the antiform (figs. 14, 15; pls. 5, 6) and the early–late Pliocene

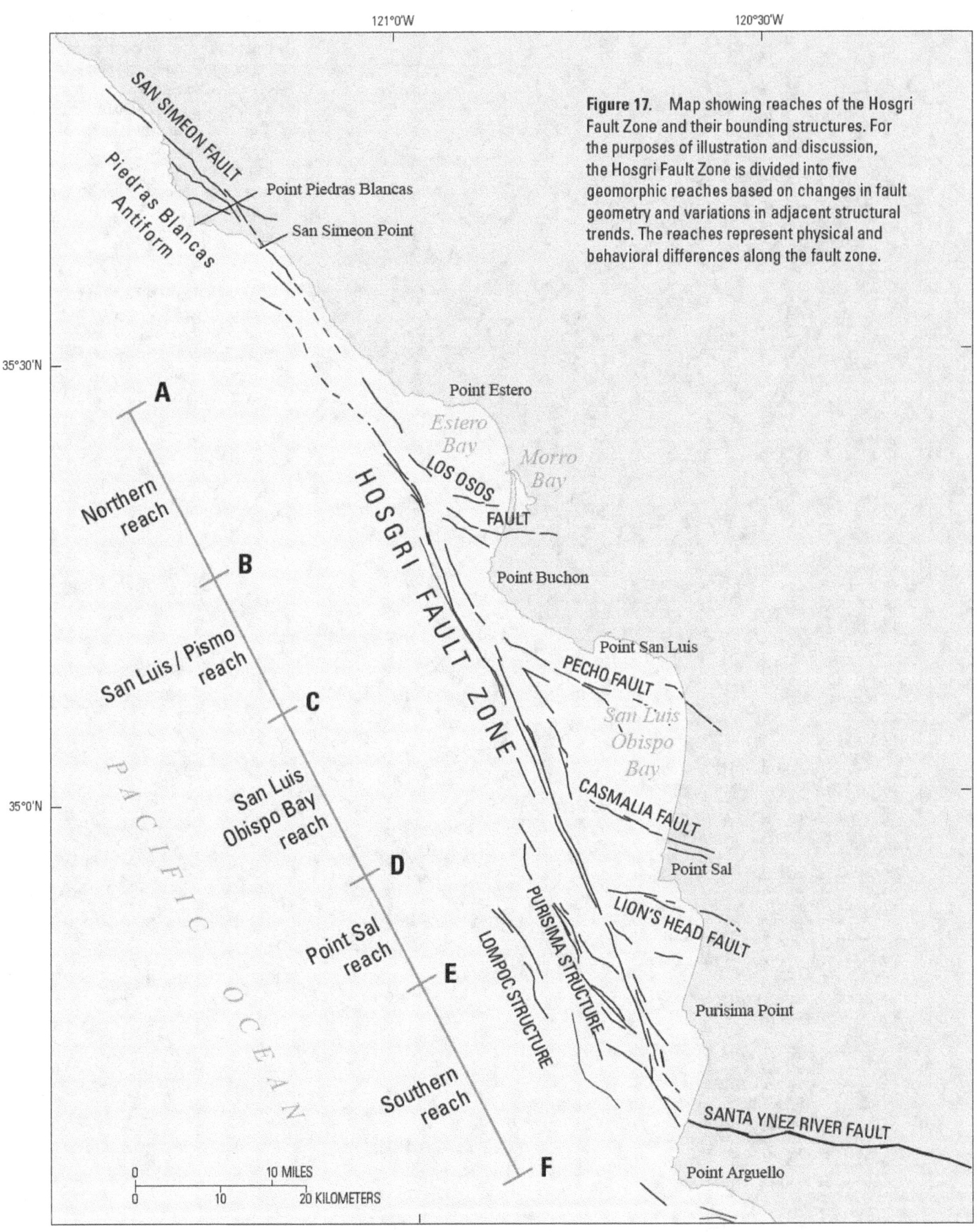

Figure 17. Map showing reaches of the Hosgri Fault Zone and their bounding structures. For the purposes of illustration and discussion, the Hosgri Fault Zone is divided into five geomorphic reaches based on changes in fault geometry and variations in adjacent structural trends. The reaches represent physical and behavioral differences along the fault zone.

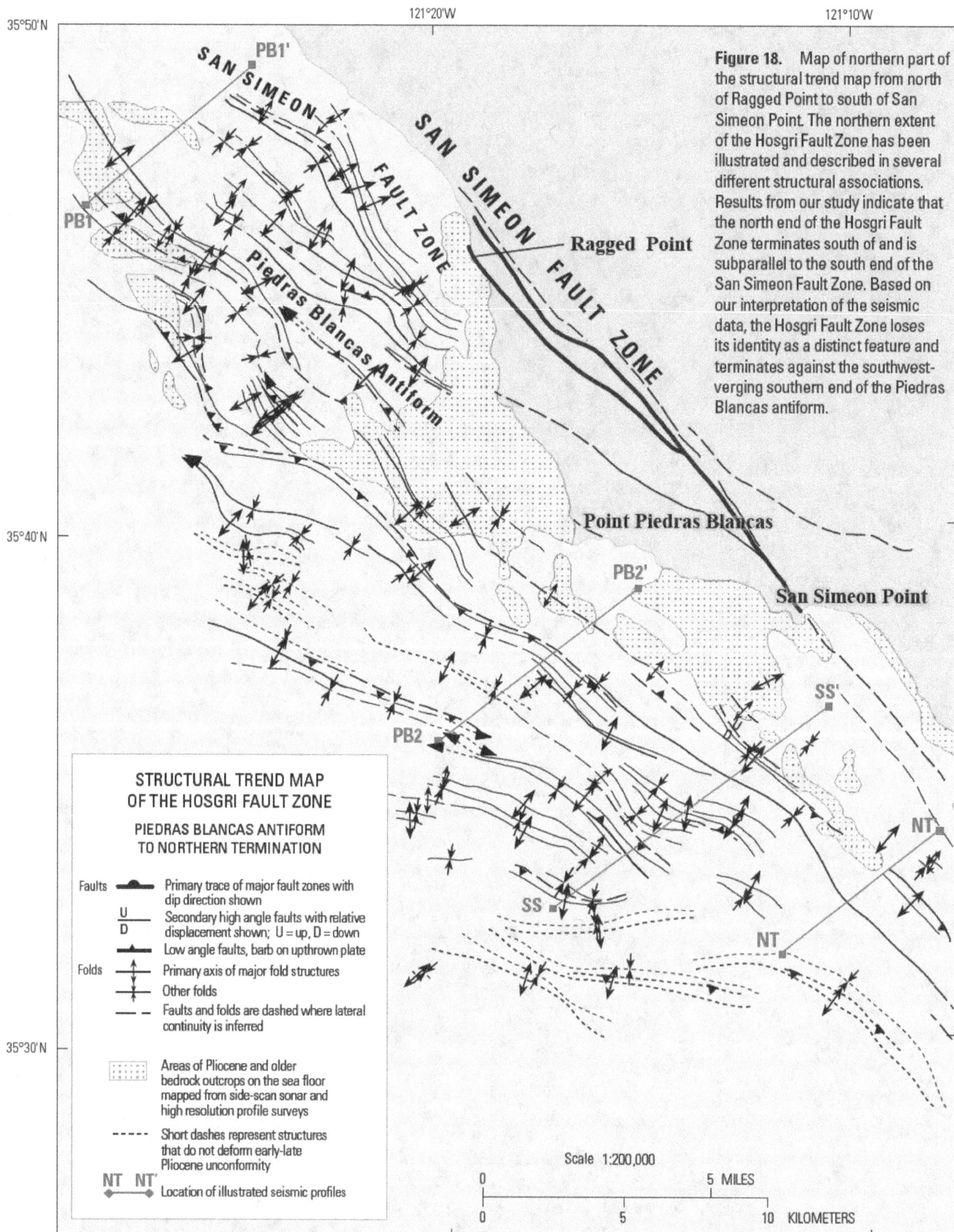

Figure 18. Map of northern part of the structural trend map from north of Ragged Point to south of San Simeon Point. The northern extent of the Hosgri Fault Zone has been illustrated and described in several different structural associations. Results from our study indicate that the north end of the Hosgri Fault Zone terminates south of and is subparallel to the south end of the San Simeon Fault Zone. Based on our interpretation of the seismic data, the Hosgri Fault Zone loses its identity as a distinct feature and terminates against the southwest-verging southern end of the Piedras Blancas antiform.

STRUCTURAL TREND MAP
OF THE HOSGRI FAULT ZONE

PIEDRAS BLANCAS ANTIFORM
TO NORTHERN TERMINATION

Faults
— Primary trace of major fault zones with dip direction shown
U/D — Secondary high angle faults with relative displacement shown; U = up, D = down
— Low angle faults, barb on upthrown plate

Folds
— Primary axis of major fold structures
— Other folds
— — Faults and folds are dashed where lateral continuity is inferred

Areas of Pliocene and older bedrock outcrops on the sea floor mapped from side-scan sonar and high resolution profile surveys

- - - - Short dashes represent structures that do not deform early-late Pliocene unconformity

NT NT' Location of illustrated seismic profiles

Scale 1:200,000

0   5 MILES

0   5   10 KILOMETERS

unconformity abuts the structure on the southwest and west sides (fig. 16, pl. 7). Modeling of possible detachment sources for the folds within the antiform indicates both northeast- and southwest-verging detachments in the upper 1 to 2 km of section. A major detachment that would encompass the entire antiform is not imaged on the seismic records.

North of Point Piedras Blancas, the primary axis of the antiform is subparallel to the strike of the San Simeon Fault Zone (fig. 18). In this area, the individual folds and thrust faults that form the offshore part of the antiform are also mapped as subparallel (±10°) to the San Simeon Fault Zone. South of Piedras Blancas, the folds of the antiform begin to converge with the San Simeon Fault Zone and, southwest of San Simeon Point, the strike of these features fans out to substantially more westward directions with strikes ranging from N. 46° W. to N. 85° W. The individual folds and faults are generally 2 to 7 km in length; however, one synclinal axis along the southwest flank of the structure extends for 15 km. Shallow thrust faults dip toward the axis of the antiform both on the northeast and southwest sides of the structure. On

the distal southwest flank of the feature, southwest-dipping thrust faults are observed. Based on the seismic imaging shown on profile PB1–PB1' (fig. 19), the primary vergence of the northern part of the structure is to the southwest. The region encompassed by the Piedras Blancas antiform has been uplifted and locally folded in early Pliocene time, as indicated by the deformation of the top of Miocene unconformity (figs. 15, 19–22), as well as by the abutment of the relatively un-deformed early–late Pliocene unconformity against the top of Miocene unconformity (figs. 16, 19).

Seismic profile PB1–PB1' (fig. 19) crosses the north end of the antiform (fig. 18). It shows a broad anticline presumably caused by slip on the southwest-verging thrust fault within the pre-Miocene basement rocks. Although the fold appears quite broad (3–4 km), its length is only 7 km, but it may extend another 7 km to the southeast as a more complex structure composed of several folds (fig. 18). The fault-propagation fold observed in figure 19 involves the pre-Miocene basement rocks, Miocene rocks, and lower Pliocene rocks. The latter are observed on the northeast side of the fold between shotpoints

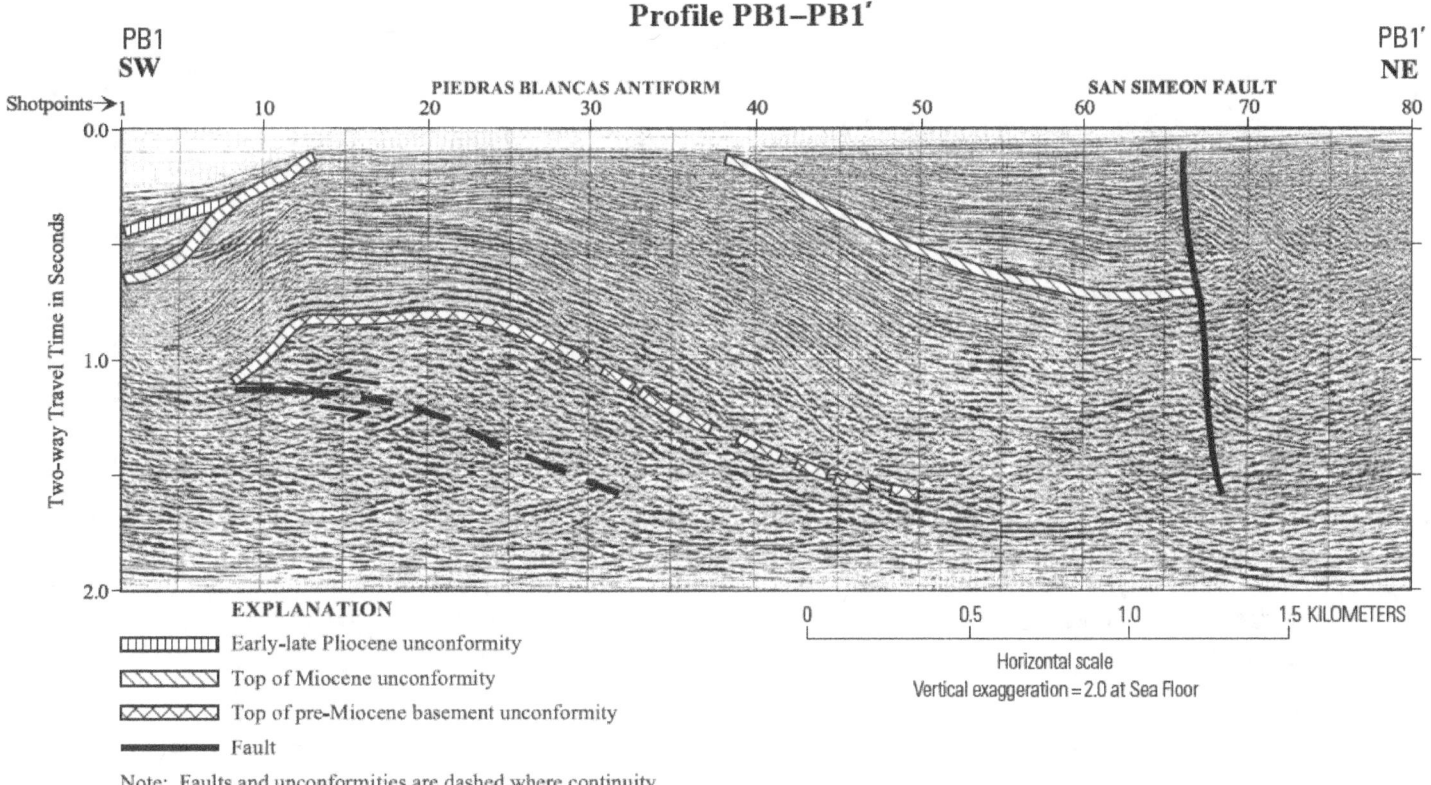

Profile PB1–PB1'

EXPLANATION

⬚⬚⬚⬚ Early-late Pliocene unconformity

⬚⬚⬚⬚ Top of Miocene unconformity

⬚⬚⬚⬚ Top of pre-Miocene basement unconformity

━━━ Fault

Note: Faults and unconformities are dashed where continuity is inferred. Arrows show direction of relative displacement on low-angle detachments.

0   0.5   1.0   1.5 KILOMETERS

Horizontal scale
Vertical exaggeration = 2.0 at Sea Floor

Figure 19.   Seismic profile PB1–PB1' is north of Ragged Point. It is part of line CM86-85 shown on plate 1. The profile images a fold on the north side of the Piedras Blancas antiform (fig. 18). The geometry of the structure shows a southwest-verging, fault-propagation fold occurring within basement rocks. The early–late Pliocene unconformity onlaps the fold, but the top of Miocene unconformity was planed off during the late Wisconsin sea-level lowstand and subsequent sea-level rise. Seafloor slope changes between shotpoints 10 and 20 suggest that the fold and underlying fault may still be active. The fault near shotpoint 65 is interpreted to be a northwest offshore extension of one of the San Simeon Fault Zone strands between Point Piedras Blancas and Ragged Point.

40 and 65 and on the southwest flank between shotpoints 1 and 7. Miocene and lower Pliocene rocks have been eroded from the top of the fold and the early–late Pliocene unconformity abuts the structure on the southwest flank. Seafloor slope changes on the southwest end of the record suggest that the fold is still an active structure. A high-angle fault is interpreted in the profile at about shotpoint 66. This fault is interpreted to be a possible offshore trace of the west branch of the San Simeon Fault Zone. It is shown as a dashed line on figure 18 immediately northeast of the synclinal axis.

Seismic profile PB2–PB2' (fig. 20) crosses the south end of the antiform (fig. 18). Profile PB2–PB2' is on the southwest flank of the antiform. The central area of the antiform uplift is on the northeast side of the profile and continues to the northeast off the east end of the profile. A relatively shallow northeast-verging thrust fault is responsible for minor deformation in the vicinity of shotpoint 20. This fault is best seen on the unannotated profiles (figs. B1–B20)

provided in appendix B. However, evidence for a southwest-verging thrust fault similar to that seen on the north side of the antiform (fig. 19) is lacking in this profile. West of shotpoint 55, there is no evidence for a high-angle fault, similar to the type seen farther south, that would represent the northwest extension of the Hosgri Fault Zone. High-angle faults may exist on the profile to the northeast of shotpoint 65, but they are not major structures because they cannot be traced between seismic lines only 1 to 2 km apart.

Seismic profile SS–SS' (fig. 21) is southwest of San Simeon Point and approximately 7 km southeast of profile PB2–PB2' (fig. 20). This profile is from a deeper penetration, lower vertical resolution seismic system than that used to acquire profile PB2–PB2'; nevertheless, coherent images of reflections below the pre-Miocene basement unconformity are missing. The overall appearance of the geology between the two profiles is similar despite the added energy and higher CDP fold of the deep penetration line. The folds in

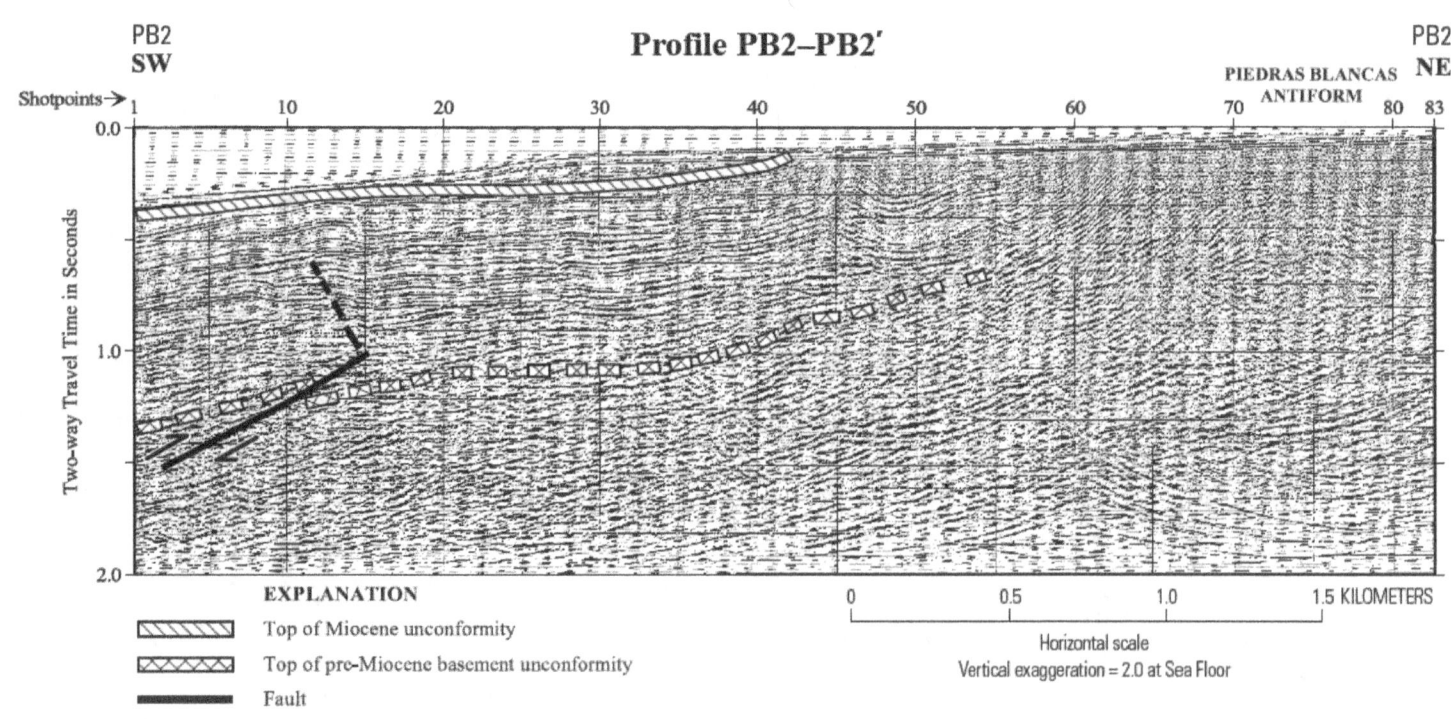

Figure 20. Seismic profile PB2–PB2' (line CM86-69 on pl. 1) is on the southwest side of the Piedras Blancas antiform (fig. 18). The main part of the antiform begins on the east side of the profile and continues east of the profile. The early–late Pliocene unconformity onlaps the structure west of the profile (fig. 16, pl. 7) and the top of Miocene unconformity has been planed off across the top of the structure. The thin wedge of sediments immediately overlying the top of Miocene unconformity west of shotpoint 42 may be Holocene sediment forming a prograding wedge. We interpret a small-displacement northeast-verging thrust fault at the west end of the profile that breaks the top of pre-Miocene basement unconformity and deforms the overlying Miocene strata. No evidence of a major southwest-verging thrust fault beneath the antiform is seen on this record although it may be deeper than 2.0 s (maximum extent of the record).

the Miocene rocks appear to have been formed above the top of pre-Miocene basement unconformity that acted as a detachment surface. Relatively minor northeast-verging thrust faults are interpreted to cause minor offsets in the top of pre-Miocene basement unconformity. These thrust faults cannot be traced to adjacent seismic lines and thus are not indicated on figure 18. No evidence for a high-angle fault is seen west of shotpoint 240. A possible fault at shotpoint 230 is not seen on adjacent seismic lines.

Seismic profile NT–NT' (fig. 22) is at the southwest end of the folds associated with the Piedras Blancas antiform. West of shotpoint 25, the Miocene rocks appear relatively undeformed but then are abruptly folded upward northeast of that point. The top of pre-Miocene basement unconformity is at a depth of about 1 km at shotpoint 25 but is interpreted to rise near the surface near shotpoint 50. A southwest-verging thrust fault within the basement rocks is interpreted to be

the cause of the uplift. This fault is not directly observed on the seismic data but is inferred based on the geometry of the fold. Cores N-25A, E, and F (pl. 2, table 4) confirm the Miocene age of the rocks between shotpoints 30 and 50. The northwest projection of the Hosgri Fault Zone seen on profiles to the south (pl. 4) would cross profile NT–NT' between shotpoints 15 and 35.

There is no evidence of continuous high-angle-fault traces of the type associated with the Hosgri Fault Zone to the south, along the southwest or west flank of the antiform. Examination of plate 4 and figure 18 indicates that, in order to extend around the Piedras Blancas antiform, the Hosgri Fault Zone is required to make a sharp westward bend and rollover into a shallow thrust fault. There is no direct connection between the steeply dipping northern reach of the Hosgri Fault Zone and the thrust faults beneath the Piedras Blancas antiform.

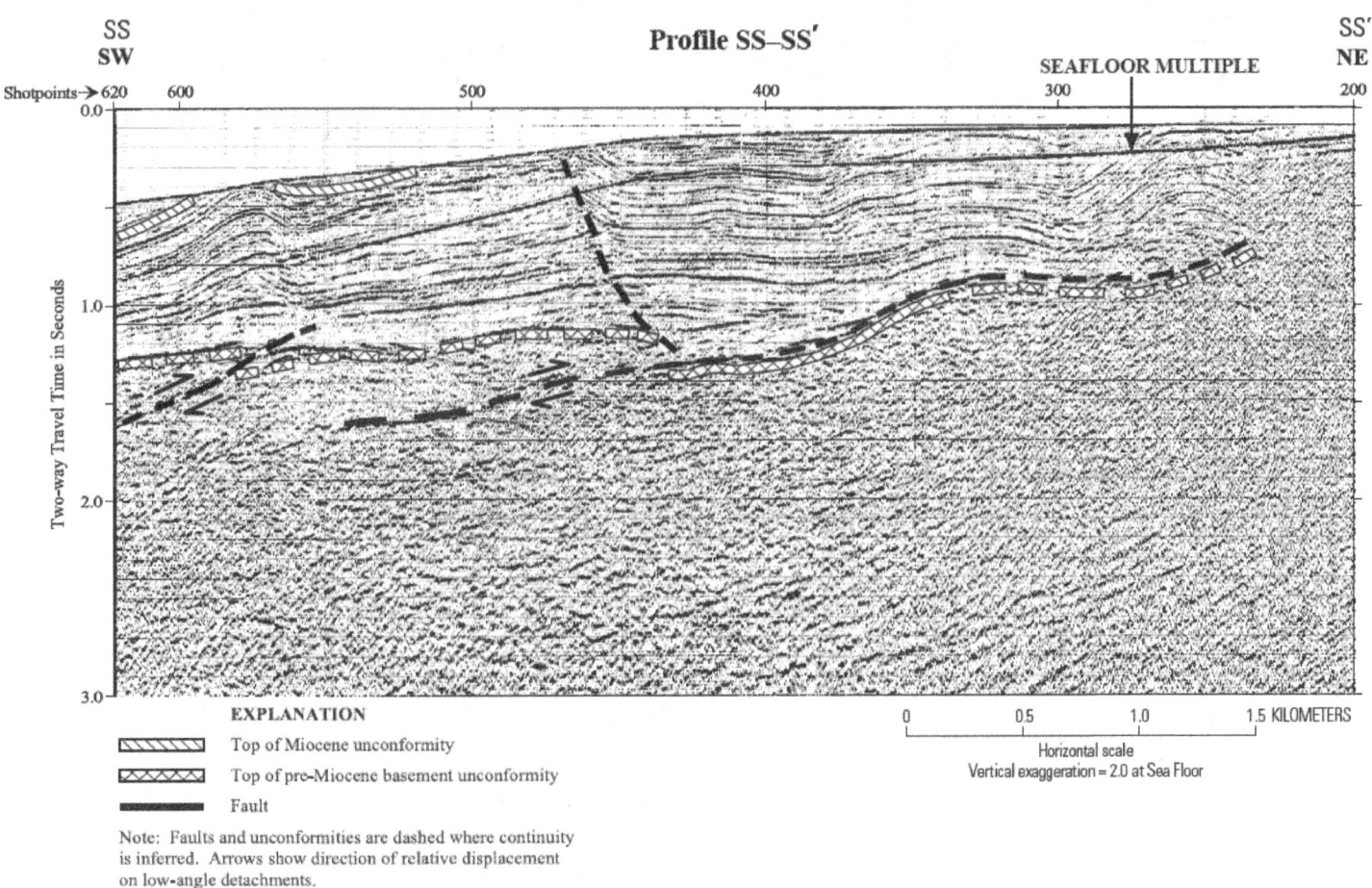

Figure 21. Seismic profile SS–SS' (line W484 on pl. 1) is southwest of San Simeon Point. It crosses the southwest limb of the Piedras Blancas antiform (fig. 18). The upper part of the section consists of a series of small folds and associated faults. The early–late Pliocene unconformity onlaps the antiform structure to the west of the profile (fig. 16, pl. 7). There is no evidence of a near vertical fault trace commonly associated with the Hosgri Fault Zone, nor is there evidence of a deeper, southwest-verging detachment seen on the north side of the antiform (fig. 19). Note the strong, linear seafloor multiple image extending across most of the profile.

Profile NT–NT′

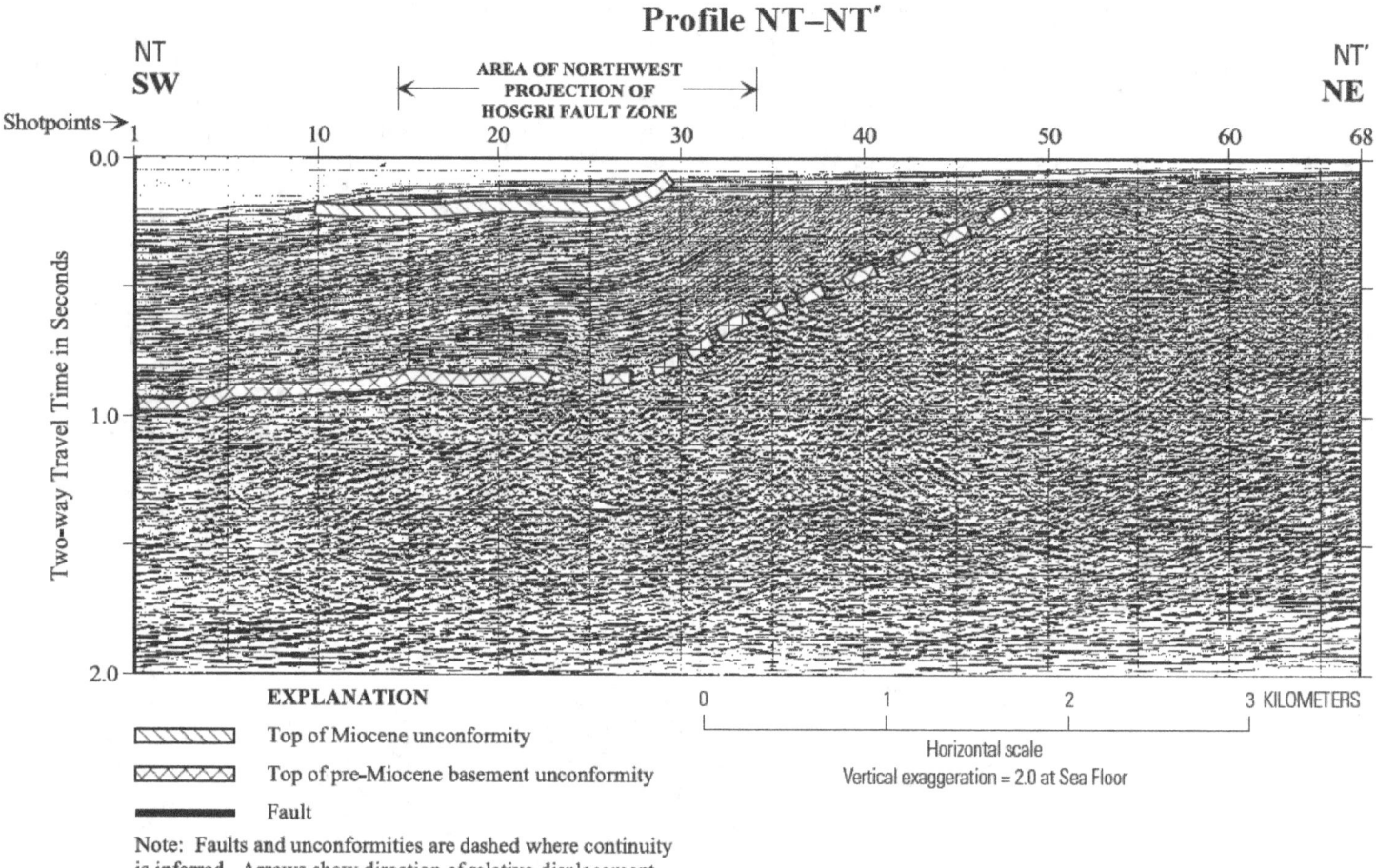

EXPLANATION

⬒ Top of Miocene unconformity

⬒ Top of pre-Miocene basement unconformity

▬ Fault

Note: Faults and unconformities are dashed where continuity is inferred. Arrows show direction of relative displacement on low-angle detachments.

Figure 22. Seismic profile NT–NT′ (line CM86-57 on pl. 1) is offshore Cambria. It crosses the southeast end of the folds associated with the Piedras Blancas antiform (fig. 18). It is similar to profile SS–SS′ except that the Miocene section exhibits fewer small folds. The northwest extension of the Hosgri Fault Zone would cross this line west of shotpoint 25, but there does not appear to be evidence for a near-vertical fault trace that cuts through the Miocene section in that area. Minor faults could lie within the basement rocks east of shotpoint 50, but this is an area of poor quality seismic data.

Figure 23. Map showing the structural trend (pl. 4) of the Hosgri Fault Zone, northern and San Luis Pismo reaches. The map includes the northern reach of the Hosgri Fault Zone that extends south to the intersection of the Los Osos Fault Zone and the San Luis/Pismo reach that extends to the intersection with the Pecho Fault (fig. 17). In this area, there are four main traces of the Hosgri Fault Zone (bold) and numerous subsidiary faults that merge with the main Hosgri Fault traces at depth. The main traces vary in length from 8 km at the north end of the fault zone to 22 km for the trace that forms the San Luis/Pismo reach. The individual traces overlap for lengths of 2 to 3 km and are generally offset 200 to 600 m in the overlap zones. The detail mapping of the traces is facilitated by high-resolution survey data (of the type shown in fig. 9) that are at closer line spacings than the CDP data (pl. 1). Seismic profiles A–A′ to E–E′ depict the fault zone and adjacent structures in these reaches and are shown on figures 24 through 28.

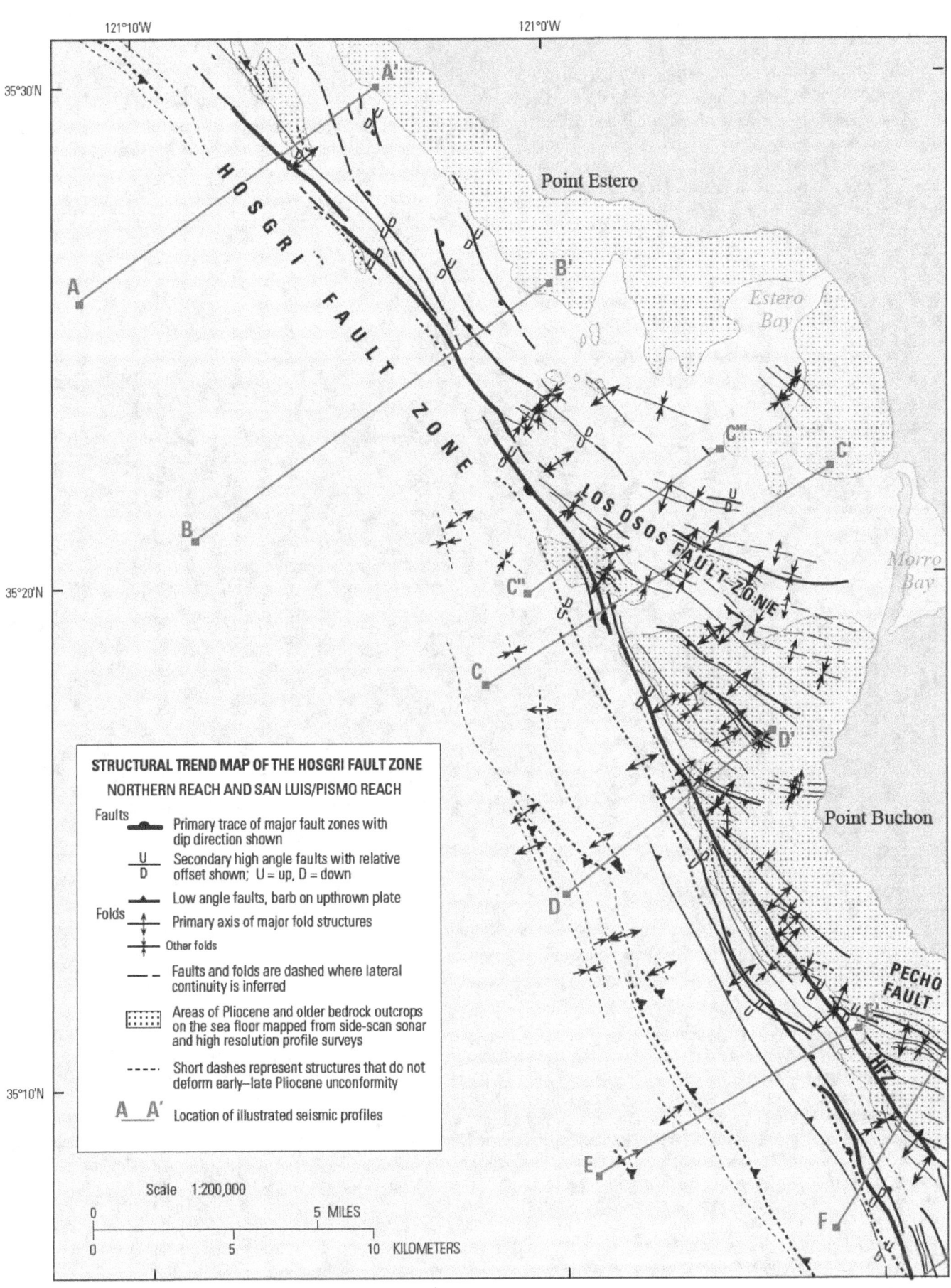

121°10'W

121°0'W

35°30'N

Point Estero

A'

B'

Estero
Bay

H O S G R I

C'''

C'

Morro
Bay

F A U L T

LOS OSOS FAULT ZONE

A

B

35°20'N

C''

C

Z O N E

D'

Point Buchon

D

STRUCTURAL TREND MAP OF THE HOSGRI FAULT ZONE

NORTHERN REACH AND SAN LUIS/PISMO REACH

Faults

Primary trace of major fault zones with
dip direction shown

U
—
D

Secondary high angle faults with relative
offset shown; U = up, D = down

Low angle faults, barb on upthrown plate

Folds

Primary axis of major fold structures

Other folds

Faults and folds are dashed where lateral
continuity is inferred

Areas of Pliocene and older bedrock outcrops
on the sea floor mapped from side-scan sonar
and high resolution profile surveys

Short dashes represent structures that do not
deform early–late Pliocene unconformity

A____A'   Location of illustrated seismic profiles

PECHO
FAULT

HFZ

E'

35°10'N

E

F

Scale   1:200,000

0   5 MILES

0   5   10 KILOMETERS

Northern Reach

The northern reach of the Hosgri Fault Zone trends N. 46° W. for 20 to 22 km from the intersection with the Los Osos Fault Zone in Estero Bay to the northern termination of the Hosgri Fault Zone southwest of Cambria (fig. 23, pl. 4). The salient features of this reach include the northern termination of the fault zone, the postulated pull-apart basin between the Hosgri and San Simeon Fault Zones (Hanson and others, 2004), and the intersection with the Los Osos Fault Zone.

The Hosgri Fault Zone extends the entire length of the northern reach from north of profile A–A' to immediately south of profile C–C' on figure 23. A relatively high data density of both high-resolution and moderate-penetration CDP seismic reflection data integrated with analog subbottom profile and sparker data allows for detailed mapping of the fault zone in this reach. The main fault zone is mapped as three noncontinuous, overlapping 8- to 13-km-long strands. The strands overlap each other for a nominal distance of 2 km with right steps of 200 to 300 m between the southern and central traces and between the central and northern traces, respectively.

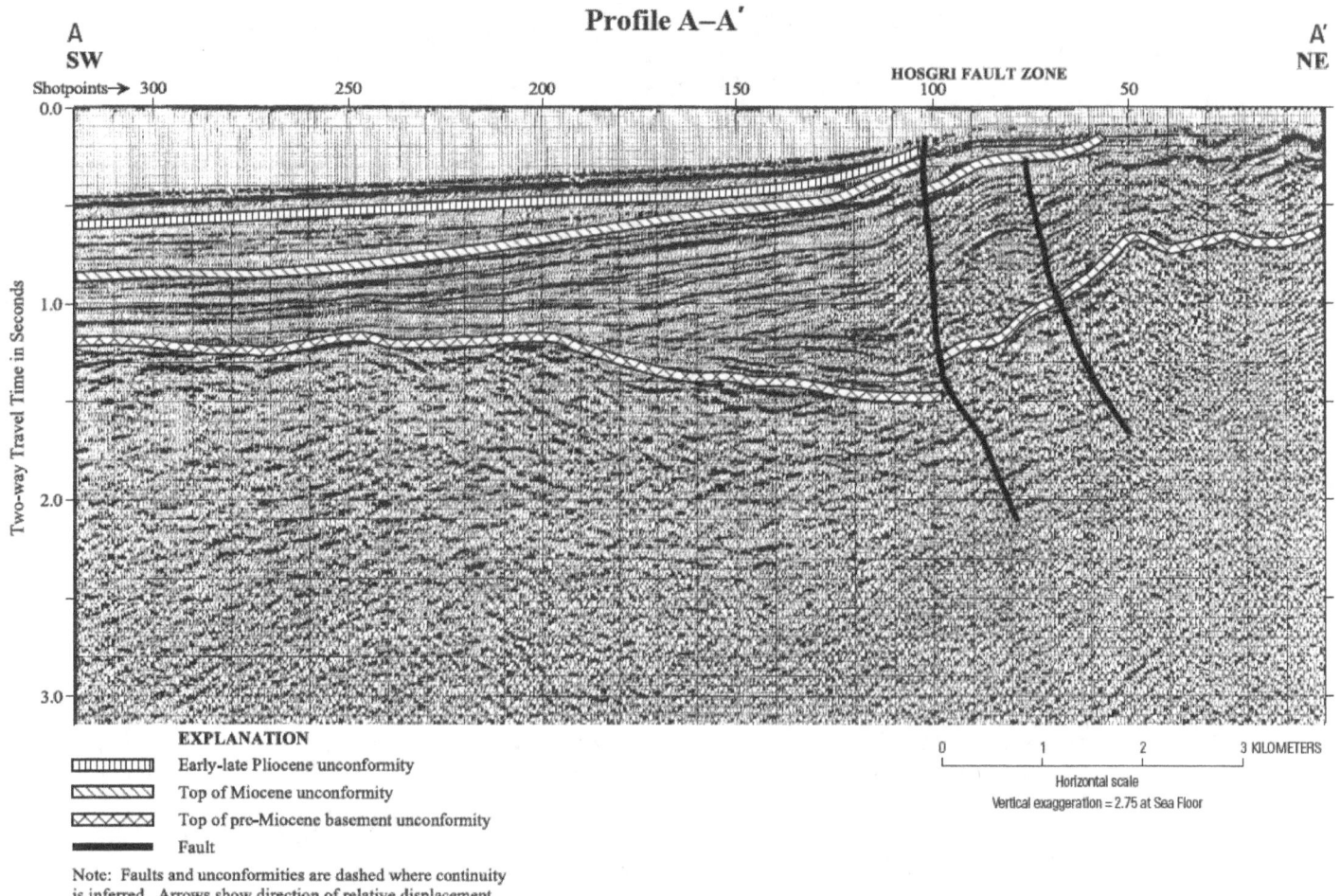

Profile A–A'

EXPLANATION

▥ Early-late Pliocene unconformity

▨ Top of Miocene unconformity

▧ Top of pre-Miocene basement unconformity

▬ Fault

Note: Faults and unconformities are dashed where continuity is inferred. Arrows show direction of relative displacement on low-angle detachments.

Horizontal scale
Vertical exaggeration = 2.75 at Sea Floor

Figure 24. Seismic profile A-A' crosses the Hosgri Fault Zone near its north end. It is part of line W74A on plate 1. Two traces of the fault zone are marked. Additional minor faulting may be present between shotpoint 75 and the northeast end of the line. The western trace of the Hosgri Fault Zone at shot point 100 is interpreted to be the main trace at this location. It is interpreted to penetrate to the vicinity of the seafloor, and the early–late Pliocene unconformity is interpreted to terminate at the fault. The eastern trace, at shotpoint 75, does not appear to offset a near-surface reflector interpreted as the top of Miocene unconformity. Both traces are near vertical in the upper one second of the record but dip to the northeast at depth. Note the opposite sense of displacement of the top of Miocene and top of pre-Miocene basement unconformities across the western trace. Folding of Miocene rocks occurs east of the Hosgri Fault Zone and in a narrow band as much as 500 m wide west of the fault. The identification of the near-surface units on the seismic data east of the Hosgri Fault Zone is based on cores, diver observations, and onshore geologic mapping (pl. 2, fig. 5). A core in the vicinity of shotpoint 90 was identified as upper Miocene to lower Pliocene siltstone (table 4), and shoreline outcrops east of the line are mapped as Franciscan Complex. The seismic reflection data indicate that rocks inferred to be early Miocene age (shotpoint 170–100 at 1.1–1.5 s) onlap an old basement high at the west half of the line (shotpoints 200 to 300) and dip gently to the northeast into the Hosgri Fault trace.

Four interpreted seismic profiles are used to illustrate the properties of the Hosgri Fault Zone in the northern reach and its intersection with the Los Osos Fault Zone. Profiles A–A' and B–B' (figs. 24, 25) indicate that the primary trace on both profiles is imaged as a prominent, near-vertical discontinuity on seismic reflection records. On profile A–A', near the northern termination of the fault zone, the primary (western) trace is near vertical in the upper 1.5 s of the record (1.5–2 km). The apparent change to a steep northeasterly dip below 1.5 s is somewhat exaggerated on the seismic time-based profiles due to the effects of higher velocity rocks on the east side of the fault. On profile A–A', there

is a change in the relative sense of vertical offset between the top of pre-Miocene basement unconformity and the top of Miocene unconformity. Changes in the sense of vertical offset through time are one of the primary characteristics of strike-slip faulting (Harding, 1985, 1990; Stone, 1969; Zalan, 1987). A secondary trace of the fault zone is interpreted on profile A–A' in the vicinity of shotpoint 75. The secondary trace appears to offset some of the reflectors from the Miocene rocks but apparently has only a minor effect on the two mapped unconformities.

The changes in structural style and fault characteristics between the north end of the Hosgri Fault Zone and the

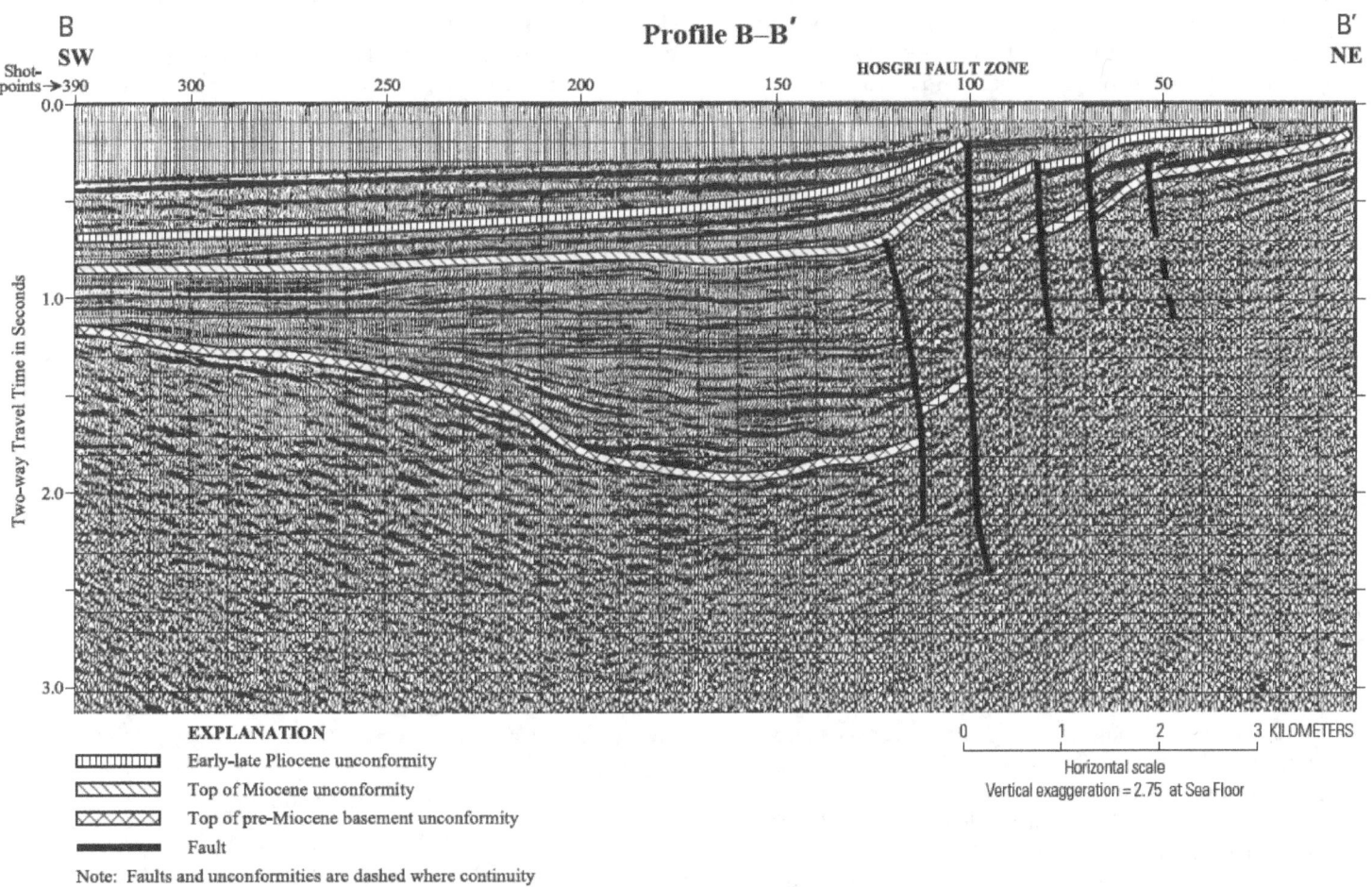

Figure 25. Seismic profile B-B' crosses the Hosgri Fault Zone south of Point Estero. It is part of line W76A on plate 1. It is parallel to, and approximately 10 km south of profile A–A'. Crosses the Hosgri Fault Zone south of Point Estero. It is part of line W76A on plate 1, and lies at the south end of the San Simeon/Hosgri pull-apart basin (Lettis and others, 1990; Hanson and others, 2004). Two near-vertical traces are interpreted between shotpoints 100 and 120. The westernmost trace (dotted fault on fig. 23) does not appear to affect the early–late Pliocene unconformity, but the main trace at shotpoint 100 is imaged on high-resolution data to offset sediment layers up to the time of the post-Wisconsin unconformity. Interpretations presented on the structural trend map (pl. 4, fig. 23) indicate that neither trace directly connects with the traces observed on profile A–A' (fig. 24). The basement rocks are up-to-the-east across both traces of the fault. The figure is inferred to indicate about 1 km of vertical displacement across the Hosgri Fault Zone. Core A4 (pl. 2, table 4) south of the east end of profile B–B' was identified as greywacke, presumably from the Franciscan Complex. West of the Hosgri Fault, the reflectors inferred to be of early Miocene age appear undeformed to a depth of 2 km (1.5–1.9 s, shotpoints 120–190) adjacent to the fault and then are uplifted and onlap the old basement high at the west end of the line (shotpoints 200–300). The overlying middle and late Miocene rocks are relatively horizontal in this area.

south end of the Piedras Blancas antiform are evident by comparison of profile A–A' (fig. 24) and profile NT–NT' (fig. 22). The overall structure displayed in the two profiles is similar. Both sections show uplift of the top of pre-Miocene basement unconformity in a northeastward direction. However in profile A–A', the flank of the uplift is disrupted, structurally complicated, and partially accommodated by two faults that can be continuously mapped to the south as members of the Hosgri Fault Zone. In profile NT–NT', the flank of the uplift shows the character of the unbroken forward limb of a fault propagation fold. In this section, the faults in profile A–A' associated with the Hosgri Fault Zone are absent. The northwest extension of the primary (western) trace of the fault zone on profile A–A' would intersect profile NT–NT' in the area between shotpoints 15 and 35. On NT–NT', minor offsets in the lower part of the Miocene section can be interpreted at shotpoint 25 as the apparent axis of a minor fold and the hinge axis of a fault propagation fold. However, neither this minor fold nor the associated fault can be continuously mapped southeastward to profile A–A'.

Profile B–B' (fig. 25) crosses the Hosgri Fault Zone approximately 10 km south of profile A–A'. The general appearance of the sedimentary basin and the western strands of the Hosgri Fault Zone have a similar appearance on the two seismic records. Both records show a near-vertical primary fault trace to 1.5 s or more. The sedimentary basin to the west deepens toward the fault zone and is relatively undisturbed except in the 0.5 to 1.0 km zone immediately adjacent to the western-most traces of the fault zone. However, the internal character of the Hosgri Fault Zone changes significantly along this reach. On profile B–B', a west-verging splay with limited lateral extent is interpreted at shotpoint 120. Compression between the splay and the main trace (shotpoint 100) is interpreted to be responsible for the folding in the Miocene rocks and the deformation of the top of Miocene unconformity and early–late Pliocene unconformity between the splay and main trace. The fault and fold geometry between the two faults is typical of a one-sided positive flower structure. Similar structures are shown on seismic images of other strike-slip faults compiled in worldwide atlases (Bally, 1983; Goudswaard and Jenyon, 1988). The splay is mapped with a vertical trace subparallel to the primary trace of the Hosgri to a depth of about 1.5 km. Below this depth, the relation of the two faults cannot be determined with certainty, and we elect to continue the trace of the splay fault downward and parallel to the main trace of the Hosgri Fault Zone, though other interpretations are possible.

San Simeon/Hosgri Pull-Apart Basin

The northeastern parts of both profiles A–A' and B–B' lie within the region interpreted by DiSilvestro and others (1990) and Lettis and others (1990) as the San Simeon/Hosgri pull-apart basin. These authors proposed that this structural feature results from the transfer of lateral slip between the San Simeon Fault Zone and the Hosgri Fault Zone. In their model

of the pull-apart basin, the San Simeon Fault Zone extends southeast from San Simeon Point and continues along, or immediately offshore from, the relatively straight coastline between Cambria and Point Estero (figs. 12, 18; pl. 4). Our maps show this extension of the San Simeon Fault Zone as a dashed feature extending southeast to offshore Cambria. This interpretation is based, in part, on high-resolution analog data of marginal quality. The analysis of cores and diver-geologist observations documenting changes in seafloor rock type (pl. 2; tables 4, 5) provide additional information on the approximate location of the southeastern offshore extension of the San Simeon Fault. South of Cambria, the fault is not imaged seismically because of its proximity to the shoreline, and no evidence of the fault is observed in the northern part of Estero Bay or farther to the southeast. Seismic imaging in this region of the bay is interpreted to be of sufficient quality to detect a southern extension of the San Simon Fault Zone if it were to exist as a significant structural feature.

The region of overlap proposed by DiSilvestro and others (1990) and Lettis and others (1990) is approximately 15 km long and 5 km wide (fig. 23; pl. 4). The area of the interpreted basin contains at least four northeast-dipping normal faults that strike north-northwest, subparallel to the Hosgri Fault Zone (fig. 23; pl. 4). Three of these normal faults are shown on profile B–B' (fig. 25). These faults are interpreted to displace the early–late Pliocene unconformity to produce a southwest-tilted half graben (fig. 25). Further, our interpretation indicates that the top of Miocene unconformity has been eroded from the east side of the Hosgri Fault Zone main trace and that upper Pliocene to Holocene deposits thicken to a maximum of 280 m at the west edge of the basin (adjacent to shotpoint 100). The relation of faulting to the Pliocene to Holocene deposition suggests contemporaneous sedimentation and faulting. On this profile, the east margin of the pull-apart basin is characterized by a gentle downwarping of sediments into the stepover region. Lettis and others (1990) and Hanson and others (2004) discuss this interpretation in greater detail.

Intersection of the Los Osos Fault Zone

The intersection of the Los Osos Fault Zone with the Hosgri Fault Zone is taken as the boundary between the northern and San Luis/Pismo reaches. Lettis and Hall (1990, 1994) describe the onshore Los Osos Fault as an active southwest-dipping to vertical reverse or thrust fault bounding the northeast margin of the San Luis Range. Profiles C"–C''' and C–C' (figs. 26, 27) cross both the Hosgri Fault Zone and the Los Osos Fault Zone (fig. 23). The junction of the Los Osos Fault Zone and the Hosgri Fault Zone forms the ridge shown in the top part of figure 10. The Los Osos Fault Zone also is associated with discontinuities in dip and small seafloor steps displayed in profile C"–C''' (fig. 26) near shotpoint 39. These seafloor morphologies suggest that both faults may be active in this area. The extension of the primary trace of the Hosgri Fault Zone to the seafloor is also apparent on this profile at shotpoint 25. The near-surface rocks east of the primary trace of the fault are identified as probable Monterey Formation (core

A–103; tables 4, 5) and have the seismic appearance of tightly folded, thinly bedded, and faulted rocks, typical of Monterey Formation onshore outcrops in some areas. Both profiles C″–C‴ and C–C′ image the splays on the west side of the primary trace of the Hosgri Fault Zone that join the primary trace at depth, forming what appears to be a one-sided flower structure. Shallow thrust faults on the west side of the main trace are also common in the reaches to the south.

Profiles C″–C‴ and C–C′ are 2 to 3 km apart and cross structurally similar parts of both the Hosgri and Los Osos Fault Zones. However, they differ greatly in their imaging capabilities. These differences relate to the use of different CDP seismic reflection systems with different imaging objectives. Profile C″–C‴

(fig. 26) is from the high-resolution CDP survey run by Comap Alaska for PG&E and was collected using a small-volume water gun and a relatively short cable designed for high-resolution near-surface imaging. Profile C–C′ (fig. 27) was collected as part of the PG&E/EDGE program using a large air-gun source and a long cable array designed for imaging intermediate and deep structure. Differences in the two survey parameters are listed in table 1.

Profile C–C′ (fig. 27) shows the top of pre-Miocene basement reflector dipping toward the Hosgri Fault Zone, similar to the form seen on profiles A–A′ (fig. 24) and B–B′ (fig. 25). Profile C–C′ displays the primary trace of the fault as near vertical and extending to 2.0 s before changing dip to the northeast. Between 2.0 and 3.0 s, alternative interpretations of the dip are possible,

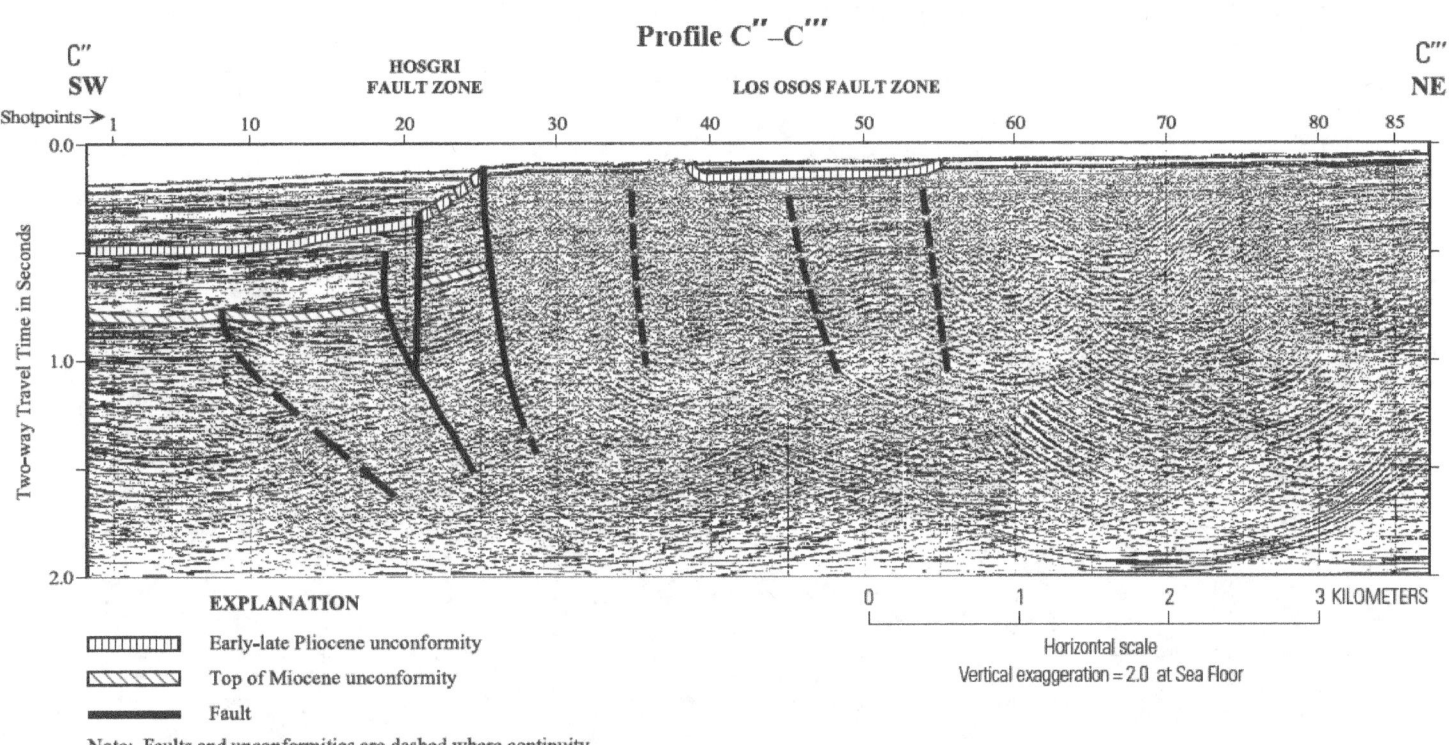

Profile C″–C‴

EXPLANATION

IIIIIIIIIII   Early-late Pliocene unconformity

NNNNNNN   Top of Miocene unconformity

▬▬▬▬▬   Fault

Note: Faults and unconformities are dashed where continuity is inferred. Arrows show direction of relative displacement on low-angle detachments.

Horizontal scale
Vertical exaggeration = 2.0 at Sea Floor

Figure 26.   Seismic profile C″–C‴ crosses the Hosgri and Los Osos Fault Zones in Estero Bay. The profile is parallel to, and approximately 4 km north of profile C–C′ (fig. 27). Profile C″–C‴ is line CM86-33 on plate 1. There are two traces of the Hosgri Fault Zone imaged on this line; the eastern trace, at shotpoint 24, is mapped as the main trace because of its greater length and apparent recent activity as interpreted from a small seafloor scarp noted on the high-resolution subbottom profile and side-scan sonar data from this area. A change in seafloor slope is also evident at shotpoint 24. The main trace is near vertical from the surface to the limits of resolution on the CDP seismic record at about 2 s (approximately 2 km depth). The western trace, at shotpoint 20, slightly deforms the early–late Pliocene unconformity but is not interpreted to extend to the surface. The data on this line were collected with a small-volume water-gun source providing higher upper frequencies than the large air gun array used on line PG&E-1 (fig. 27). The higher frequencies recorded by these data (fig. 26) provide greater resolution of the near-surface geology than seen on figure 27. East of the Hosgri Fault Zone, profile C″–C‴ images tightly folded and faulted rocks of the Los Osos Fault Zone in the upper 1 s of the record between shot points 35 and 65. Cores A-103 and A-104 (table 4) and diver samples at location D (table 5) are from the area between the Hosgri Fault Zone and shotpoint 38. Core A-103 was identified as probable Monterey Formation. Core A-104 had similar lithology to sample A-103 but its age could not be definitively determined (table 4).

including both a more vertical alignment extending to 3.0 s at shotpoint 295 and a more easterly dip placing the base of the mapped trace near shotpoint 240. Comparison of profiles C–C' and C"–C"' suggest that shallow structures east of the Hosgri Fault Zone are too tightly folded to be detected by the acquisition geometries used to collect seismic profile C–C' (fig. 27). In contrast, profile C"–C"'(fig. 26) shows Hosgri Fault Zone traces only to reflection times of 1.2 to 1.5 s but images the near-surface geology in the 0- to 200-ms range beneath the seafloor east of the fault zone.

San Luis/Pismo Reach

Along the San Luis/Pismo reach, the Hosgri Fault Zone forms the west boundary of the San Luis/Pismo structural block (Lettis and others, 2004). The north boundary of the reach is the Los Osos Fault Zone. The south boundary of the reach is the Pecho Fault, a northeast-dipping reverse fault. Both the Los Osos and Pecho Fault Zones occur in areas of tight folding and poor seismic image quality. The fault zones are identified from interpretation of grids of sparker data and other high-resolution data, which represent the faults as aligned zones of data dropout, and other forms of secondary evidence for faulting. These faults are discussed in more detail in Lettis and others (2004). Between these bounding faults, the Hosgri Fault Zone trends N. 25° W. to N. 30° W. for 20 to 22 km (fig. 23, pl. 4). The fault zone consists of two subparallel traces, with secondary folds and faults between the traces. Within the San Luis/Pismo reach, the fault zone forms a boundary between areas of contrasting structural trends. There are marked differences in the trends, lengths, and widths of structures on opposite sides of the east trace. The Hosgri Fault Zone is oblique to known thrust and reverse faults on the east that terminate against it, and it is parallel or

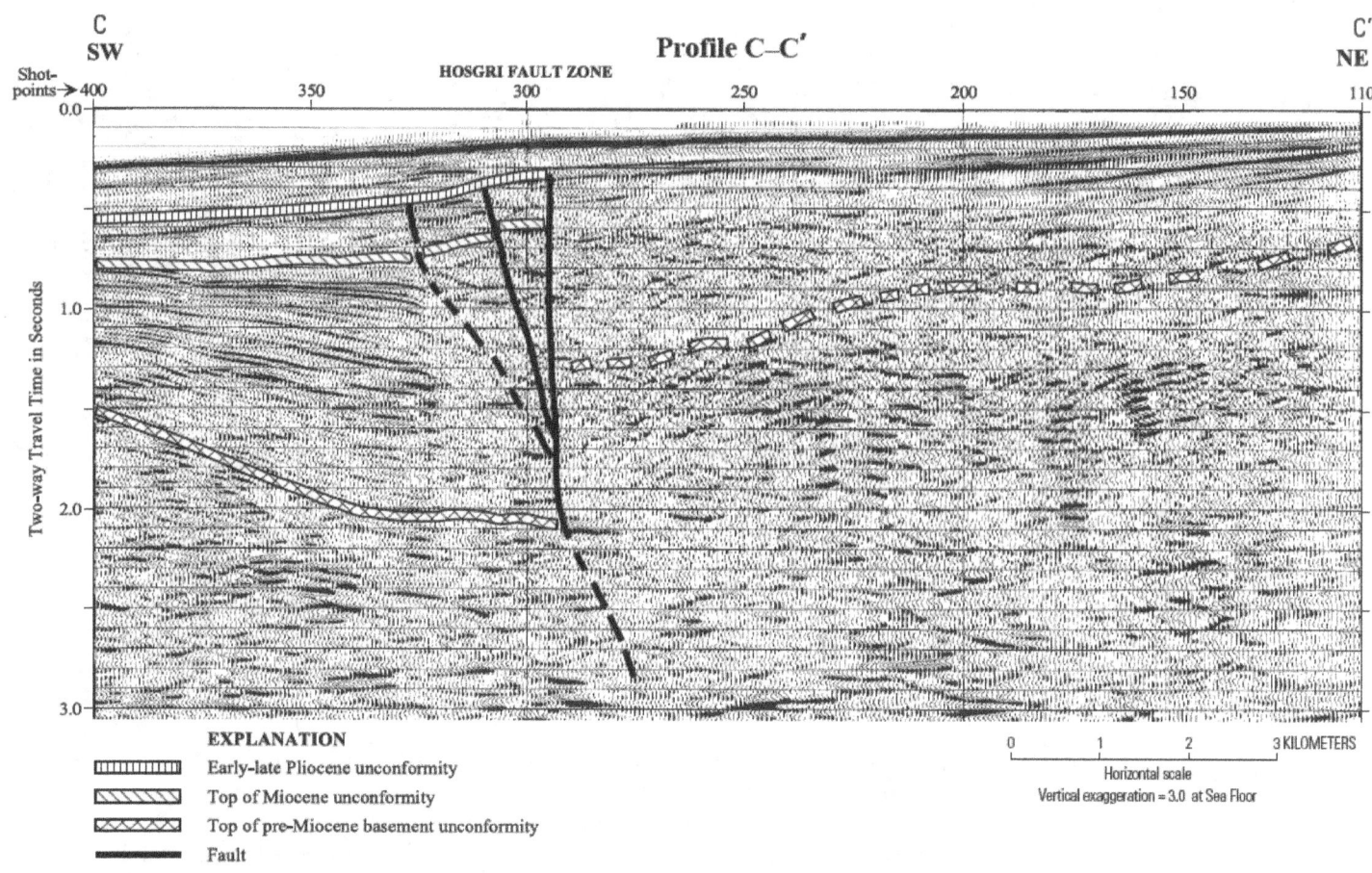

EXPLANATION

- Early-late Pliocene unconformity
- Top of Miocene unconformity
- Top of pre-Miocene basement unconformity
- Fault

Note: Faults and unconformities are dashed where continuity is inferred. Arrows show direction of relative displacement on low-angle detachments.

0   1   2   3 KILOMETERS

Horizontal scale

Vertical exaggeration = 3.0 at Sea Floor

Figure 27.   Seismic profile C–C' is the northeastern part of deep crustal survey line PGE-1 (fig. 3, pl. 1). It crosses the Hosgri Fault Zone west of Morro Bay. The main trace of the fault appears vertical to depths of 2 s (~3 km) with two interpreted splays that join the main trace at about 1.7 s. The "acoustic shadow" of the overlying fault block, rather than a separate fault, is interpreted to cause the termination of reflectors between 0.9 and 1.9 s near shotpoint 320. Due to the utilization of a low frequency response and high-energy-output air-gun array source and a long cable array for its acquisition, this line does not successfully image the shallow geology east of the Hosgri Fault Zone where shallow folding with short spatial wavelength is the dominant structural characteristic. Compare C–C' with profile C"–C"' (fig. 26).

subparallel to buried anticlines and associated detachments faults mapped on the west side of the fault.

Profiles C–C' (fig. 27), D–D' (fig. 28), and E–E' (fig. 29) show interpreted seismic sections from the San Luis/Pismo reach. Two, and sometimes three, closely spaced traces of the fault zone occur in a 2- to 3-km-wide zone (fig. 23, pl. 4). After correction for vertical exaggeration and apparent dip, the traces are vertical to near vertical in the upper 2 km of section and dip 65° to 85° NE. at depth. Two steeply dipping traces of the Hosgri Fault Zone and an associated thrust fault are shown on profile D–D'. The western main trace of the fault zone closely parallels and bisects the crest of an anticline west of Point Buchon. Artifacts forming diffraction-

like patterns are present in the upper part of this migrated profile. Similar features are also present on high-resolution analog records from the area. These features are interpreted as acoustic energy disbursed from a plume of gas-charged sediments marking the western trace of the Hosgri Fault Zone. The presence of this plume suggests that the western trace is acting as a conduit for hydrocarbon escape to the ocean floor. The eastern trace apparently truncates both the top of Miocene unconformity and early–late Pliocene unconformity. It is considered to be the primary and active trace from south of profile C–C' to beyond the intersection with the Pecho Fault at the southeast corner of figure 23.

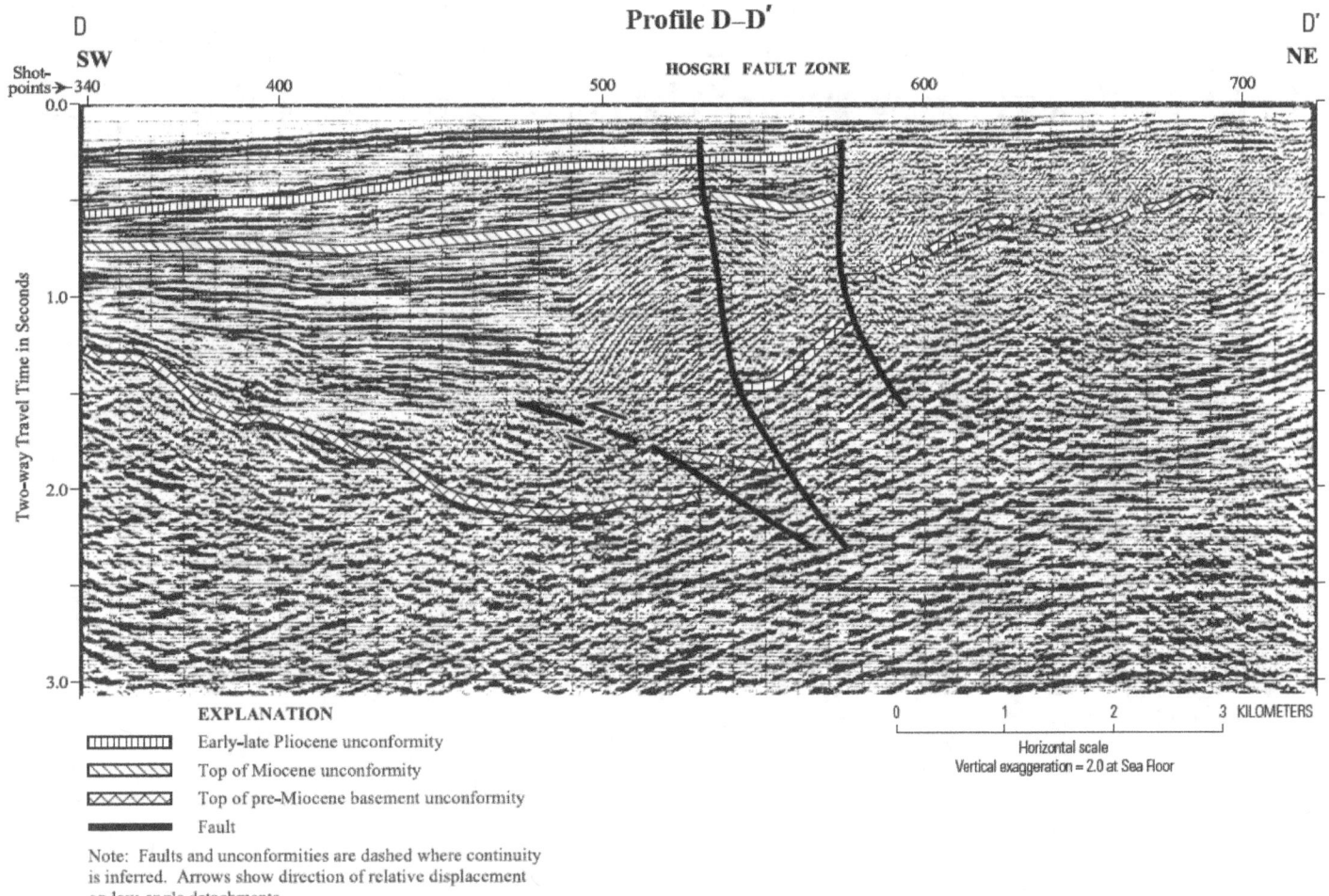

EXPLANATION

- Early–late Pliocene unconformity
- Top of Miocene unconformity
- Top of pre-Miocene basement unconformity
- Fault

Note: Faults and unconformities are dashed where continuity is inferred. Arrows show direction of relative displacement on low-angle detachments.

Figure 28. Seismic profile D–D' crosses the Hosgri Fault Zone west of Point Buchon. It is line GSI-85 on plate 1. There are three faults shown on the profile and the structural trend map (fig. 23). The western fault is a thrust fault that appears to intersect the western trace of the Hosgri Fault Zone (shotpoint 530) below 2.0 s. Both of the two Hosgri Fault traces are near vertical in the upper 1 to 1.5 s (1.0–1.4 km) of the record but dip to the northeast below those depths. The anticline associated with the thrust fault appears to be truncated by the top of Miocene unconformity. The western trace of the Hosgri Fault Zone, at shotpoint 530, is nearly coincident with the axis of the anticline at the location of the profile and is interpreted to offset the unconformity. The western trace appears to terminate at or near the early–late Pliocene unconformity. Based on high-resolution data (fig. 10), the eastern trace at shotpoint 575 is the active trace of the fault zone extending to the seafloor. East of the Hosgri Fault Zone, Miocene rocks are uplifted, eroded, and exposed at the seafloor. Rock types identified in the two shallow cores collected in the vicinity of the east half of this profile (A-113 and A-115 on pl. 2 and table 4) were identified as probable Monterey Formation or the equivalent of Miocene age (McCulloch and others, 1985).

The apparent vertical separation of basement across the fault is consistently up on the east along the entire San Luis/Pismo reach (fig. 14, pl. 5). The top of pre-Miocene basement is vertically separated across the multiple traces of the Hosgri Fault Zone by approximately 0.75 to 1.0 s (900 m to 1,200 m) of two-way travel time. Deformation of younger strata along this reach reflects continuing uplift of the adjacent San Luis/Pismo structural block. Estimated amounts

and rates of vertical deformation of the top of Miocene and early–late Pliocene unconformities along this reach are presented by Hanson and others (2004). Discontinuous west-facing seafloor scarps (fig. 10, bottom) on both traces of the Hosgri Fault Zone at the south end of the reach suggest late Quaternary activity.

There is a 10° westward deflection in the trend of the Hosgri Fault Zone at the north end of the San Luis/Pismo

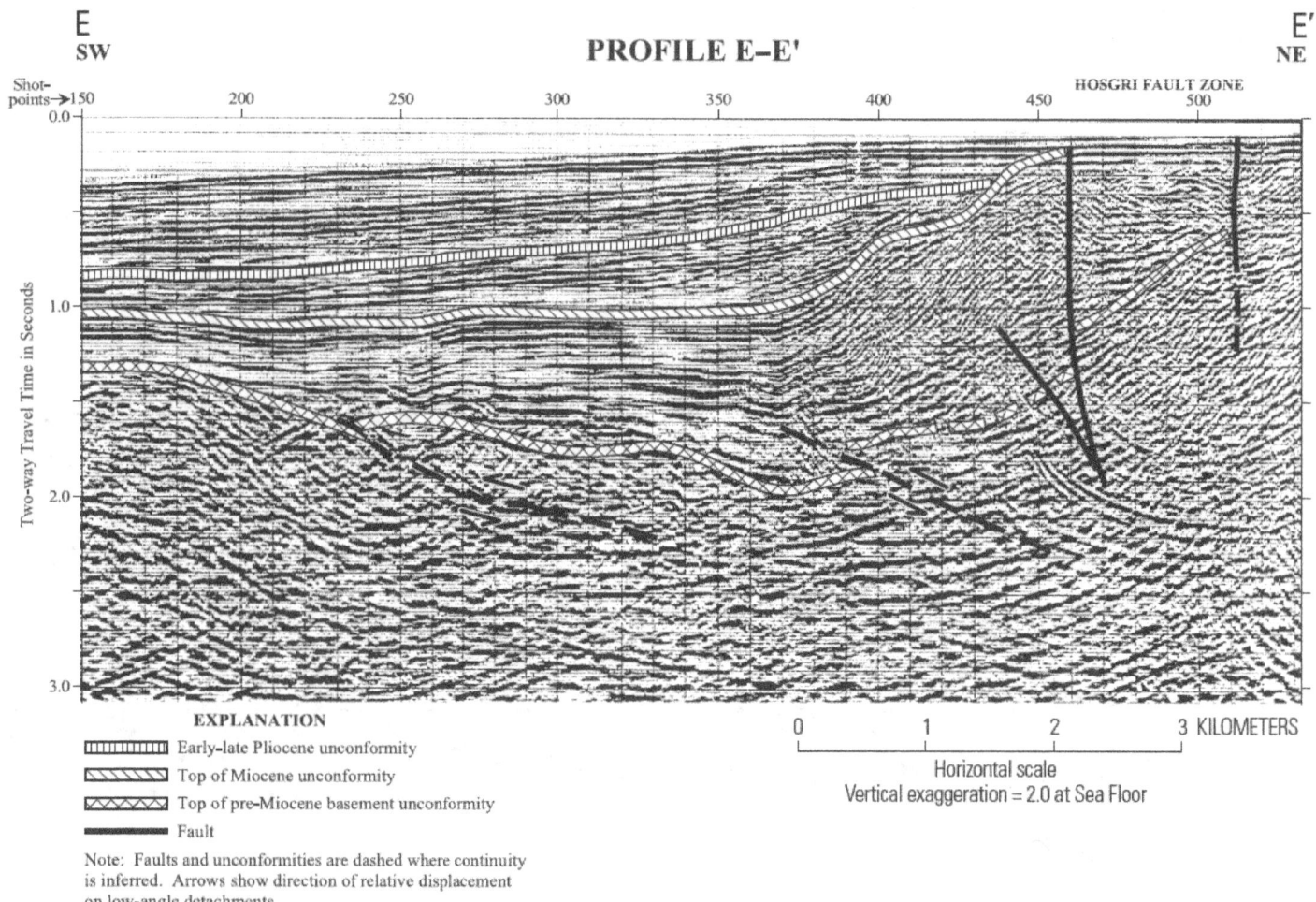

PROFILE E–E'

EXPLANATION

Early–late Pliocene unconformity

Top of Miocene unconformity

Top of pre-Miocene basement unconformity

Fault

Note: Faults and unconformities are dashed where continuity is inferred. Arrows show direction of relative displacement on low-angle detachments.

Horizontal scale
Vertical exaggeration = 2.0 at Sea Floor

Figure 29.   Seismic profile E–E' is at the south end of the San Luis/Pismo reach, north of the intersection between the Hosgri Fault Zone and the Pecho Fault. It is line GSI-87 on plate 1. There are two traces of the Hosgri Fault Zone shown on this profile. Both traces appear near vertical to 1.0 s; however, the west trace, at shotpoint 460, dips slightly to the northeast below this level. Both traces appear to extend nearly to the seafloor, and high-resolution seismic data, diver observations, and cores (pl. 2; tables 4, 5) suggest the zone between the traces, and the area east of the east trace, consists of tightly folded Miocene rocks, possibly Monterey Formation, overlain by thin patches of Holocene sediment. Two thrust faults are interpreted west of the Hosgri Fault Zone. The downdip extent of the thrusts is not imaged below 2.5 s on the seismic data, and the location of the thrust faults is based, in part, on analyses of the associated folds. The minor folding associated with the west thrust between shotpoints 280 and 320 appears to affect the top of Miocene unconformity but not the early–late Pliocene unconformity or the seafloor. This west thrust is subparallel to the top of pre-Miocene basement unconformity mapped immediately to the west and may utilize the unconformity as a detachment surface. The east thrust fault is interpreted to be responsible for the uplift of the anticline west of the Hosgri Fault Zone and may be responsible for a slight seafloor bulge beginning around shotpoint 350.

reach, near the intersection of the Los Osos Fault Zone (fig. 23, pl. 4). This change in direction is coincident with the northwest termination of a broad fold complex that subparallels the fault zone and deforms and uplifts the early–late Pliocene and top of Miocene unconformities directly west of the Hosgri Fault Zone across most of the reach. This fold is evident on both profiles D–D' (fig. 28) and E–E' (fig. 29). We interpret the axis of the fold to be cut by the west trace of the Hosgri Fault Zone on profile D–D' (fig. 28), and the east limb of this fold is truncated by the west trace on profile E–E' (fig. 29).

This fold complex is interpreted to be the result of imbricate thrusting associated with the same compressional stresses that formed the Purisima and Lompoc structures to the south. The causal thrust fault shows an apparent dip of about 35° to 45° to the northeast and as it descends northeastward it approaches, but does not intersect, the west trace within the depth of resolution ability of the seismic records in the area.

Absence of significant deformation on the early–late Pliocene unconformity in the north and central parts of the reach suggests that the principal episode of folding ended prior to deposition of upper Pliocene sediments in that area and also implies localized, episodic folding in this region. The early–late Pliocene unconformity has a gradual basinward slope west of the Hosgri Fault Zone, both in the northern and southern parts of the reach (profiles C–C', D–D', E–E'). At the north end of the reach, the fold does not exist or is only a very narrow feature between two strands of the Hosgri Fault Zone (fig. 26). In the central part of the reach, there appears to be little deformation of the early–late Pliocene unconformity above the fold and the west trace of the Hosgri Fault Zone (fig. 28). However, on profile E–E', both the sediments and the seafloor reflect post-Pliocene deformation above the fold (fig. 29).

San Luis Obispo Bay Reach

South of the intersection with the Pecho Fault, the primary trace of the Hosgri Fault Zone steps west 2 km and extends 62 km to the southeast as a continuous feature. The San Luis Obispo Bay reach is defined as the 23-km-long part of this trace from its intersection with the Pecho Fault, across San Luis Obispo Bay, to its intersection with the Casmalia Fault Zone (fig. 30, pl. 4). Profiles F–F' (fig. 31), G–G' (fig. 32) and H–H' (fig. 33) illustrate the Hosgri Fault Zone in this reach. Profile F–F' is from the high-resolution Comap Alaska CDP survey, G–G' is from a moderate-penetration petroleum industry CDP exploration survey, and H–H' is from the deep-penetration PG&E/EDGE survey. The three illustrations reflect contrasting views of the eastern offshore Santa Maria Basin and Hosgri Fault Zone from surveys collected with different source and recording parameters.

Profile F–F' (fig. 31) crosses the northern part of the reach and shows the principal traces of the Hosgri Fault Zone, as well as the trace of the Pecho Fault. The latter may be the offshore extension of the postulated Santa Maria Valley Fault shown on some geologic maps of the area (for example, Jennings, 1977). However, a direct connection cannot be made on high-resolution seismic data in San Luis Obispo Bay, because the Santa Maria Valley Fault is buried in the onshore area adjacent to the mapped location of the Pecho Fault.

Along the San Luis Obispo Bay reach, the Hosgri Fault Zone strikes N. 15–20° W. and consists of a continuous fault that forms the primary trace of the Hosgri Fault. This trace is vertical to steeply east dipping (80° to 90°) in the uppermost 1.5 to 2 s (1 to 1.5 km) of its vertical extent and appears to dip to the northeast at depth as shown on profiles G–G' (fig. 32) and H–H' (fig. 33).

The main eastern trace of the Hosgri Fault Zone extends into the San Luis Obispo Bay reach, from the San Luis/Pismo reach to the north, and subparallels the western trace for 10 km (fig. 30). Within the 2- to 3-km-wide zone of overlap between the two main traces of the Hosgri Fault Zone, several short discontinuous faults are mapped (fig. 30). This zone of overlap between the west and east traces forms a right en echelon stepover in which upper Pliocene and Miocene strata dip to the southwest and appear to be down-dropped in a half-graben (profile F–F', shotpoints 23 to 46, fig. 31). The half-graben is interpreted to be a small pull-apart basin formed as horizontal slip transfers from the west trace to the east trace. High-resolution analog data show that the west trace and the discontinuous east trace locally displace the late Wisconsin unconformity, demonstrating recent activity along this reach.

South of the right en echelon stepover, two faults with rapidly changing arcuate strikes are mapped (pl. 4). They form a 12-km-long zone of faulting that is subparallel to the west trace. These faults are interpreted to join the Hosgri at depth as illustrated on profile H–H'. Uplift and folding of the Miocene and lower Pliocene rocks 1 km west of these faults are inferred to be related to the northward development of compression between the east and west traces, which is manifested as a positive flower structure in the fault zone as shown in profile H–H'.

An important attribute of the San Luis Obispo Bay reach is the interpretation of apparent reversal in the vertical sense of separation across fault traces within the Hosgri Fault Zone and along strike across the entire fault zone. Similar reversals are also observed farther south along the southern reach as shown on figure 14 and plate 5. In profiles F–F' (fig. 31) and G–G' (fig. 32), the top of Miocene unconformity is displaced up to the east, whereas in profile H–H' (fig. 33) it is interpreted to be down on the east. The mapping of the top of Miocene unconformity between profiles G–G' and H–H' is controlled by a number of wells (pl. 6, table 7). On profile H–H', there is also a reversal of sense of displacement between the early–late Pliocene unconformity and top of Miocene unconformity (both down to the east) and the top of pre-Miocene basement unconformity (up to the east). Along this profile, well control exists on both sides of the Hosgri Fault Zone.

On the west side of the Hosgri Fault Zone in the southern half of the reach, an anticline or southwest-dipping monocline parallels the west trace (fig. 29, pl. 4). This anticline is at about shotpoint 360 on profile G–G' (fig. 32)

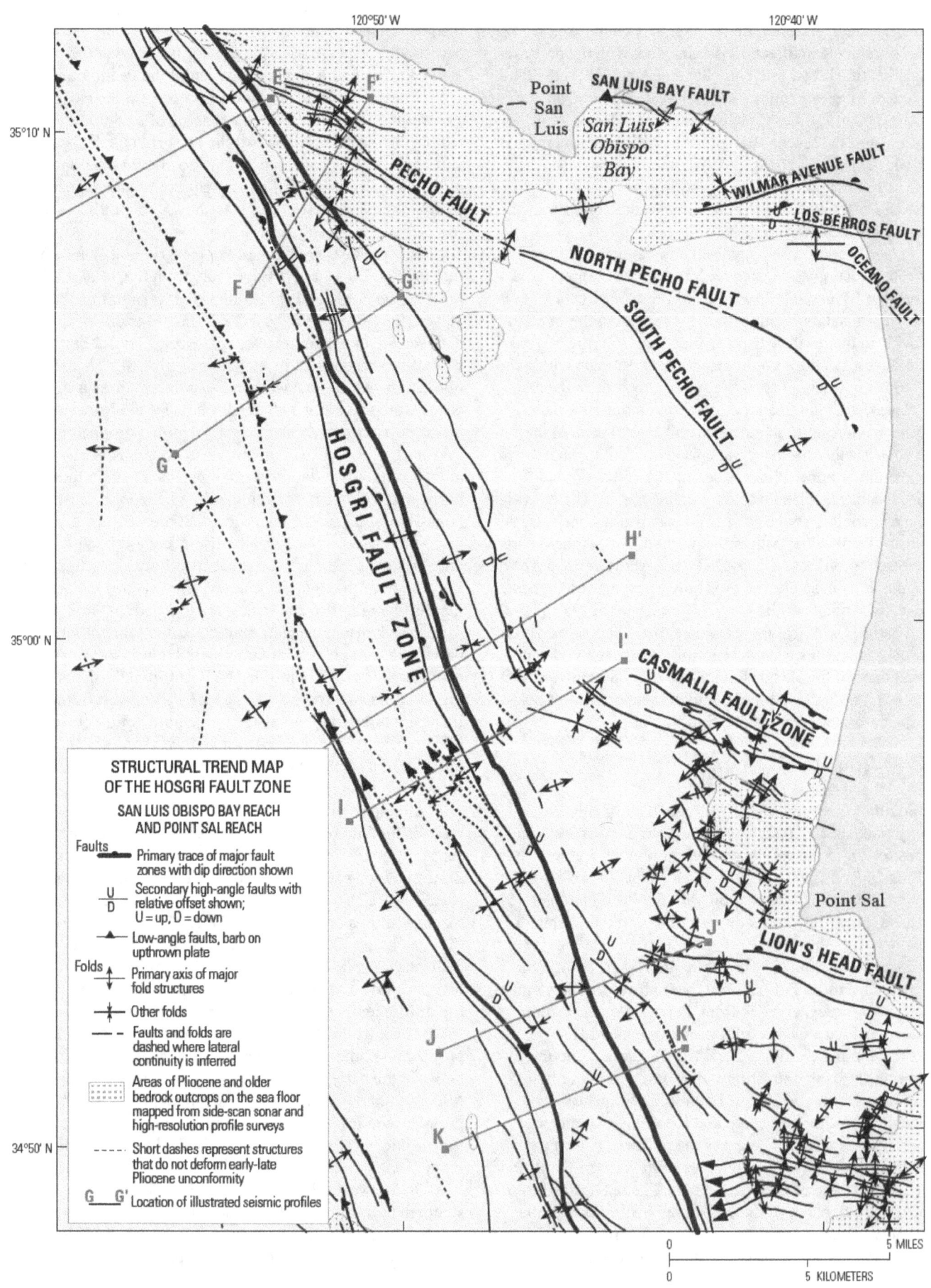

STRUCTURAL TREND MAP
OF THE HOSGRI FAULT ZONE

SAN LUIS OBISPO BAY REACH
AND POINT SAL REACH

Faults
— Primary trace of major fault
zones with dip direction shown

U/D Secondary high-angle faults with
relative offset shown;
U = up, D = down

▲ Low-angle faults, barb on
upthrown plate

Folds
↕ Primary axis of major
fold structures

╫ Other folds

— — Faults and folds are
dashed where lateral
continuity is inferred

▦ Areas of Pliocene and older
bedrock outcrops on the sea floor
mapped from side-scan sonar and
high-resolution profile surveys

- - - Short dashes represent structures
that do not deform early-late
Pliocene unconformity

G——G' Location of illustrated seismic profiles

Figure 30. Map showing part of the structural trend map (pl. 4) that includes the San Luis Obispo Bay and Point Sal reaches (fig. 17). It extends from the intersection of the Pecho Fault in the north to the projected intersection with the Lion's Head Fault in the south. The projected intersection of the Hosgri and Casmalia Fault Zones is considered the division between the two reaches. At the north end of the San Luis Obispo Bay reach, there are two main traces of the Hosgri Fault Zone. The east trace, that is considered the main trace in the San Luis/Pismo reach to the north, terminates just south of Profile G–G', while the west trace extends continuously from north of profile F–F' to south of the Lion's Head Fault intersection. The east and west traces overlap for approximately 10 km between profiles E–E' and the end of the east trace south of profile G–G'. Detailed mapping of the traces is facilitated by high-resolution survey data (of the type shown in fig. 10) that is at closer line spacings than the CDP data (pl. 1). Seismic profiles F–F' to J–J' depict the fault zone and adjacent structures in these two reaches and are shown on figures 31 through 35.

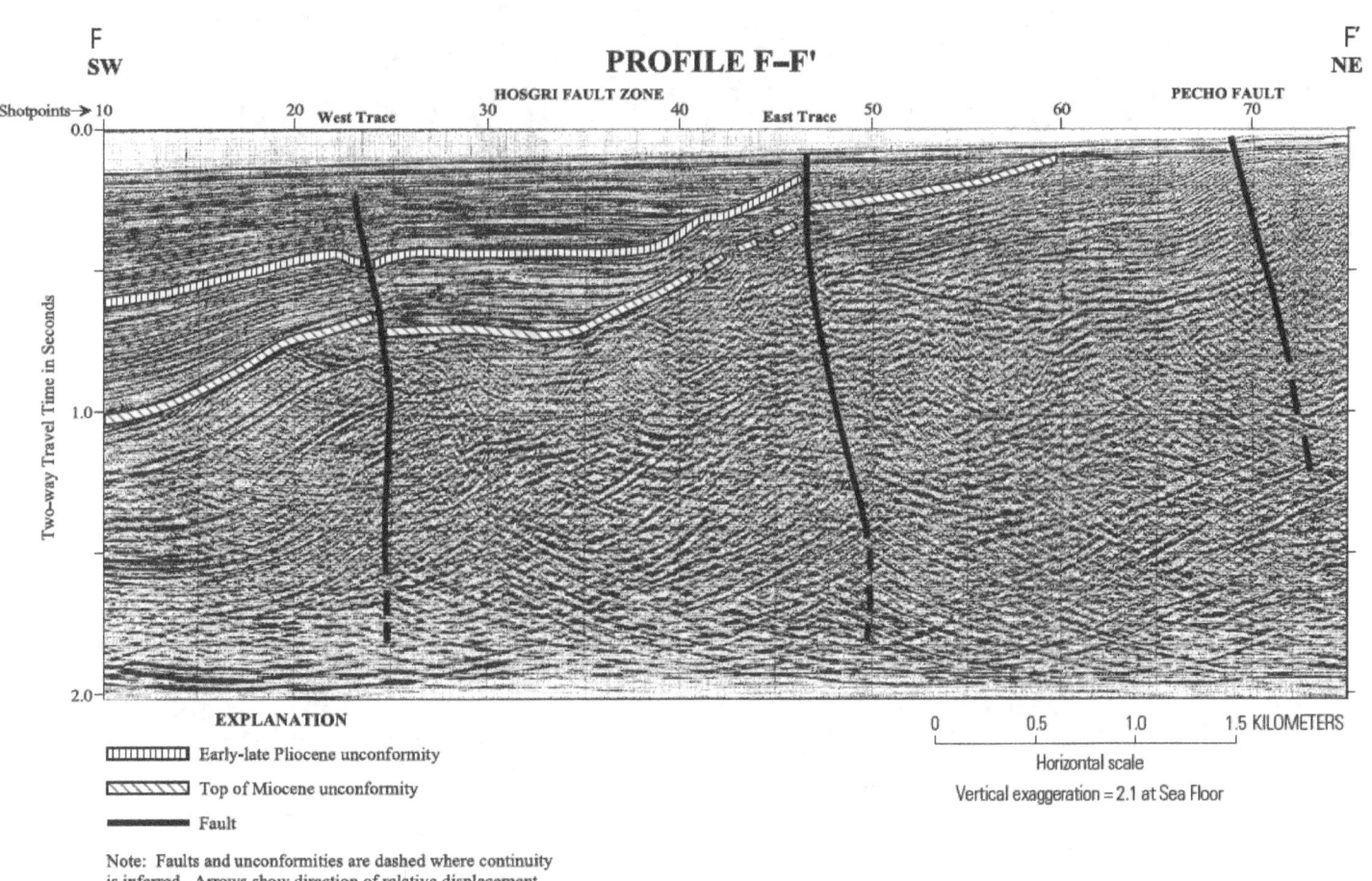

Figure 31. Seismic profile F–F' crosses the Hosgri Fault Zone and the Pecho Fault west of Point San Luis. It is a high-resolution image of the two main Hosgri Fault Zone traces and associated structures within the upper 1.5 to 2.0 s (≈1.5–2.0 km) of the section. It is line CM86-117 on plate 1. The line is 4 to 5 km south of profile E–E' and trends more northerly than E–E' (fig. 30). On profile F–F', both traces of the Hosgri Fault Zone appear to displace folds in the Miocene rocks. The east trace shows evidence of Holocene activity whereas the west trace shows evidence of activity into the Quaternary. The increase in the thickness of the lower Pliocene section across the west trace suggests that the apparent sense of vertical displacement changed between early and late Pliocene. Core and diver observations indicate that both Miocene and Franciscan Complex rocks crop out on the seafloor northeast of the Pecho Fault.

and shotpoint 480 on profile H–H' (fig. 33). We have identified a subhorizontal detachment associated with this fold at or near the basement rock contact. This fold appears to have formed during the late Miocene to middle Pliocene episode of crustal shortening that is recognized elsewhere in the offshore Santa Maria Basin (McCulloch, 1987; Clark and others, 1991; McIntosh and others, 1991; Meltzer and

Levander, 1991). A progressive decrease in the amount of fold deformation of Miocene and lower Pliocene sediments is shown clearly on profile G–G'. The early–late Pliocene unconformity has a basinward slope but apparently only a minor warp over the fold on profile G–G' (fig. 32). On profile H–H' (fig. 33), the early–late Pliocene unconformity is warped, but reflectors at 0.5 s and higher appear flat and

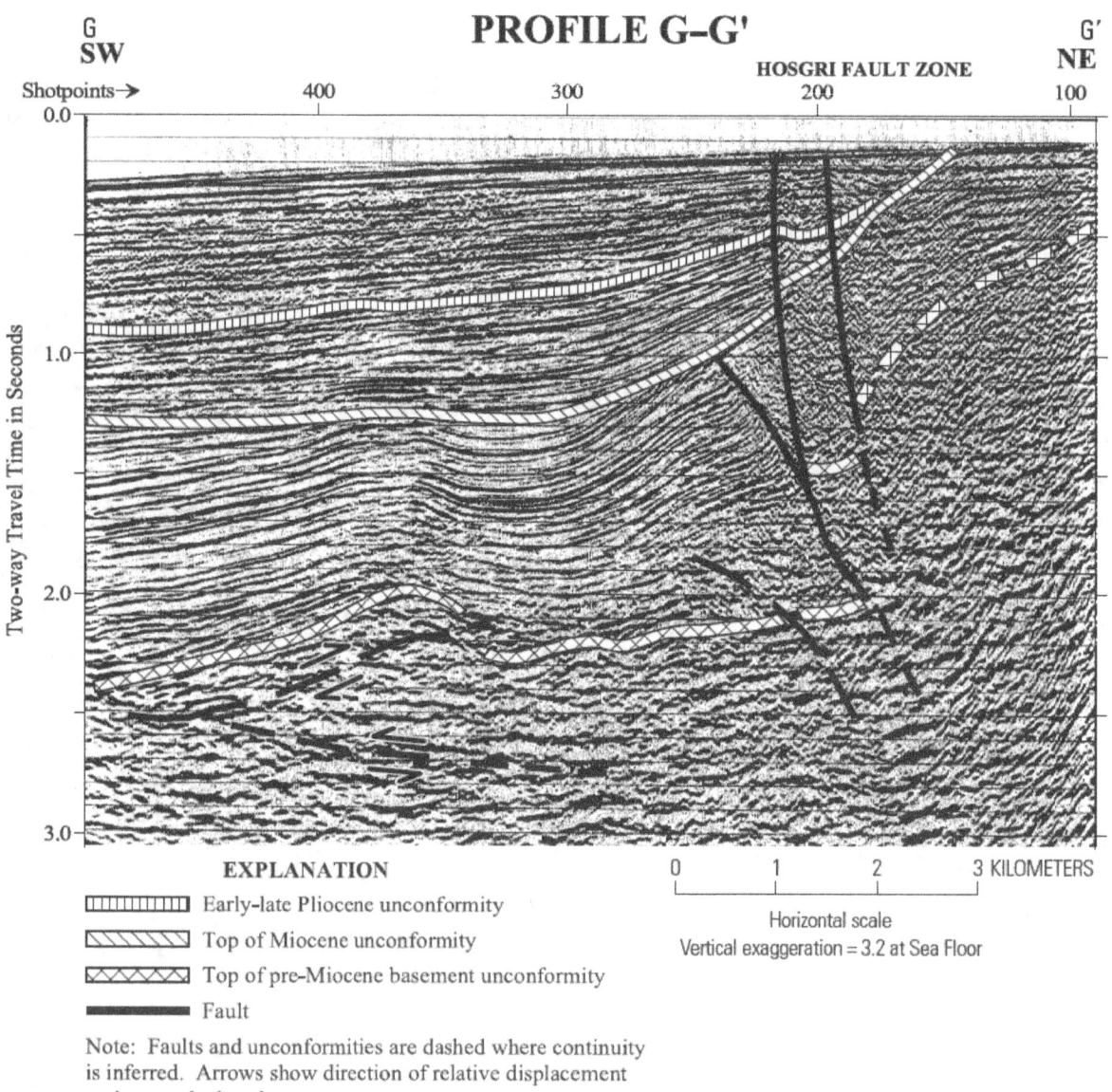

PROFILE G–G'

EXPLANATION

▦ Early-late Pliocene unconformity

▨ Top of Miocene unconformity

▧ Top of pre-Miocene basement unconformity

━━ Fault

Note: Faults and unconformities are dashed where continuity is inferred. Arrows show direction of relative displacement on low-angle detachments.

Figure 32.   Seismic profile G–G' is southwest of Point San Luis and crosses the west trace of the Hosgri Fault Zone. Profile G–G' is line J-126 on plate 1. Two closely spaced fault traces are shown near shotpoint 200. Both traces appear to reach the seafloor and are steeply dipping in the upper 1.5 s (≈1.5 km). They dip steeply northeast below 1.5 s and may join at depth though no evidence of this exists in the seismic imaging. Inactive thrust or reverse fault splays are shown immediately southwest of the western trace and also appear to join the western trace at depth. The anticlinal fold below 1.3 s at shotpoint 360 appears to be caused by a thrust fault that displaces the top of pre-Miocene basement unconformity. The location of the faults is modeled from the location and form of the associated folds.

undeformed. These observations are interpreted to indicate the activity of the fold and associated thrust fault decrease in a northward direction and are probably not currently active in the area north of profile H–H′. These anticlinal folds are part of the northward-plunging Purisima structure depicted on the maps of the three unconformities (pls. 5–7; figs. 14–16). The detachment responsible for the Purisima structure lies within the seismic basement, and its intersection with the Hosgri Fault Zone is not imaged on the profiles in this reach.

Point Sal Reach

The Point Sal reach is the 12- to 14-km-long section of the Hosgri Fault Zone between the intersections of the Casmalia Fault Zone and the Lion's Head Fault Zone (figs. 17, 29; pl. 4). Onshore, the Casmalia Fault Zone has also been labeled on published maps as the Orcutt Frontal Fault (Clark, 1990), Casmalia Fault (Lettis and others, 1990), and Pezzoni Fault (Hall, 1978) and as combinations of these names. Along this reach the Hosgri Fault Zone forms the west boundary of

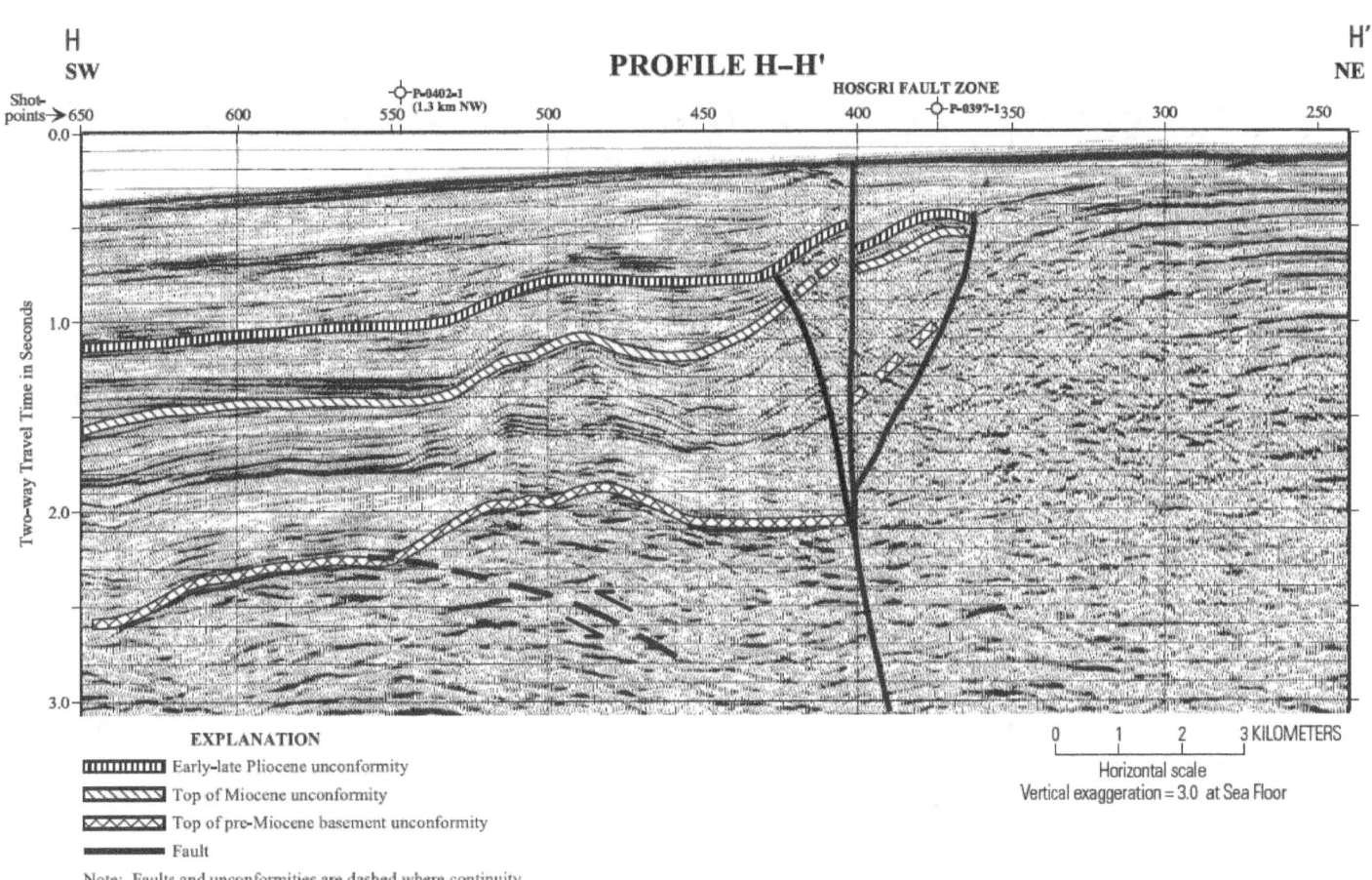

Figure 33. Seismic profile H–H′ is part of line PGE-3, one of the deep crustal survey lines (fig. 3, pl. 1). The western trace of the Hosgri Fault Zone is interpreted to be a three-branch flower structure extending over a 3-km-wide zone of disruption above 1.0 s. The main trace of the fault appears to be near vertical to 3.0 s, with a slight northeastward dip below 2.4 s. Two wells are close to the seismic line and the data from these wells (table 7) were used to help identify the mapped unconformities on both sides of the fault zone. The anticlinal structure between shotpoints 450 and 550 is near the northernmost extent of the 35-km-long zone of continuous west-verging thrust faulting (pl. 5) that is interpreted to be associated with the Purisima structure farther to the southeast. Seismic line PGE-3 does not adequately image the geology east of the Hosgri Fault Zone, because it is a deep crustal survey line that has a relatively low frequency energy source and a large horizontal spacing of its recording array.

the Point Sal high, a region of elevated basement rock within the Casmalia block that itself is uplifted between the Casmalia and Lion's Head Fault Zones (Lettis and others, 2004). This region of elevated basement is well defined by potential field data (Rietman and Beyer, 1982; McCulloch and Chapman, 1977). Profiles I–I' (fig. 34) and J–J' (fig. 35) show the Hosgri Fault Zone and adjacent structures at the north and south ends of the reach.

The structural trend map (fig. 30, pl. 4) shows that, along this reach, the Hosgri Fault Zone consists of a single strand that is the southward continuation of the western trace of the Hosgri Fault Zone mapped in the San Luis Bay reach. In the Point Sal Reach, the Hosgri Fault displays a near-vertical dip in the upper 1.5 s of the seismic records. At greater depths the dip decreases and rotates to the northeast.

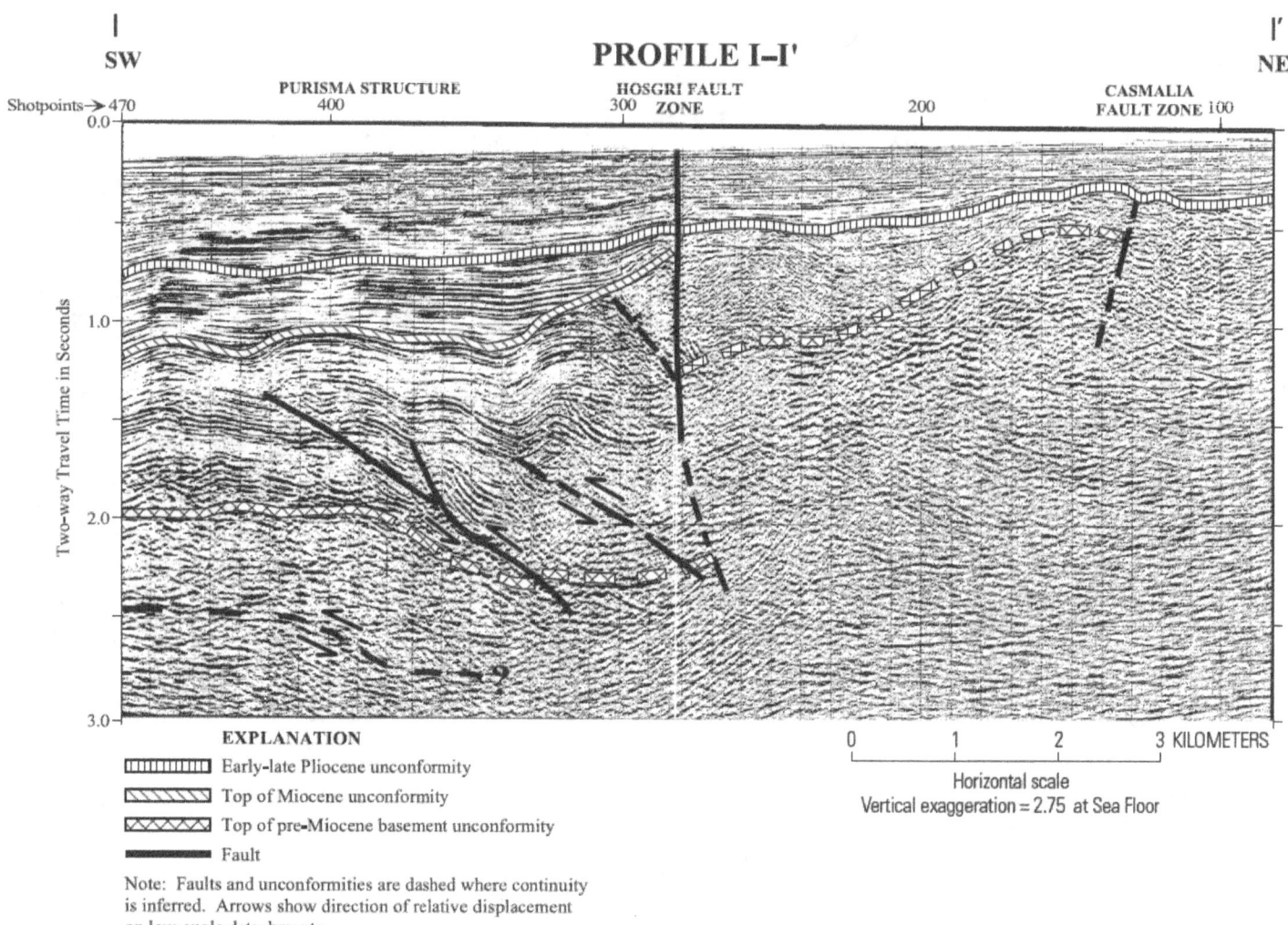

Figure 34.   Seismic profile I–I' crosses the Hostri and Casmalia Fault Zones northwest of Point Sal. It is line 45-202 on plate 1. The upper unconformity shown on the east side of the Hosgri Fault Zone appears to separate upper Pliocene and younger rocks from underlying Miocene rocks, and the lower Pliocene section may be missing. In this area, there is 0.5 s of post-lower Pliocene section at the Hosgri Fault Zone and more than 0.7 s of this section at shotpoint 400 farther to the west. The early–late Pliocene unconformity is apparently not vertically offset by the fault. On the west side of the fault, there are several tight folds between the Hosgri Fault Zone and the main fold of the northernmost extension of the Purisima structure (pl. 4). The rapid increase of rock thickness section between the top of pre-Miocene basement unconformity and the top of Miocene unconformity between shotpoints 375 and 300 may be the result of structural thickening caused by minor imbricate thrust faults associate with these folds. This is one of the profiles displayed by Crouch and others (1984) to support their interpretation of the Hosgri Fault Zone as a thrust fault. Snyder (1987) shows an alternative model of this profile that attributes the folding to bedding-plane slippage within the Miocene rocks rather than to major thrusting postulated by Crouch and others (1984).

The two illustrated seismic profiles crossing the Hosgri Fault Zone in this reach (figs. 34, 35) show a series of well-defined thrust faults on the west side of the fault zone. On profile I–I' (fig. 34), the northward-dipping Purisima structure is evident as a series of low-amplitude folds and thrust faults that display only minor influence on the structure of the early–late Pliocene unconformity. Upper Pliocene and younger horizons above the unconformity dip basinward and are either flat lying or only mildly deformed. However,

where thrust faults break Miocene rocks, these rocks show strong compressional deformation. The faulting is inferred to originate within the pre-Miocene basement or along the top of pre-Miocene basement unconformity, which may act as a detachment fault in this area. On profile I–I', the early–late Pliocene unconformity is not vertically offset across the Hosgri Fault. However, a vertical zone of disrupted reflectors are imaged coincident with the upward projection of the fault and may indicate the extension of the fault to the surface as a

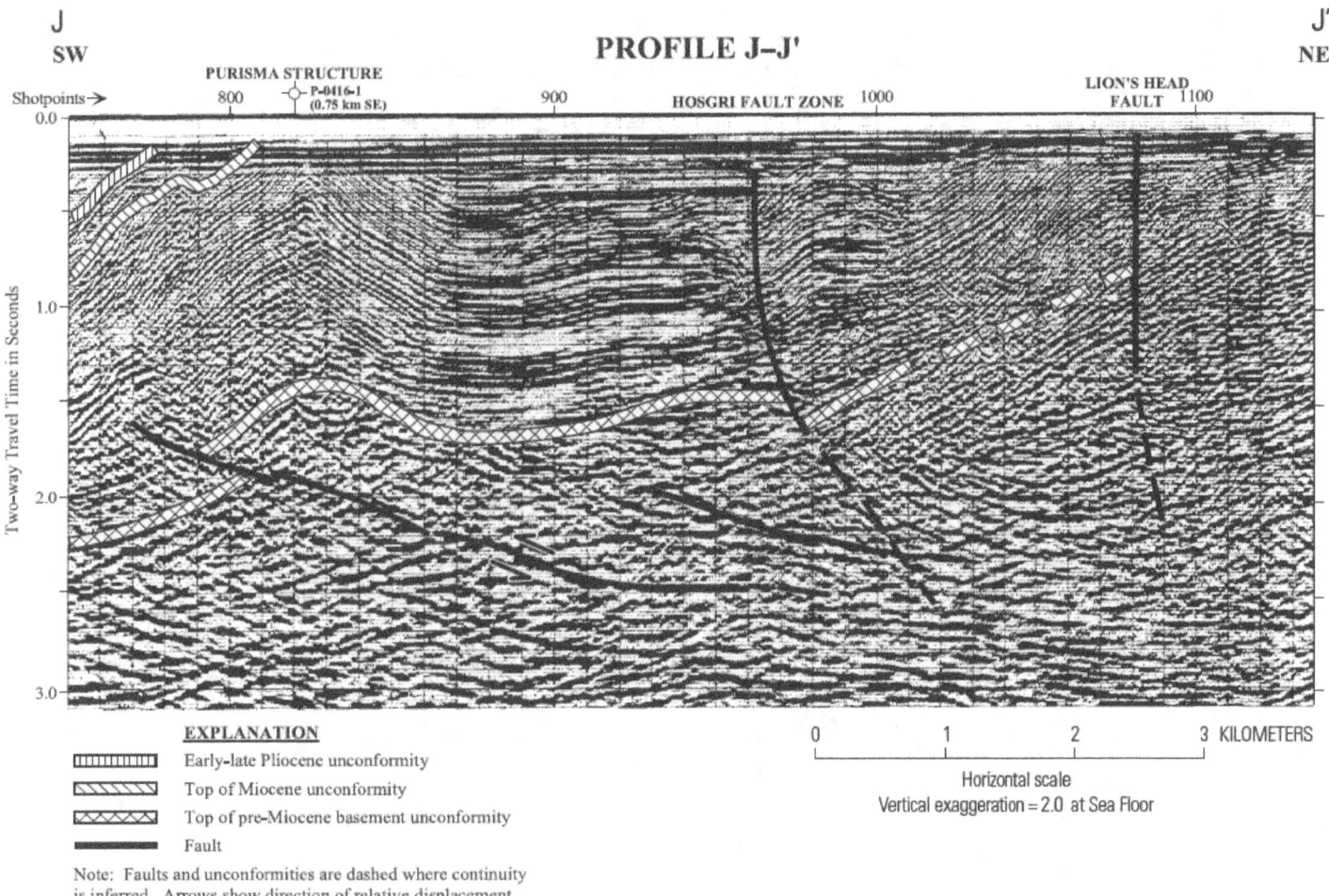

Figure 35. Seismic profile J–J' is offshore from Point Sal and shows the Purisima structure, Hosgri Fault Zone, and Lion's Head Fault. The profile is line GSI-107 on plate 1. The primary trace of the Hosgri Fault Zone is continuous with the primary trace of the fault zone shown on section I–I' (fig. 34). At this profile, the Hosgri Fault trace dips to the east below 1.2 s. A comparison between profiles J–J' and I–I' (fig. 34) suggests uplift of the entire section spanned by Profile J–J' as evidenced by the lack of the early–late Pliocene unconformity on profile I–I'. There is apparently little vertical displacement on the pre-Miocene basement surface at the Hosgri Fault Zone. Numerous high-amplitude reflections occur within the basement complex in the southern reach as illustrated below 2.0 s on this profile. The origin of these reflection events is not indicated by our data set. Possible sources are sediment and metasediment horizons, low-angle fault planes, and seismic processing artifacts. On profile J–J' the existence of a low-angle detachment within the basement rocks is implied by the modeling of the Purisima fold structure.

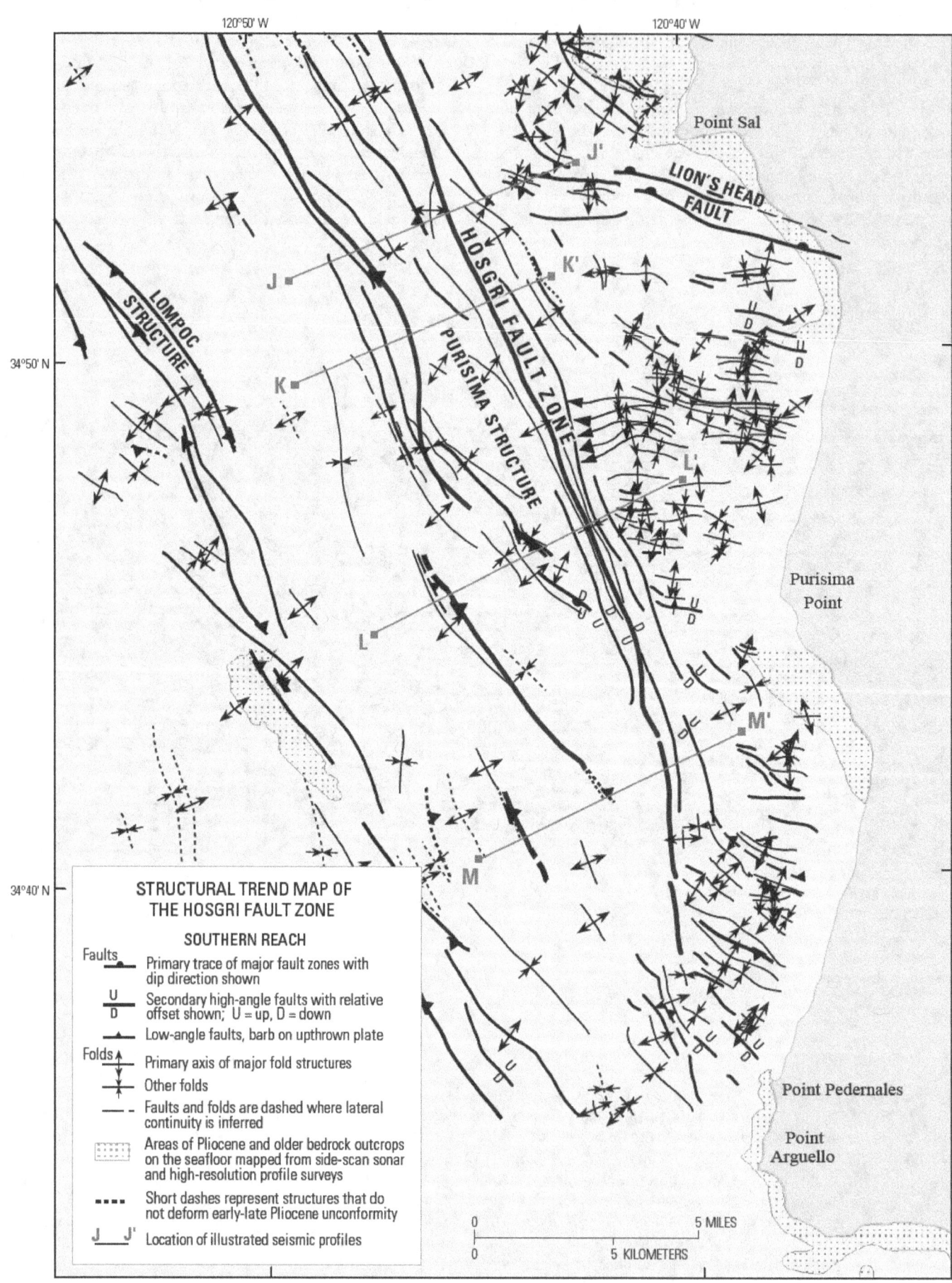

STRUCTURAL TREND MAP OF
THE HOSGRI FAULT ZONE

SOUTHERN REACH

Faults
— Primary trace of major fault zones with
dip direction shown

$\frac{U}{D}$ Secondary high-angle faults with relative
offset shown; U = up, D = down

— Low-angle faults, barb on upthrown plate

Folds
— Primary axis of major fold structures

— Other folds

— Faults and folds are dashed where lateral
continuity is inferred

Areas of Pliocene and older bedrock outcrops
on the seafloor mapped from side-scan sonar
and high-resolution profile surveys

Short dashes represent structures that do
not deform early-late Pliocene unconformity

J___J' Location of illustrated seismic profiles

0   5 MILES

0   5 KILOMETERS

small vertical-displacement feature. The lack of displacement at the early–late Pliocene unconformity is not necessarily indicative of lack of activity on the Hosgri Fault, but the fault may be dominantly lateral slip in character in this area, resulting in coincidental alignment of horizons.

East of the Hosgri Fault Zone, the top of Miocene unconformity and lower Pliocene rocks have been eroded, placing upper Pliocene and younger rocks in contact with Miocene rocks across the Hosgri Fault Zone as displayed in Profile I–I′. The strata deposited before the early–late Pliocene unconformity are intensely folded and form a zone of complex faults and folds east of the fault zone as shown on plate 4 and figure 30. Profile I–I′ extends northeastward into southern San Luis Obispo Bay. This profile shows 250 to 400 m of nearly flat-lying upper Pliocene to Holocene sediments in this area. The offshore part of the Casmalia Fault Zone appears to have deformed the early–late Pliocene unconformity, but northeast of shotpoint 170 the overlying sediments appear horizontal and buttress against the uplift observed in the unconformity.

Profile J–J′ (fig. 35), at the boundary between the Point Sal reach and the southern reach, presents a substantially different image of the Purisima structure and Hosgri Fault Zone than seen at the north boundary of the reach. Miocene rocks of the Purisima structure are exposed at the seafloor, suggesting the fold was eroded during a recent sea-level lowstand. However, within the resolution of the seismic data, there does not appear to be any seafloor displacement since that time. Both the top of Miocene unconformity and early–late Pliocene unconformity also are eroded from above the Hosgri Fault Zone.

Numerous subhorizontal reflectors are evident within the pre-Miocene basement rocks on profile J–J′ (fig. 35). The origin of these features is not identified and they may have multiple sources. On profile J–J′, some of the reflectors are interpreted to be thrust faults responsible for the Purisima structure and other folds, and others are inferred to be the signatures of sedimentary or metasedimentary rock units

within the pre-Miocene basement. Many of the apparent broad subhorizontal features at depth are artifacts of the seismic processing. Attempts to map these subhorizontal reflectors have not been successful, because the intrabasement reflectors cannot be correlated between adjacent seismic lines. Therefore, it is difficult to specify a definitive geologic origin for these features.

Southern Reach

The southern reach of the Hosgri Fault Zone is 24 to 26 km long and extends from the intersection of the fault zone with the Lion's Head Fault to its termination 4 km northwest of Point Pedernales (fig. 36). The fault zone strikes N. 20° W. along the northern part of this reach to a location about 5.5 km west of Purisima Point, where its strike bends toward the south to a bearing of N. 7° W. The fault continues along this trend to its southern termination. Features associated with the Hosgri Fault Zone in this reach are the Purisima structure fold complex, reversals in sense of vertical displacement, and the presence of a 20-km-long region along which flower structures dominate the fault-zone geometry. The reach also includes the southern termination of the fault zone, where it breaks into short, en echelon traces and dies out (fig. 36, pl. 4). Profiles K–K′ (fig. 37), L–L′ (fig. 38), and M–M′ (fig. 39) illustrate the Hosgri Fault Zone and adjacent structures in the reach.

On profile K–K′, we interpret the Hosgri Fault Zone as a series of four strands that join at depth to form a flower structure (Harding, 1985). The primary trace of the fault is near vertical in the upper 1.0 s of the record and then is interpreted to dip to the northeast. Younger rocks (Miocene and younger) have been eroded off the top of the Purisima structure and to the east. A very slight change in seafloor slope in the vicinity of shotpoint 900 may indicate post-Wisconsin activity on the Hosgri Fault Zone in this area.

One of the prominent structural features in the southern reach is the Purisima fold complex located west and subparallel to the Hosgri Fault Zone. This is a zone of uplift that geometrically varies, from north to south, from a 2-km-wide discrete anticline (profile J–J′, fig. 35,) separated from the Hosgri Fault Zone to a 5-km-wide region of uplift with multiple folds that upwarps and converges into, and is terminated by, the fault zone (profiles K–K′, fig. 37, and L–L′, fig. 38). The northern part of the Purisima structure is interpreted to result from fault-bend folding generated by a single thrust fault imaged on profiles J–J′ and K–K′ between shotpoints 800 and 900 and 750 and 850, respectively. However, to the south, the structure is interpreted to be underlain by two west-verging thrust faults, which are responsible for the formation of multiple folds as shown in profile L–L′ and plate 5.

The cross-sectional appearance of the Purisima structure changes significantly from profile to profile. This is due to the presence of northwest-trending cross folding superimposed on the primary Hosgri-parallel trend of the

Figure 36. Map showing part of the structural trend map (pl. 4) that includes the southern reach of the Hosgri Fault Zone (fig. 17). It extends from the intersection of the Lion's Head Fault in the north to the interpreted south end of the Hosgri Fault Zone directly north of Point Pedernales. In this reach the folding on the east side of the Hosgri Fault Zone becomes tighter and more discontinuous. Fold axes are more closely spaced, have shorter aerial extent, and display a more westerly trend than those to the north. A major thrust fault, inferred to be the causal fault of the Purisima structure, lies west of the Hosgri Fault Zone. Seismic profiles K–K′ to M–M′ depict the fault zone and adjacent structures in this reach and are shown on figures 37 through 39.

uplift. Profile J–J' cuts the Purisima structure at a location where its shape is dominated by Hosgri-parallel fault-bend folding and its east flank is well developed. Profile K–K', approximately 3.5 km to the south, crosses the structure in a location where its line of section strikes obliquely across a major northwest-trending cross fold, which locally nullifies the east flank of the Purisima trend's primary Hosgri-parallel fold trend. Farther south, profile L–L' traverses the structure in a location where Hosgri-parallel folding is again dominant (fig. 15, pl. 5). The Purisima structure ends abruptly 2 km north of profile M–M' (fig. 16, pl. 6). The only vestige of its

folding on this profile is a zone of uplift bounding the west side of the primary trace of the Hosgri Fault.

Profile M–M' (fig. 39) is at the south end of the Purisima structure where it merges with the Hosgri Fault Zone. The profile crosses the fault zone approximately 7 km to the southwest of Purisima Point (fig. 36). We interpret the fault zone as a narrow flower structure that offsets the top of pre-Miocene basement unconformity. The fault appears to have deformed, but not offset, the top of Miocene unconformity and lower Pliocene sediments above the unconformity. The top of pre-Miocene basement unconformity regionally

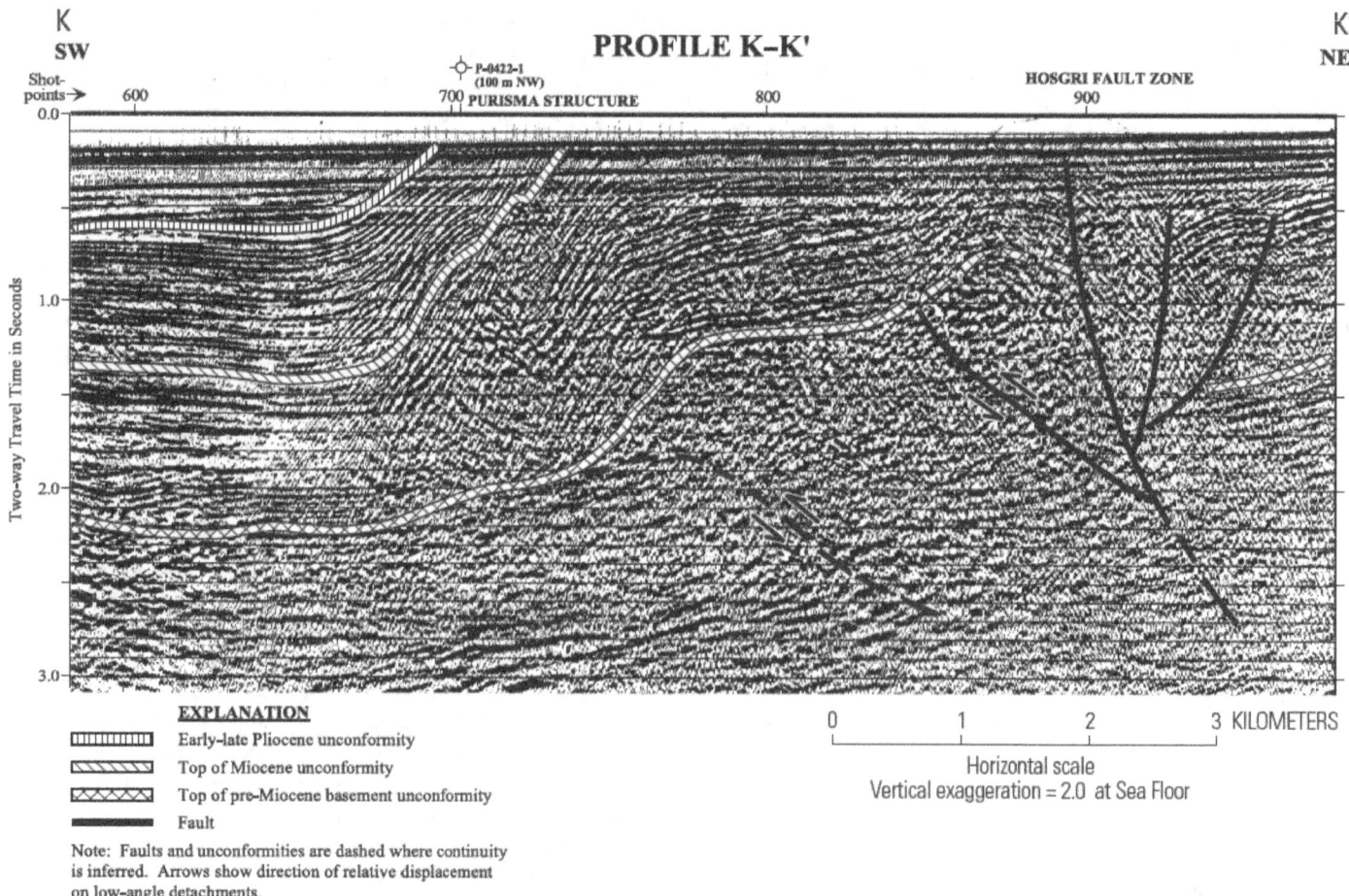

Figure 37.   Seismic profile K–K' crosses the Purisima structure and the Hosgri Fault Zone at the north end of the southern reach. It is line GSI-112C on plate 1. The Hosgri Fault Zone is interpreted as a flower structure with the side branches joining the main trace between 1.5 and 2.0 s reflection time (approximately 2.0 to 2.5 km depth). In this area, the sense of displacement reverses on the top of pre-Miocene basement unconformity. Uplift is on the southwest side of the Hosgri Fault Zone in contrast to profile J–J', 4 km to the north, that shows little basement vertical offset and all profiles farther north, where the basement is uplifted on the northeast side of the fault zone. Additional evidence confirming this reversal of basement-rock displacement across and along the Hosgri Fault Zone is discussed in the text. We interpret both the early–late Pliocene and top of Miocene unconformities to be eroded off the top of the Purisima structure and across the Hosgri Fault Zone. The intrabasement reflectors noted on profile J–J' (fig. 35) are also present below 2.5 s on this profile.

dips into the fault zone as documented in the profiles from north of Point Sal. A relatively flat, northeast-dipping intrabasement reflector beginning at 2.2 s beneath shotpoint 320 may be a detachment responsible for the folding beneath and west of shotpoint 400. The continuity of this reflector appears broken in several places, around shotpoint 450 and between shotpoints 570 and 600. It is not clear whether this reflector correlates with the event at 2.4 s on the east side of the Hosgri Fault Zone or the one at 2.9 s. It is also possible that strike-slip motion has juxtaposed the events and there is no correlation at all of deep events across the Hosgri Fault Zone at this location.

Two reversals in the sense of vertical separation in the top of the pre-Miocene basement unconformity are interpreted across the Hosgri Fault Zone along the 30-km

reach spanned by profiles I–I' (north of Point Sal) and M–M' (south of Purisima Point). The amount of vertical separation across the unconformity reverses from about 1 km with the east side up on profile I–I' to 0.2 km with the east side down 10 km to the south on profile J–J'. Farther south on profile K–K', the east-side-down separation increases to about 0.7 km and again diminished to 0.3 km, 9 km farther south on profile L–L'. In the 10-km-long reach between profiles L–L' and M–M', the sense of displacement of the unconformity again reverses to 0.5 km with east side up. West of the Hosgri Fault Zone, the reflection signature interpreted as the top of pre-Miocene basement unconformity is relatively easily mapped, and its location is substantiated by numerous wells along the west side of the fault zone. East of the fault zone, seismic signatures are more difficult to interpret and,

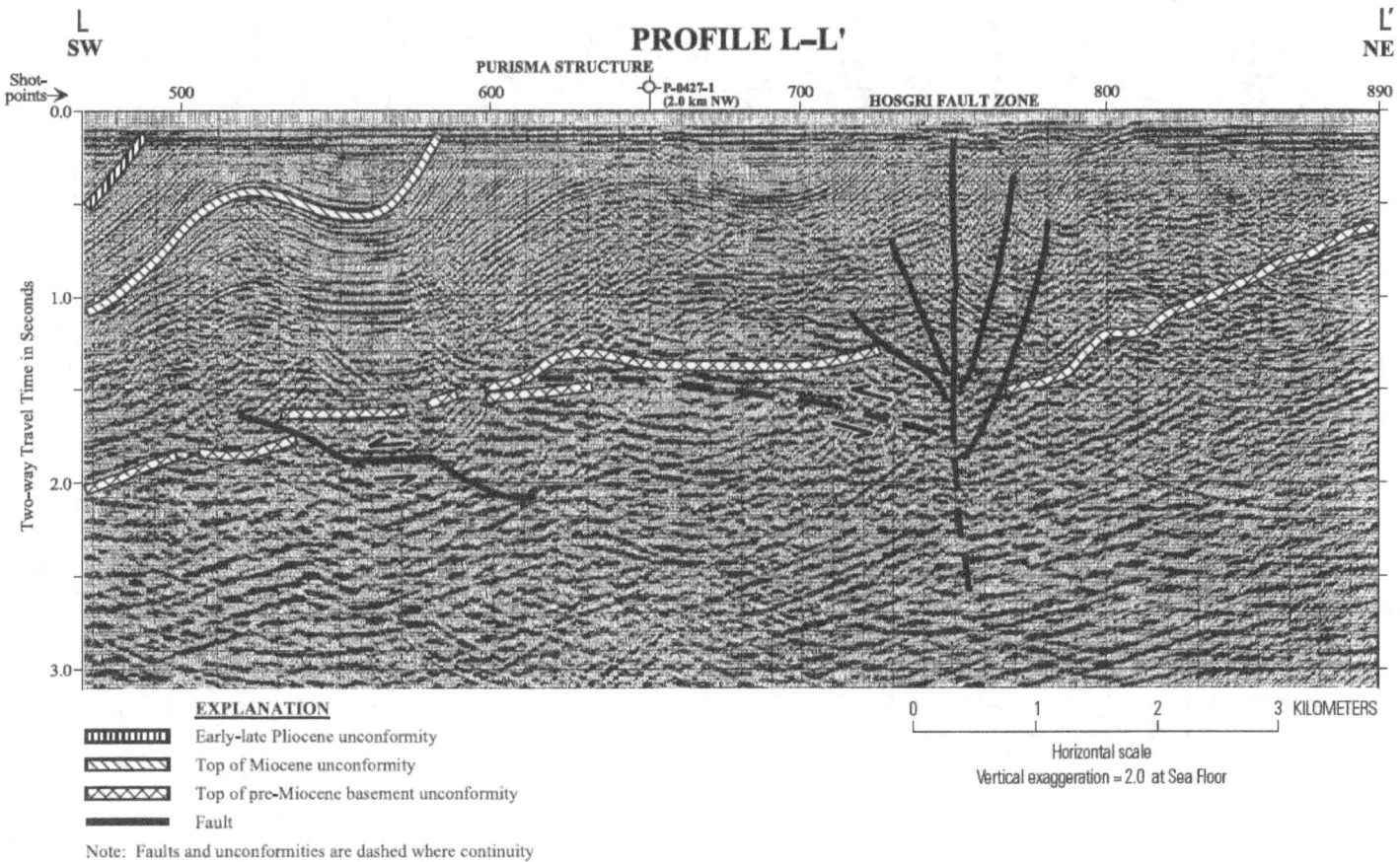

Figure 38. Seismic profile L–L' crosses the Purisima Structure and Hosgri Fault Zone west of Purisima Point. It is line GSI-118 on plate 1. The Hosgri Fault Zone is interpreted as a flower structure with the branches joining the main fault at about 1.5 s (approximately 2 km depth in Miocene rocks). The top of pre-Miocene basement unconformity rises to the east but has only minor apparent vertical offset at the Hosgri Fault Zone. The intra-basement reflectors noted on profiles J–J' (fig. 35) and K–K' (fig. 37) are also present on this profile. Both the early–late Pliocene and top of Miocene unconformities are not present east of the west flank of the Purisima Structure. This is also true for the approximate 12.5 km reach southeastward from profile J–J' (figs. 15, 16). This is confirmed by data from well 0427-1 (table 7).

on this side of the fault, wells are sparse. Confirmation of the seismic interpretations of east-side-down basement regions is provided by the coincidence of these regions with magnetic and gravity anomalies (McCulloch and Chapman, 1977; Rietman and Beyer, 1982; Sauer and Mariano, 1990).

The southern reach of the Hosgri Fault Zone is interpreted to display characteristics of flower structures (Harding, 1985). Similar to other reaches of the fault zone, multiple traces are mapped along the southern reach. However, the nature of these traces differs at depth from the relations documented between the east and west traces to the north. In the southern reach, the multiple traces in the upper 1.0 s of the seismic profiles are interpreted as branches of flower structures that join the primary trace at depths of 1.5 to 2 s. In this reach, a 2-km-wide region of near-surface fault traces characterize the fault zone rather than a single dominant (primary) trace. The deeper parts of the fault zone are projected to 2.5 to 3.0 s on profiles K–K' through M–M' and are inferred to show east dip ranging from 65° to 85° in this time range.

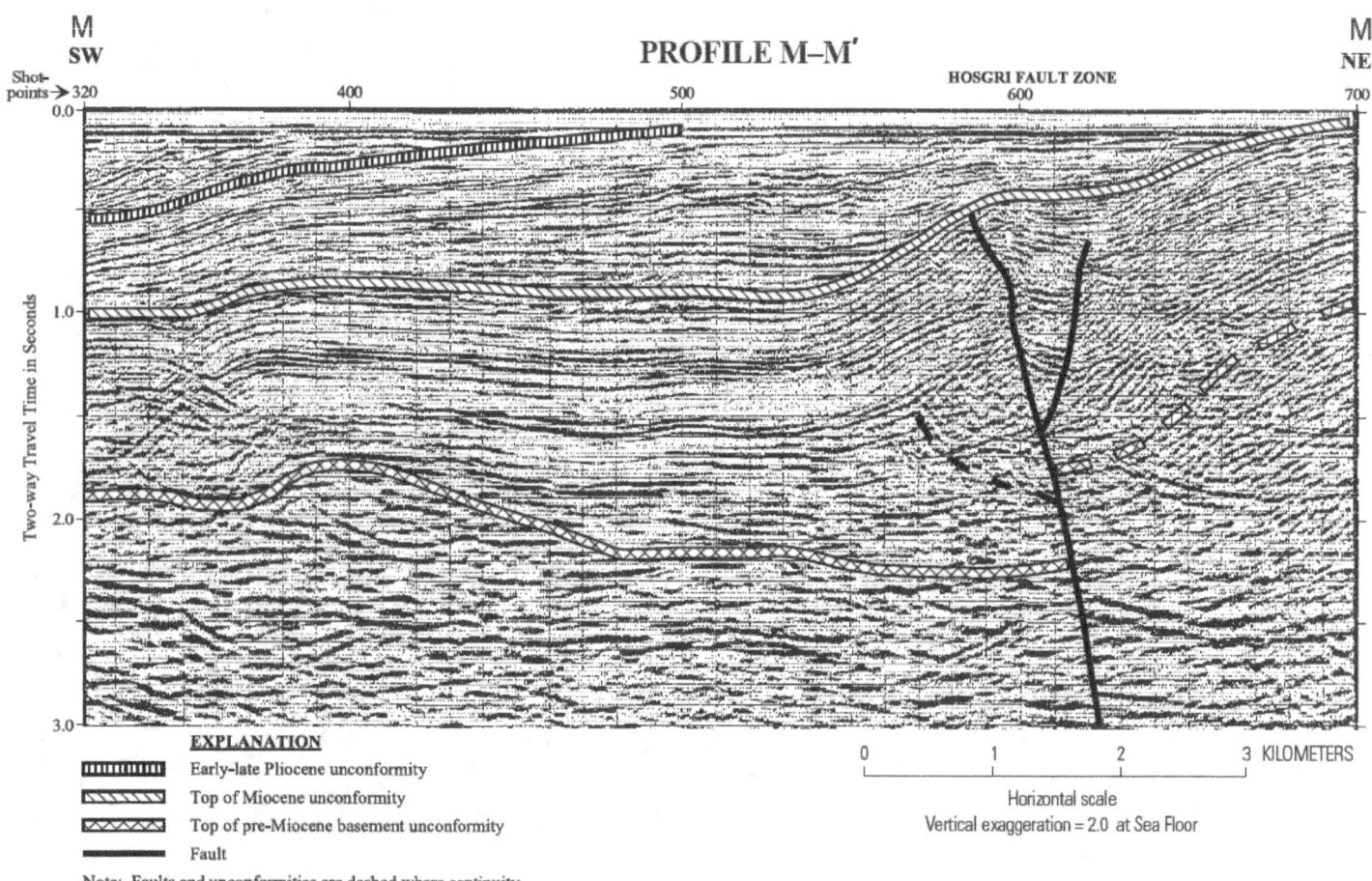

Figure 39. Seismic profile M–M' crosses the Hosgri Fault Zone south of Purisima Point. It is line GSI-123 on plate 1. Significant changes in the character of the fault zone have occurred between profiles L–L' and M–M'. The top of pre-Miocene basement unconformity west of the fault dips eastward into the Hosgri Fault Zone similar to profiles A–A' to I–I' and is up on the northeast side of the fault. The Hosgri Fault Zone appears to be a flower structure, but the main branch is near vertical to 3.0 s and does not have the northeast dip observed in profiles J–J' (fig. 35) and K–K' (fig. 37). The top of Miocene unconformity is mappable across the entire section, and though it is deformed above the Hosgri Fault Zone, it is not broken by it. The lower Miocene reflectors appear to onlap the top of pre-Miocene basement unconformity between shotpoints 400 and 500. A prominent gently northeastward-dipping intrabasement reflector is present at 2.3 to 2.6 s between shotpoints 320 and 550. This reflector appears to be either offset by a vertical fault or discontinuous between shotpoints 550 and the Hosgri Fault Zone at shotpoint 620.

South of the Point Sal high, between Point Sal and Purisima Point, the Hosgri Fault Zone separates east-west-trending folds on its east side from the major northwest-trending folds on the west side that is dominated by the Purisima and Lompoc structures (pls. 5, 6, 7). South of Purisima Point, the folding on the east side of the fault zone swings to a more northwesterly direction until, at the south end of the Hosgri Fault Zone, the strike of folding on both sides of the fault is subparallel and trends northwest (fig. 36, pl. 4).

Characterization of the Hosgri Fault Zone

We characterize the geometry and displacement history of the Hosgri Fault Zone using integrated analysis of more than 10,000 km of high-resolution and moderate- to deep-penetration CDP seismic reflection data from the eastern offshore Santa Maria Basin. These data are evaluated along the entire length of the fault zone, as well as beyond its north and south terminations. Our analyses identify along-strike changes in downdip geometry, sense of vertical separation, number and complexity of traces, intra-fault-zone structures, and other factors required to assess the deformational style and recency of activity of the Hosgri Fault Zone. In this manner, we are able to integrate local structural or stratigraphic anomalies into a comprehensive assessment of the fault zone. We integrate the CDP data with information from near-surface, high-resolution geophysical surveys, data from 29 offshore wells, seafloor cores, and observations and samples by diver-geologists. The use of these data sets allows us to identify near-surface geologic units and to map three basin-wide unconformities throughout the eastern offshore Santa Maria Basin and across the Hosgri Fault Zone. The unconformities are used to establish the recency and sense of displacement along and across the various traces of the fault zone.

Regional Framework

The Hosgri Fault Zone forms the east boundary of the offshore Santa Maria Basin and separates regions having strongly contrasting structural orientations. The fault zone is a complex, narrow, linear, 110-km-long zone of deformation that is associated with a region of central California that has experienced, within Neogene time, both extension and transpression (McCulloch, 1987). As a result, many of the features of the region, including the Hosgri Fault Zone, have their origin in a complex history of reactivation, reversal of movement, and rotation of preexisting structures.

The fault zone is part of a well-documented, regional, coastal California right-slip fault system that includes the San Simeon, Sur, and San Gregorio Fault Zones (Graham and Dickinson, 1978; Sedlock and Hamilton, 1991, Dickenson and

others, 2005). It is the southernmost member of this system, and right slip is apparently transferred between the Hosgri Fault Zone and the southern San Simeon Fault Zone via fault geometries suggesting a right-releasing stepover.

The fault zone has decoupled the late Neogene structural evolution of the offshore basin from its onshore counterpart. Fold axes and fault trends west of the Hosgri Fault Zone are subparallel to the fault. Structural axes east of the fault zone are oblique to its trend and vary in strike from east-west to northwest-southeast. In this model, right-slip displacements on the east side of the Hosgri Fault Zone are progressively absorbed southward by crustal shortening in the form of east-west-oriented folding and reverse faulting (Lettis and others, 2004). Near the latitude of Point Pedernales, right-lateral displacement across the fault zone is reduced to zero by this mechanism, and the coastal California right-slip fault system ends (Cummings and Johnson, 1994; Sorlien and others, 1999a). South of Point Arguello, the regional structural grain of the Western Transverse Ranges province trends west-north-westerly and is unbroken across the southward projection of the Hosgri Fault Zone as shown in the figures of Fisher (1987).

Structural Characteristics

Observations from the Structural Trend Map

The Hosgri Fault Zone extends approximately 110 km, from near Point San Simeon on the north to its southern termination near Point Pedernales. We do not interpret the fault zone to continue to the north around the Piedras Blancas anticlinorium, as was originally shown by Hoskins and Griffiths (1971). The fault zone aligns with a coastal system of strike-slip faults (fig. 1), and it is related to the San Simeon Fault Zone via a right en echelon stepover geometry south of Point San Simeon. Lettis and others (1990) and Hanson and others (2004) interpret this stepover to be a pull-apart basin formed between the two faults.

The strike of the Hosgri Fault Zone changes along its length. The 21-km-long section of the fault zone north of Morro Bay strikes N. 45° W., the 25-km-long segment of the fault from the latitude of Morro Bay to a point about half-way between Point Buchon and Point San Luis strikes N. 35° W., the central 60 km trends approximately N. 25° W., and the southern 10 km of the fault zone strikes N. 7° W. The more northerly trends of the central and southern parts of the fault zone are associated with compressional folding within the offshore Santa Maria Basin west of the fault zone (pls. 4, 5).

There are major discordances in the alignment of structures across the Hosgri Fault Zone except at its extreme north and south terminations. Structures to the west of the north end of the fault zone are subparallel to the Hosgri and San Simeon Fault Zones, as are the active normal faults in the basin between the two fault zones. From Point Estero to Point Sal, the divergence in strike between structures on

Table 8. Summary descriptions of geomorphic reaches of the Hosgri Fault Zone.

Reach	Location and structural blocks[1]	Strike and length	Geomorphic expression from geophysical and bathymetric data
Northern	Intersection with Los Osos Fault Zone north to San Simeon Hosgri step-over	N. 46 W. 20 to 22 km	Limited topographic expression; local seafloor scarps and disruption of late Wisconsin sediment basin
San Luis/ Pismo	Intersection with Pecho Fault north to intersection with Los Osos Fault Zone. Hosgri Fault Zone forms western boundary of San Luis/Pismo structural block	N. 25–30 W. 20 to 22 km	Discontinuous seafloor scarps; both traces displace the late Wisconsin unconformity; west trace associated with seafloor scarps and inflection points. Central zone contains small sediment-filled grabens. East trace forms boundary between deformed bedrock outcrops to the east and sediment-covered basin to the west
San Luis Obispo Bay	Intersection with Casmalia Fault Zone north to intersection with Pecho Fault. Hosgri Fault Zone forms western boundary of Santa Maria Valley structural block	N. 15–20 W. 23 km	Limited topographic expression; sediment covered over entire reach; west trace and several of the eastern traces locally displace the late Wisconsin unconformity but not the sea floor
Point Sal	Intersection with southern trace of Lion's Head Fault Zone north to intersection with Casmalia Fault Zone. Hosgri Fault Zone forms western boundary of Casmalia structural block	N. 20–22 W. 12 to 14 km	Little to no topographic expression; western trace displaces post-late Wisconsin sediment basin in manner consistent with right slip
Southern	Southern termination near Point Pedernales north to southern trace of Lion's Head Fault Zone. Hosgri Fault Zone forms western margin of Vandenberg/Lompoc structural block	N. 23–25 W. changes to N. 7 W. south of Purisima Point 24 to 26 km	Limited to no topographic expression; local seafloor disruption and deformation of post-late Wisconsin sediments

[1]Structural blocks are defined in Lettis and others (2004).

[2]Seismicity from October 1987 to February 1997 is discussed in McLaren and Savage (2001).

opposite sides of the fault zone averages 30°. Between Point Sal and Purisima Point, this divergence increases to as much as 90°. Between Purisima Point and the south termination of the fault, this divergence gradually decreases. South of the mapped termination of the Hosgri Fault Zone near Point Pedernales, the east-west structural trends do not change orientation across the southern projection of the fault. Faults that obliquely approach the Hosgri Fault Zone from the east include the southwest-dipping Los Osos Fault north of Point Buchon (Lettis and Hall, 1990), the northeast-dipping Pecho Fault at Point San Luis (Lettis and others, 1990), the southwest-dipping Casmalia Fault north of Point Sal, and the northeast-dipping Lion's Head Fault south of Point Sal (Clark, 1990) (faults are labeled on pl. 4 and fig. 17). Although these faults approach the Hosgri Fault Zone at angles of 30° to 50°, as they near the fault zone they generally bend northward and become subparallel to the fault zone at their west ends. This complicated structural pattern contributes to the masking of

any evidence for the displacement of older structures that can serve as piercing points for measuring lateral slip.

Between Point Buchon and Point San Luis, the Hosgri Fault Zone consists of two major traces, referred to as the east trace and west trace. The designated primary fault trace shifts from the east trace north of Point Buchon to the west trace south of Point San Luis. Additional minor traces exist that are parallel or subparallel to these primary traces but are much shorter in length. Intra-fault-zone deformation between the two primary traces and between the primary and minor traces includes structures reflecting both localized crustal shortening and extension. For example, there are two major areas of intra-fault-zone extension and subsidence along the Hosgri Fault Zone at right en echelon steps in the primary traces. These areas of subsidence include the region between the north end of the Hosgri Fault Zone and the southern projection of the San Simeon Fault and the depression of strata between the two primary traces at the northern end

Table 8. Summary descriptions of geomorphic reaches of the Hosgri Fault Zone.—Continued

Geophysical data observations	Seismicity[2]
• One primary fault trace, near-vertical, dips greater than 80° NE. • Short west-verging splays merge with near-vertical trace at a depth of 1 to 2 km (one-sided flower structure) • Sense of vertical separation reverses within a single section and along strike • Right-releasing stepovers have extensional deformation (for example, San Simeon/Hosgri pull-apart basin)	Relatively active; historical seismicity down to 9 km; focal mechanisms indicate right slip on NNW-trending plane
• Two discontinuous vertical to near-vertical faults (east trace and west trace) within a 2- to 3-km-wide zone • Low-angle, west-vergent fault west of western trace • West trace vertical in upper 1 km; dips 65–70° E. at depths of 3 to 4 km • East trace dips 70–80° NE. • Low-angle fault dips 35–45° NE. in near-surface; dip increases to 60° NE. at 2 to 3 km • A major change in structural trend occurs across the east (main) trace	Relatively active; historical seismicity down to 12 km; focal mechanisms indicate right slip on NNW-trending plane
• Fault zone is complex, with a primary western trace and multiple en-echelon eastern traces • Relatively continuous west trace is vertical in upper 1 to 2 km, dips 60–75° NE. to a depth of 4 km • Low-angle fault dips 30±10° NE., increasing to 60° NE. or more at depth • Fault splays diverge upward (flower structures) • Abrupt thinning of Miocene section across fault • Apparent vertical separation of Cenozoic strata across main fault trace varies from 0 to 100 m • Right-releasing step-over between west and east traces south of Pecho Fault • Sense of vertical separation reverses within a single section	Relatively quiescent
• Two parallel, high-angle faults in a zone 1 km wide • Series of low-angle, west-vergent folds (including Purisima structure to the west) • Western high-angle trace is continuous and appears to be near vertical (70–90° NE.) to depths in excess of 2 km • Abrupt thinning of Miocene section across main trace • Fault splays diverge upward (flower structure) • Sense of vertical separation reverses within a single section and along strike • Locally, youngest (Pliocene and Pleistocene) deposits are displaced down on the east	A few historical earthquakes were between depths of 6 and 7 km
• Multiple fault traces • Change in fault trend south of Purisima Point • West trace continuous south past Purisima Point; discontinuous south of change in fault trend • East trace discontinuous, not present south of change in fault trend • Fault splays diverge upward from western trace (flower structure) • Sense of vertical separation reverses along strike • Fault dips 75° E. north of Purisima Point and becomes vertical to the south	Relatively quiescent; a few historical earthquakes were concentrated near Point Pedernales at depths of 5 to 9 km

of San Luis Obispo Bay (pl. 4). Areas of localized crustal shortening within the Hosgri Fault Zone are present at left en-echelon steps or left bends in the primary trace. For example, there is localized monoclinal folding immediately east of the fault zone in the south-central part of Estero Bay, where the fault trace steps about 0.25 km west to form an abrupt left-restraining bend that extends 5 km (pl. 4).

Late Quaternary crustal shortening occurs west of the Hosgri Fault Zone. A series of folds and thrust faults that subparallel the fault zone are present in the southern part of the offshore Santa Maria Basin. These structures include the Purisima and Lompoc fold and fault trends (pls. 4–7) and the Queenie structure (Clark and others, 1991) to the northwest (fig. 1, pls. 5–7). Active crustal shortening also occurs north of the northern projection of the Hosgri Fault Zone along the Piedras Blancas structure, where many folds and thrust faults are mapped. In contrast, no evidence exists for active crustal shortening in a 10-km-wide zone to the west of the central

and northern extent of the Hosgri Fault Zone between San Luis Obispo Bay and Cambria. In this area, active folding and faulting (pls. 5–7) is restricted to the Hosgri Fault Zone and the areas to the east.

We divide the Hosgri Fault Zone into reaches based on distinct changes in behavioral and physical characteristics of the fault zone and adjacent structures (fig. 17, table 8). The attributes that change between the reaches include variations in strike, trace geometry, downdip geometry, amount and sense of vertical separation, types of structural terrains that it juxtaposes, displacement history, and instrumentally recorded seismicity.

Within each reach, we have identified a primary trace based on linear continuity, depth of fault imaging on the seismic records, and recency of activity. Locally, secondary traces parallel the main trace within a 2- to 4-km-wide zone and often merge with the main trace at depth. There is no single main trace that is continuous through all the reaches. Rather, the primary traces of the fault zone form a series of right en-echelon steps with great local complexity in the regions of overlap. At the boundaries between some of the reaches, the primary zone of recent deformation may locally transfer between the west and east traces of the fault zone. In these areas of slip transfer, localized zones of extensional features are present at right releasing steps and zones of contractural features are present at left-restraining steps.

Evidence for Lateral Displacement

Piercing points, such as offset folds, unique rock formations, or smaller scale entities such as channels or other geomorphic features, are commonly used in onshore studies to identify and assess the extent of lateral slip. No piercing points have been determined in the shallow-shelf environment of the eastern offshore Santa Maria Basin. Not even features as geologically unique as the hypabyssal intrusives of the Morro Rock-Islay Hills complex (Ernst and Hall, 1974) can be traced across the fault zone, in either the seismic reflection data used in this study or the available potential-field data of McCulloch and Chapman (1977), Rietman and Beyer (1982), or Sauer and Mariano (1990) that encompasses these features.

Adding to the difficulty in detecting the strike-slip characteristics of the Hosgri Fault Zone is the intrinsic bias of two-dimensional rendering of the faults within the zone. Due to their two-dimensional nature, the CDP seismic reflection lines used in this study only image the combined effects of contractional and extensional deformation. Only through inference can we identify lateral slip. To overcome this bias we interpreted data along the entire fault zone to evaluate the presence or absence of secondary structures indicative of strike-slip deformation.

Harding (1985, 1990), Lemiszki and Brown (1988), Stone (1969, 1989), Sylvester (1988), Withjack and Meisling (1987), and Zalan (1987) provide criteria for identifying strike-slip faulting using seismic reflection and subsurface structural data. The primary criteria include (1) a long, narrow, linear fault zone associated with known lateral-slip faults; (2) the separation of contrasting structural trends across the fault zone; (3) localized extensional and compressional deformation at releasing or restraining bends, respectively; (4) changes in the sense and magnitude of vertical separation in the fault zone, both along strike and vertically upsection; and (5) the presence of flower-type structures. Harding (1990) and Stone (1969) emphasize the use of both map and section views of a fault zone to assess faulting style and point out the pitfalls of relying on only a few lines of evidence. In addition, Bally (1983) and Goudswaard and Jenyon (1988) published seismic reflection profiles from known strike-slip faults. These illustrations show that strike-slip faults commonly are associated with compressional folds and changes in downdip geometry with depth and illustrate some of the forms that such features can display when compression occurs across lateral-slip faults. Nur and Boccaletti (1990) summarized the results of an international workshop on strike-slip

tectonics. They indicated that a common observation in many diverse geographical areas of strike-slip faulting is mixed-mode faulting, which is the contemporaneous or sequential occurrence of strike-slip faulting and other types of faulting in a single tectonic setting. They also reached the conclusion that the "traditional view that strike-slip faulting involves only, or mostly, translation of fault-bounded blocks must give way to the inclusion of block rotation as an ubiquitous aspect of distributed deformation".

Although the seismic reflection data used in this study do not permit us to estimate the maximum amount of lateral slip on the Hosgri Fault Zone, we have identified several features, in both map and section view, that are indicative of lateral-slip faulting according to Harding (1985, 1990) and Stone (1989):

(1) **The long, narrow, linear character of the fault zone and its association with known lateral-slip faults—** Our mapping documents a long (110 km), narrow, fault zone having a linear trace. Lettis and others (2004), Dickinson and others (2005), and Hanson and others (2004) provide evidence that the Hosgri Fault Zone is the southernmost member of the regional, coastal California right-slip fault system that includes the San Simeon, Sur, and San Gregorio Fault Zones. Lateral displacements along these faults are well documented, although the total amount of lateral displacement is still under discussion (Graham and Dickenson, 1978; Sedlock and Hamilton, 1991; Dickinson and others, 2005).

(2) **The separation of contrasting structural trends across the fault zone—**Our mapping demonstrates a strong change in structural trend and character across the trace of the Hosgri Fault Zone. Variations in structural orientation across the fault zone range from 90° at its south end to subparallel at its north end as illustrated on plate 4. In addition, the seismic profiles presented in figures 24 through 39 illustrate the dramatic change in degree of deformation and change in style of folding across the fault zone.

(3) **Localized extensional and compressional deformation at releasing or restraining bends—**At its northern end, right slip is transferred to the Hosgri Fault from the San Simeon Fault Zone via the San Simeon/Hosgri pull-apart basin (Lettis and others, 1990; Hanson and others, 2004). Profiles A–A′ and B–B′ (figs. 24, 25) extend into this structure. Hanson and others (2004) present a seismic image across the pull-apart basin as their figure 11A. Another zone of extensional deformation is coincident with the change in strike of the fault zone near Point Buchon (figs. 23, 30; pl. 4). At this location, the primary zone of deformation in the fault zone shifts from the east trace of the fault zone to the west trace of the fault zone across an apparent extensional (down-dropped) zone documented by profiles E–E′ and F–F′ (figs. 29, 31).

(4) **Changes in the sense and magnitude of vertical separation both along strike of the fault zone and vertically, upsection, within the fault zone—**Profiles I–I′ through M–M′ (figs. 34–39) display variations in sense of displacement along strike in Miocene and younger sediments, as well as reversal of displacement at the level of the top of

pre-Miocene unconformity. These data demonstrate changes in basement displacement from down on the west, to no displacement, to up on the west, and back to down on the west within a distance of less than 20 km. In addition, upsection changes in apparent vertical separation may be seen on several of the profiles including A–A' (fig. 24), G–G' (fig. 32), H–H' (fig. 33), and I–I' (fig. 34).

(5) **Symmetrical and asymmetrical flower structures**— Profiles H–H' (fig. 33), I–I' (fig. 34), K–K' (fig. 37), L–L' (fig. 38), and M–M' (fig. 39) are interpreted as having geometries of various forms of flower structures. Profile I–I' (fig. 34), for example, shows upward-diverging fault splays on the west side of the fault zone that form an asymmetrical flower structure. The other referenced profiles show upward-diverging fault splays on both sides of the Hosgri Fault Zone that form symmetrical flower structures.

Downdip Geometry

Seismic images of the Hosgri Fault Zone on the CDP records used in this study are generally limited to the upper 2 s of data, although on some records it is possible to extend the trace to 2.5 to 3 s. These reflection times translate into a depth range of 2.5 to 3 km with an occasional record showing the fault zone to a depth of about 4 km. The greatest error in accuracy of fault location at depth results from difficulty in recognition of the fault signature within the Franciscan basement rocks. When the fault is within higher velocity basement rocks, it appears to penetrate less deeply than when it is within slower rocks. On an east-dipping fault trace, the increase in velocity across the fault zone can cause 5° to 10° of decrease or "pull-up" in the apparent dip of the trace at depth.

Throughout its length, the Hosgri Fault Zone is imaged as vertical to near vertical in the upper 1 s (1 km) of seismic data. In the northern reach (profiles A–A' to D–D', figs. 24–28), this vertical dip is interpreted to reflection times of 1.5 to 2.0 s (2 to 2.5 km). South of Point Buchon (profiles E–E' to I–I'; figs. 29, 31–34), the main trace of the Hosgri Fault Zone has a steep northeasterly dip below depths of 1 to 1.5 km. The observed dips are in the range of 60° to 75° after correction for velocity pull-up effects. Analyses by others also support the near-vertical downdip geometry of the Hosgri Fault Zone. Worden (1992), Pullammanappallil and Louie (1994), and Shih and Levander (1994) have imaged the fault using advanced processing methods applied to the deep crustal CDP seismic line RU-3, acquired in 1986 (Meltzer and Levander, 1991), and concluded that the fault is near vertical to steeply northeast dipping.

Low-angle thrust faults associated with folding west of the Hosgri Fault Zone are present in the southern subbasin of the offshore Santa Maria Basin, south of San Luis Obispo Bay. These thrust faults generally dip northeastward, toward the Hosgri Fault Zone. Locally, the Hosgri Fault Zone either truncates or offsets shallow thrusts (1.5 s or less) within the Miocene sedimentary units, as illustrated on profiles I–I', L–L', and M–M' (figs. 34, 38, 39). Deeper detachments have been interpreted on several profiles. These inferred faults are below the depth at which we can confidently use the seismic data presented to determine their structural relation to the Hosgri Fault Zone. However, based on the concept of strain partitioning along transpressive plate margins (Lettis and Hanson, 1992; Christie-Blick and Biddle, 1985), any subhorizontal faults present in the region probably intersect the Hosgri Fault Zone at depth and accommodate the convergent component of slip along the fault zone. Alternatively, the available data cannot preclude that low-angle faulting is the result of thrusting that, in part, predated the development of the current Hosgri Fault Zone and, rather than merging with the fault zone, is cut by it. In either case, if the subhorizontal seismic-reflection events are thrust faulting, only minor (<0.5 km) offset or crustal shortening is apparent where they extend into the Tertiary section and display mappable seismic signatures. Thus, these low-angle and reverse faults appear to be subordinate to the Hosgri Fault Zone in terms of their apparent vertical displacement.

Southern Termination

Other authors have studied the southern termination of the Hosgri Fault Zone. Cummings and Johnson (1994) interpreted the CSLC seismic data sets between Point Arguello and Point Sal and concluded that the Hosgri Fault Zone terminates in the Point Pedernales area. They interpreted their data to show that, south of Purisima Point, the Hosgri Fault Zone decreases in both vertical and right-slip displacement, turns east, and splays towards the Santa Ynez River Fault Zone. Steritz (1986) and Steritz and Luyendyk (1994) studied several proprietary data sets in the Point Arguello region and concluded that the Hosgri Fault Zone continues to the south around Point Arguello and terminates north of Point Conception. They indicate that the continuation involves significant changes in both the strike and style of faulting.

Although faulting undoubtedly continues around Point Arguello, our observations indicate that it does not have the continuity or trend that characterize the Hosgri Fault Zone throughout its 110-km length from offshore Cambria, in the north, to offshore Point Pedernales in the south (fig. 12, pl. 4). The interpretations of both Steritz (1986) and Sorlien and others (1999b) provide support for a change in character of faulting from Point Arguello southward. Steritz, to establish his extension of the Hosgri Fault Zone between Point Arguello and Point Conception, mapped the zone as a series of west-trending faults having primarily a reverse sense of slip. These characteristics contrast markedly with the character of the fault zone between Purisima Point and Point Pedernales, and we consider this contrast in mapped characteristics to support our conclusion of a termination of the Hosgri Fault Zone offshore Point Pedernales.

Seismic 3–D imaging presented by Fisher (1987) in his figure 9 also is in accord with our findings. This imaging clearly illustrates the rapid change in direction of the regional structural grain between Point Arguello and Point Conception. It displays a band of unbroken northwest- to west-trending folds crossing any southward projection of the Hosgri Fault Zone that does not parallel the easterly swing of the coastline between Point Arguello and Point Conception. The data and maps presented by Fisher (1987) strongly suggest that no significant faulting on trend with the Hosgri Fault Zone extends beyond Point Arguello.

Structure Contour Maps of the Unconformities

Top of Pre-Miocene Basement Unconformity

The elevation of the pre-Miocene basement unconformity within the mapped area ranges from less than –500 m to greater than –3,000 m. (fig. 14, pl. 5). The shallowest basement contours are in areas within or east of the Hosgri Fault Zone. Basement is deepest in the southern part of the basin in a depression extending for about 30 km subparallel to the fault zone and ranging between 5 km and 25 km west of the fault zone. This depression is bounded by the projections of Point San Luis and Point Sal westward along a line approximately parallel to the Hosgri Fault Zone. Another deep occurs at the northwest corner of the map, 50 km north of the northern end of the fault zone, offshore from Cape San Martin.

The pre-Miocene-basement-unconformity surface has a general northwest trend that is superimposed on older, broad northeast-trending folds. These older northeast trends have amplitudes of 1,000 m or more and, thus, we consider them a significant structural element in the region of the offshore Santa Maria Basin encompassed by this study. A northeast-trending anticline is evident in the southern part of the map 20 km west of Purisima Point (fig. 14, pl. 5). This feature has a strike of approximately N. 35° E. Other indications of this trend may be associated with the deep in the reach between Point Sal and Point San Luis and in a more northerly trending high, cresting 15 km west of the Hosgri Fault Zone adjacent to Point Estero. The Amberjack high is another basement high congruent with these trends; it was identified by Crain and others (1985) in the reach between Point Arguello and Point Conception immediately south of the mapped area. These trends appear to be strongly overprinted by Hosgri-parallel compressional folding in the region south of Point San Luis, though the crest of the Lompoc structure and the Purisima structure appear to align with the northeast-trending high west of Purisima Point.

The Hosgri Fault Zone displaces the pre-Miocene basement unconformity along its entire length from Point Pedernales north to San Simeon Point. The maximum vertical offset occurs between Point Sal and southern Estero Bay with lesser offsets at the northern and southern ends of the fault zone. From Point Sal north, the displacement is east side up. Between Point Sal and Purisima Point, the displacement of the unconformity alternates between a west-side-up and west-side-down geometry, as discussed

in the previous section of this paper. This change in sense of displacement across the fault zone, observed on reflection profiles, is also reflected in the marine gravity and aeromagnetic maps of the offshore Santa Maria Basin (McCulloch and Chapman, 1977; Rietman and Beyer, 1982; Sauer and Mariano, 1990).

The unconformity is also displaced by thrust faults that underlie the Queenie, Lompoc, and Purisima structures in the southern part of the offshore Santa Maria Basin and by thrust faults on the flanks of the Piedras Blancas structure on the northern reaches of the basin. The unconformity is less deformed in the central part of the basin west of the Hosgri Fault Zone than in the north and south. The pre-Miocene basement surface is more irregular and, in several areas, not congruent with the two younger, overlying unconformities (pls. 6, 7; figs. 15, 16).

Top of Miocene Unconformity

Throughout the mapped area south of Cambria, the structural trend of the top of Miocene unconformity is to the northwest, parallel or subparallel to the trend of the Hosgri Fault Zone. North of the Hosgri Fault Zone, the unconformity trend is more to the northwest, where it is uplifted and eroded along an axis coincident with basement expression of the Piedras Blancas structure.

The elevation of the top of Miocene unconformity within the mapped area ranges from seafloor to deeper than –1,300 m (fig. 15, pl. 6). The deepest area is in the southern part of the basin, coincident with the southern part of the pre-Miocene basement unconformity depression west of Point Sal. The top of Miocene unconformity displays the northeast-trending anticline noted in the previous section, located 20 km west of Purisima Point, as well as vestigial evidence of the north-trending pre-Miocene basement high offshore from Point Estero.

Within the mapped area, the only fault that both cuts and displaces the top of Miocene unconformity is the Hosgri Fault Zone, which displays an east-side-up sense of displacement throughout the mapped region. Displacement across individual fault traces within the fault zone generally ranges between 50 to 150 m with a significant part of the total relief across the Hosgri Fault Zone resulting from folding of the entire basement and sedimentary section.

The unconformity has been eroded across the crest of the three major anticlinal structures in the southern part of the basin—the Purisima, Lompoc, and Queenie structures. The uplifts result, in part, from the same thrust-fault complexes that are inferred from the borehole and seismic data presented in this paper (see well 415-1 and seismic line GSI-106 on pl. 3) to displace the top of pre-Miocene basement unconformity beneath these structures. However, as a result of horizontal displacement along the thrusts, the axes of folds in the top of Miocene unconformity are not congruent with the structures observed in the underlying pre-Miocene-unconformity surface. For example, the axis of the Queenie anticlinal fold at the level of the top of Miocene unconformity (fig. 15, pl. 6) lies 2 to 3 km east of the crest of the top of pre-Miocene basement high (fig. 14, pl. 5), where it corresponds to the location of a top of pre-Miocene basement basin (Clark and others, 1991).

Early–Late Pliocene Unconformity

The elevation of the early–late Pliocene unconformity within the mapped area ranges from seafloor to deeper than −1,000 m (fig. 16, pl. 7). The deepest area is in the southern part of the basin, northwest of Point Sal. In a manner similar to the structure of the top of Miocene unconformity, this surface also displays the northeast trend south of Point Sal and the Hosgri-parallel overprinting of this feature by thrust-related folding west of the Hosgri Fault Zone. Also, the basin between Point San Luis and Point Sal remains observable at the level of the unconformity.

Similar to the top of Miocene unconformity, the only fault that both cuts and displaces the early–late Pliocene unconformity is the Hosgri Fault Zone. Folding of the unconformity occurs primarily by warping in fault-bend folds associated with thrust faults and by buttressing against the more strongly folded flanks of the underlying top of Miocene unconformity. Offset of the early–late Pliocene unconformity across individual fault strands within the Hosgri Fault Zone is generally 50 m or less.

In conformance to trends in the top of Miocene unconformity, the structural trend of the early–late Pliocene unconformity is primarily to the northwest parallel or subparallel to the trend of the Hosgri Fault Zone. The unconformity has been eroded from, subcrops against, or outcrops over the crests of the three anticlinal structures in the southern part of the basin (Queenie, Lompoc, and Purisima structures, pl. 7). Between Point Sal and Point Estero, the unconformity is relatively undeformed and slopes gently to the southwest. In the northern part of the mapped area, the unconformity abuts against the southwestern flank of the Piedras Blancas structure and appears to have been eroded on the northwest side. Remnants of the unconformity may exist on the east side of the Hosgri Fault Zone. However, because of the lack of well data and continuity of seismic expression, these remnants cannot be directly correlated with the unconformity within or on the west side of the fault zone.

Tectonic History

McCrory and others (1995) summarize the complex late Cenozoic tectonic evolution of the offshore Santa Maria Basin and the Hosgri Fault Zone. The large volume of structural and stratigraphic data compiled and analyzed in this study provides evidence bearing on the tectonic history of both the basin and the fault zone. The primary sources for our analyses

of the tectonic history are maps of the unconformities and the detailed descriptions of the geometry of the Hosgri Fault Zone and the fault termination modes at the northern and southern ends. Using these sources, we further develop and describe the tectonic history with emphasis on the east side of the offshore Santa Maria Basin and the evolution of the Hosgri Fault Zone. Our analyses indicate an early extensional history for the basin followed by regional uplift and westward tilting in the northern part of the study area and a complex interplay of compression and wrench tectonics in the central and southern parts of the area. The description of the tectonic history of this area is divided into five overlapping stages:

- Development of older northeast-trending structures
- Extensional deformation and development of eastward-tilted half graben
- Uplift and westward tilting
- Transpression along the Hosgri Fault Zone
- Compression west of the Hosgri Fault Zone

Northeast-Trending Structures

The oldest structural features documented in our study are the broad northeast-trending folds that modulate the elevation of, and are overprinted by, the later strike-slip features associated with the Hosgri Fault Zone and the northwest-trending compressional features west of the fault zone. These older structures have amplitudes of 1,000 m or more and were present during the deposition of the strata between the pre-Miocene basement unconformity and top of Miocene unconformity. This is documented by the 700 m to 1,000 m of thinning between these surfaces over the crest of the northeast-trending folds south of Point Sal (pls. 5, 6). This northeast-trending folding is interpreted to have initiated after pre-Miocene basement unconformity (after 23 Ma) with a cession of major deformation before the formation of the top of Miocene unconformity (6.0–5.3 Ma). The broad northeast-trending anticline 20 miles west of Purisima Point (pl. 5) and the adjoining basin to the northwest are present on all three unconformity maps. The lack of significant thinning between the top of Miocene and early–late Pliocene unconformities over the crest of the fold suggests minimal deformation after the formation of the top of Miocene unconformity. Because of the extensive thinning across this feature between formation of the two older unconformities, differential compaction may also have played a role in generating antiform structures in the younger strata.

Extensional Deformation and Eastward-Tilted Half Graben

Extensional deformation is evidenced on the seismic reflection profiles from the northern and central parts of the offshore Santa Maria Basin. Structural and stratigraphic relations displayed west of the Hosgri Fault Zone for over 60 km from the latitudes between profiles A–A′ to H–H′ on plate 4 suggest the presence of a sediment-filled, eastward-tilted half graben opening toward the present location of the Hosgri Fault Zone. Seismic images of the sediments display onlap and internally conformable depositional patterns that suggest a period of broad regional deformation during which the eastward-tilting and the northwest-trending folds developed. This style of deformation is inferred to have continued until some time between the end of deposition of the Monterey Formation and the development of the top of Miocene unconformity.

The half graben, described by McCulloch (1987), is observed from immediately south of Cape San Martin southward beyond Point Sal in the data presented in this report. The relation of the eastern-bounding fault of the half graben to the location of the Hosgri Fault Zone cannot be precisely determined from our data. However, thick sequences of Miocene strata extend substantially east of the Hosgri Fault Zone near Point Buchon and in the western parts of the onshore Santa Maria Basin (pl. 2, fig. 8). The extent of these Miocene marine sedimentary rocks suggest that the location of the present Hosgri Fault Zone may be tens of kilometers west of the east boundary of the half graben in these areas.

South of Point Sal, the eastward-thickening sedimentary section between the top of pre-Miocene basement unconformity and the top of Miocene unconformity is displayed in profiles J–J′ through M–M′ (figs. 35, 37–39). These profiles suggest that the half graben was the dominant pre-top of Miocene unconformity structure in this area and may have developed after the formation of the northeast-trending folds. Well data from the southern part of the offshore Santa Maria Basin indicate that Miocene sediments in the graben span the period from about 23 to 5.3 Ma (table 7; figs. 6, A1).

Uplift and Westward Tilting

At the northern end of the Hosgri Fault Zone, regional westward tilting may be inferred from comparison of profiles A–A′ and B–B′ (figs. 24, 25). This tilting occurred after the top of Miocene unconformity formed and continues to increase to the north until the east-dipping basement contact of the half graben is rotated horizontal (profiles S–S′ and NT–NT′; figs. 21, 22). This westward tilting is considered to be in response to deformation associated with the formation of the Piedras Blancas antiform and (or) the formation of the north-trending basement high that is 15 km offshore from Point Estero. Both of these basement features are shown on plate 5. The conformable nature of the stratigraphic horizons imaged on profiles A–A′ and B–B′ (figs. 24, 25) above the top of Miocene unconformity indicates that the timing of the westward tilting is primarily post-top of Miocene unconformity in age (<5.3 Ma) and may be continuing today.

South of Point Sal, the top of pre-Miocene basement unconformity and the top of Miocene unconformity are both uplifted and tilted westward. This tilting is seen on profiles J–J′ through L–L′ (figs. 35, 37, 38). The uplift of the eastern edge of the original half-graben appears to be in response to thrust faulting responsible for the Purisima and Lompoc structures and flower-type structures associated with the Hosgri Fault Zone in this region. The maximum uplift of the unconformities coincides with the intersection of the projection of the northeast-trending basement high in this area (pls. 5–7). Alternatively the half graben may have formed after these structures, causing their axes to plunge to the east. A similar scenario can also explain the relations of the half graben to north-trending folding observed at the north end of the Hosgri Fault Zone.

Transpression along the Hosgri Fault Zone

During the late stages of subsidence of the half graben, extensional faulting, which is inferred to have produced the half graben, changed to transpressional motion in response to changes in plate motion and the opening of the Gulf of California. The timing of onset of transpressional tectonics cannot be accurately determined from the data presented here. However, it can be stated that significant folding did not begin in the northern part of the basin until after the end of Monterey Formation deposition about 6 Ma, as suggested by the conformable character of these sediments on profiles A–A′ and B–B′ (figs. 24, 25). In fact, along the trace of these profiles, significant deformation did not begin until after the time of formation of the top of Miocene unconformity at about 5.3 Ma.

Large-scale post-top of Miocene unconformity deformation is confined to the vicinity of the Hosgri Fault Zone in the northern part of the basin; it grows in intensity and expands away from the fault zone toward the south. By the latitude of Point Sal and profile J–J′ (fig. 35), the top of Miocene unconformity is uplifted and eroded approximately 4 km west of the Hosgri Fault Zone. A similar pattern of deformation exists for the early–late Pliocene unconformity. This unconformity is more intensely deformed in the southern part of the basin than in the north. Hanson and others (2004) analyzed these unconformities in detail to compute rates of deformation along the fault zone. Lettis and others (1990) and Hanson and others (2004) suggest that lateral slip has been transmitted across the San Simeon/Hosgri stepover at least since the formation of the early–late Pliocene unconformity at about 3.5 to 2.8 Ma.

From the time of onset of transpressional motion along the Hosgri Fault Zone, the fault is interpreted to have uncoupled the stresses creating the Hosgri-parallel folding that is dominant west of the fault zone from the stresses that are responsible for the more westerly trending folding east of the fault zone. The parallelism of structural trends at both the north and south ends of the Hosgri Fault Zone and the disparity of structural trends across the central and south-central reaches of the fault zone are compatible with a model invoking progressively increasing southeastward buckling of rocks on the northeast side of the fault. This buckling (and associated lateral displacement along the Hosgri Fault Zone) is inferred to reach a maximum in the reach between Point San Luis and Purisima Point and to rapidly diminish to zero at the south end of the fault north of Point Pedernales. The space problem produced by such a model is not addressed in this paper but can be partially ameliorated by successive southward wedging and rotation of crustal blocks along the San Simeon, Nacimiento, Oceanic, West Huasna, Lion's Head, and associated onshore fault systems (fig. 1).

Compression West of the Hosgri Fault Zone

Within the southern reach, major folds have developed west of the Hosgri Fault Zone in the southern offshore Santa Maria Basin (fig. 35, pl. 4). The relative timing of the folding can be determined by examining the geometric relation of the opal-CT to quartz transformation zone to the folds and the extent of involvement of this transformation zone in the folding. Figure 11 illustrates the basic relations of this silica-phase transformation to the relative timing of the formation of geologic structures. The following observations suggest, at least for the south end of the Hosgri Fault Zone, that structures are younger westward and southward from Point Sal:

- North of Point Sal, on the east side of the basin near the Hosgri Fault Zone, the transformation zone is relatively undeformed, indicating that major folding terminated prior to formation of the transformation zone.

- A major episode of folding spanned the time of formation of the transformation zone in the western and central parts of the basin near the Queenie structure (Clark and others, 1991).

- South of Point Sal, the east edge of the basin has undergone a broad, step-like uplift following formation of the transformation zone. The magnitude of this uplift is between 0.25 km to 0.5 km near Purisima Point and almost 1 km at the location of profile J–J' (fig. 35) offshore Point Sal. The steps align with basement seismic images that may be interpreted as low-angle faults on some seismic profiles.

- The transformation-zone reflection is folded within the Purisima and Lompoc structures, indicating that they also formed after the transformation zone.

Recency of Activity

The moderate- and deep-penetration CDP seismic reflection lines that cross the Hosgri Fault Zone and adjacent parts of the offshore Santa Maria Basin illustrate episodes of post-late Miocene transpressional deformation. However, these records provide little direct evidence of late Quaternary fault displacement, because of the relatively low frequency response of CDP sources and processing corrections for source/receiver geometry. To provide information on recency of activity, high-resolution subbottom profiler records were used to identify deformation of post-late Wisconsin sediments. A thin veneer or local patches of post-late Wisconsin sediment are present along most reaches of the Hosgri Fault Zone and have been mapped in detail (PG&E, 1988). Displacement of the base of this sediment is indicative of late Quaternary activity. Figure 10 shows such displacement in the south-central part of Estero Bay and south of Point Buchon along the northern and San Luis/Pismo reaches of the Hosgri Fault Zone. Also, scarps are observed on side-scan sonar, echo sounder, and subbottom profiler records over many of the fault traces in areas where bedrock is exposed at the seafloor. Such features also are indicative of late Quaternary activity. Evidence of recency of activity, correlated with deeper images from the CDP records, was one of the characteristics used to identify the primary trace of the Hosgri Fault Zone. Locations along the fault zone that show evidence of late Quaternary activity are listed in table 8.

Conclusions

We provide a comprehensive geophysical assessment of the tectonic setting and behavior of the Hosgri Fault Zone, based on our integrated analyses of an extensive suite of deep, intermediate- and high-resolution seismic data combined with geological information from petroleum exploration wells, core samples, and diver-geologist samples and observations. Based on these analyses, we characterize the contemporary Hosgri Fault Zone as an active, transpressional, convergent right-oblique slip-fault zone that extends southeastward approximately 110 km from a location 6 km offshore from Cambria to a point 5 km northwest of Point Pedernales. The fault zone separates two tectonic domains of contrasting styles and orientations of crustal deformation. These domains are the offshore Santa Maria Basin and the onshore Los Osos-Santa Maria domain (Lettis and others, 2004). Seismic images indicate that the major fault strands within the fault zone display vertical to steeply northeast-dipping fault planes to a depth of 2 to 3 km. We further conclude that, below this depth level, available seismic imaging is not sufficiently coherent to provide reliable interpretations. Displacements of the base of post-Wisconsin sediments are observed on high-resolution seismic records, and a pressure ridge and several seafloor scarps are imaged on side-scan sonar, echo sounder, and sub-bottom profiler records. These features suggest late Quaternary offset at several locations along the fault zone.

A strong component of lateral slip along the fault zone is indicated by the linearity of the fault traces and reversals of vertical separation, both along the strike of the fault zone and updip within the fault zone. Further supporting a dominant component of lateral slip are localized regions of extensional and compressional deformation occurring at locations with fault geometries indicative of releasing and restraining stepovers, respectively. Clearly defined areas exist within which the fault zone terminates. Definable northern and southern terminations and the lack of evidence for major detachments or continuous thrust faulting associated with the fault zone suggest that both lateral displacements and horizontal compressional movement along the Hosgri Fault Zone have been relatively limited during latest Neogene time.

Acknowledgments

This investigation originated as part of the Diablo Canyon Long Term Seismic Program conducted by Pacific Gas and Electric Company (PG&E) under the direction of Lloyd S. Cluff. All of the seismic data used in this study is either owned by PG&E or in the public domain. The authors thank PG&E for its support and permission to publish the data.

The collection and analyses of these data began in 1985 and, in the initial phases of the investigation, many individuals participated in the data analyses and mapping tasks. Gerald Shiller, Laurel DeSilvestro, Timothy Hall, and Charles Branch worked on the interpretation and integration of the high-resolution data sets. David Smith and Michael Angell analyzed the fault-fold relations and modeled the low-angle faults. Douglas Hamilton and the late Richard Jahns began their studies of the Hosgri Fault Zone in the early 1970s and identified the foundations for many of the structural concepts that have contributed to our understanding of the Hosgri Fault Zone.

Steven Lewis, Drew Mayerson, Eric Geist, and Kate Miller provided critical reviews of an early draft of this manuscript. The present manuscript is significantly different. Kathryn Hanson, Holly Ryan, Patricia McCrory, Sam Johnson, and John Barron reviewed selected parts of the report related to their professional interests. Aaron Broughton and the late Lionel Kimura from Fugro West, Inc. (now Fugro Consultants) in Ventura, California, produced the majority of the figures and plates. Margaret Keller edited the final manuscript and oversaw production of the chapter for the U.S. Geological Survey. We thank all of the illustrators, reviewers, and editors for their significant contributions. However, only the authors are responsible for any errors or omissions.

Special thanks are extended to Lloyd Cluff, Marcia McLaren, and Margaret Keller for their continued encouragement to the authors throughout the development and completion of this manuscript.

References Cited

Argus, D.F., and Gordon, R.G., 1991, Current Sierra Nevada-North America motion from very long baseline interferometry—Implications for the kinematics of the western United States: Geology, v. 19, no. 11, p. 1085–1088.

Atwater, Tanya, 1989, Plate tectonic history of the northeast Pacific and western North America, Chapter 4, *in* Winterer, E.L., Hussong, D.M., and Decker, R.W., eds., Decade of North American geology, Volume N—The Northeastern Pacific Ocean and Hawaii: Geological Society of America, p. 21–72.

Bally, A.W., ed., 1983, Seismic expression of structural style—A picture book and atlas: American Association of Petroleum Geologists Studies in Geology, series 15, v. 1–3.

Barron, J.A, 1986, Updated diatom biostratigraphy for the Monterey Formation of California, *in* Casey, R.E., and Barron, J.A., eds., Siliceous microfossils and microplankton studies of the Monterey Formation and modern analogs: Pacific Section, Society of Economic Paleontologists and Mineralogists, Book 45, p. 105–119.

Barron, J.A., and Isaacs, C.M., 2001, Updated chronostratigraphic framework for the California Miocene, *in* Isaacs, C.M., and Rullkötter, J., eds., The Monterey Formation from rocks to molecules: Columbia University Press, p. 393–395.

Barron, J.A., and Ramirez, C.J., 1992, Paleoceanographic and tectonic controls on the Pliocene diatom record of California, *in* Tsuchi, R., and Ingle, J.C., Jr., eds., Pacific Neogene—Environment, evolution, and events: Tokyo, Japan, University of Tokyo Press, p. 25-41.

Behl, R.J., and Ingle, J.C., 1998, The Sisquoc Formation-Foxen Mudstone boundary in the Santa Maria Basin, California—Sedimentary response to the new tectonic regime, *in* Keller, M.A., ed., Evolution of sedimentary basins/onshore oil and gas investigations—Santa Maria Province: U.S. Geological Survey Bulletin 1995–V, 16 p.

Berkland, J.O., Raymond, L.A., Kramer, J.C., Moores, E.M., and O'Day, M., 1972, What is Franciscan?: American Association of Petroleum Geologists Bulletin, v. 56, p. 2295–2302.

Bishop, C.C., and Davis, J.F., 1984, Correlation of stratigraphic units of North America, (COSUNA) project, southern California region correlation chart: American Association of Petroleum Geologists, Chart 1.

Buchanan-Banks, J.M., Pampeyan, E.H., Wagner, H.C., and McCulloch, D.S., 1978, Preliminary map showing recency of faulting in coastal south-central California: U.S. Geological Survey Miscellaneous Field Studies Map MF–910, 3 sheets, scale 1:250,000.

Canfield, C.R., 1939, Subsurface stratigraphy of the Santa Maria Valley oil field and adjacent parts of the Santa Maria Valley, California: American Association of Petroleum Geologists Bulletin, v. 23, p. 45–81.

Chanell, J.E.T., Rio, D., and Thunell, R.C., 1988, Miocene/Pliocene boundary magnetostratigraphy at Capo Spartivento, Calibria, Italy: Geology, v. 16, p. 1096–1099.

Christie-Blick, N., and Biddle, K.T., 1985, Deformation and basin formation along strike-slip faults, in Biddle, K.T., and Christie-Blick, N., Strike-slip deformation, basin formation and sedimentation: Society of Economic Paleontologists and Mineralogists, Special Publication No. 37, p. 1–13.

Clark, D.H., 1990, Late Quaternary deformation in the Casmalia Range, Coastal south-central California, in Lettis, W.R., Hanson, K.L., Kelson, K.I., and Wesling, J.R., eds., Neotectonics of the south-central coastal California: Friends of the Pleistocene, Pacific Cell, 1990 Fall Field Trip Guidebook, p. 299–347.

Clark, D.H., Hall, N.T., Hamilton, D.H., and Heck, R.G., 1991, Structural analysis of late Neogene deformation in the central offshore Santa Maria Basin, California: Journal of Geophysical Research, v. 96, no. B4, p. 6435–6457.

Cole, R.B., and Stanley, R.G., 1998, Volcanic rocks of the Santa Maria Province, California, in Keller, M.A., ed., Evolution of sedimentary basins/onshore oil and gas investigations—Santa Maria Province: U.S. Geological Survey Bulletin 1995–R, 35 p.

Crain, W.E., Mero, W.E., and Patterson, D., 1985, Geology of the Point Arguello discovery: American Association of Petroleum Geologists Bulletin, v. 69, no. 4, p. 537–545.

Crain, W.E., Mero, W.E., and Patterson, D., 1987, Geology of the Point Arguello field, in Ingersoll, R.V., and Ernst, W.E., eds., Cenozoic basin development of coastal California, Rubey Volume VI: Englewood Cliffs, N.J., Prentice-Hall, Inc., p. 405–426.

Crouch, J., Bachman, S.B., and Shay, J.T., 1984, Post-Miocene compressional tectonics along the central California margin, in Crouch, J., and Bachman, S.B., eds., Tectonics and sedimentation along the California margin: Pacific Section, Society of Exploration Paleontologists and Mineralogists, v. 38, p. 37–54.

Crouch, J., and Suppe, J., 1993, Late Cenozoic tectonic evolution of the Los Angeles Basin and inner California borderland—A model for core complex-like crustal extension: Geological Society of America Bulletin, v. 105, no. 11, p. 1415–1434.

Cummings, D., and Johnson, T.A., 1994, Shallow geologic structure offshore Point Arguello to Santa Maria River, central California, in Alterman I.B., McMullen, R.B., Cluff, L.S., and Slemmons, D.B., eds., Seismotectonics of the central California Coast Ranges: Geological Society of America Special Paper 292, p. 211–222.

Dibblee, T.W., Jr., 1950, Geology of southwestern Santa Barbara County, California— Point Arguello, Lompoc, Point Conception, Los Olivos, and Gaviota quadrangles: California Division of Mines and Geology Bulletin 150, 95 p.

Dickinson, W.R., Ducea, M., Rosenberg, L.I., Greene, H.G., Graham, S.A., Clark, J.C., Weber, G.E., Kidder, S., Ernst, W.G., and Brabb, E.E., 2005, Net dextral slip, Neogene San Gregorio-Hosgri Fault Zone, coastal California, geologic evidence and tectonic implications: Geological Society of America Special Paper 391, 43 p.

DiSilvestro, L.A., Hanson, K.L., Lettis, W.R., and Shiller, G.I., 1990, The San Simeon/Hosgri pull-apart basin, south-central coastal California: Eos, Transactions of the American Geophysical Union, v. 71, no. 43, p. 1632.

Dumont, M.P., 1989, The Monterey Formation and biostratigraphy—An overview, in MacKinnon, T.C., ed., Oil in the California Monterey Formation: American Geophysical Union Field Trip Guidebook T311, 28th International Geological Congress, p. 28–32.

Dumont, M.P., and Barron, J.A., 1995, Diatom biochronology of the Sisquoc Formation in the Santa Maria Basin, California, and its paleoceanographic and tectonic implications, in Keller, M.A., ed., Evolution of sedimentary basins/onshore oil and gas investigations—Santa Maria Province: U.S. Geological Survey Bulletin 1995–K, 17 p.

Dunham, J.B., and Blake, G.H., 1987, Guide to the coastal outcrops of the Monterey Formation of western Santa Barbara County, California: Pacific Section, Society of Economic Paleontologists and Mineralogists, Field Trip Book 53, p. 31–32.

Ernst, W.G., and Hall, C.A., 1974, Geology and petrology of the Cambria felsite, and new Oligocene formation, west-central California Coast Ranges: Geological Society of America Bulletin, v. 85, no. 4, p 523–532.

Ewing, J., and Talwani, M., 1991, Marine deep seismic reflection sections off central California: Journal of Geophysical Research, v. 96, no. B4, p. 6423–6433.

Fisher, T., 1987, Discovery of the Point Arguello oil field from a geophysical perspective: Society of Exploration Geophysicists, The Leading Edge, v. 6, no. 10, p. 16–21.

Gardner, G.H.F., Gardner, L.W., and Gregory, A.R., 1974, Formation velocity and density—The diagnostic basics for stratigraphic traps: Geophysics, v. 39, p. 770–780.

Goudswaard, W., and Jenyon, M.K., 1988, Seismic atlas of structural and stratigraphic features: The Hague, European Association of Exploration Geophysicists.

Gradstein, F., Ogg, J., and Smith, A., eds., 2004, A geologic time scale 2004: Cambridge, U.K., Cambridge University Press, 1 pl., 589 p.

Graham, S.A., and Dickinson, W.R., 1978, Evidence for 115 kilometers of right slip on the San Gregorio-Hosgri Fault trend: Science, v. 199, p. 179–181.

Grant, F.S., and West, G.F., 1965, Interpretation theory in applied geophysics: New York, NY, McGraw-Hill Book Co., 575 p.

Greene, H.G., and Kennedy, M.P., 1989, Geology of the south-central California continental margin: California Division of Mines and Geology, Continental Margin Geologic Map Series, Area 4 of 7, 4 sheets, scale 1:250,000.

Hall, C.A., Jr., 1973a, Geology of the Arroyo Grande quadrangle, California: California Division of Mines and Geology, map sheet 24, scale 1:48,000.

Hall, C.A., Jr., 1973b, Geologic map of the Morro Bay South and Port San Luis quadrangles, San Luis Obispo County, California: U.S. Geological Survey Miscellaneous Field Studies Map MF–511.

Hall, C.A., Jr., 1975, San Simeon-Hosgri Fault System, coastal California: Economic and environmental implications: Science, v. 190, p. 1291–1294.

Hall, C.A., Jr., 1978, Origin and development of the Lompoc-Santa Maria pull-apart basin and its relation to the San Simeon-Hosgri strike-slip fault, western California, *in* Silver, E.A., and Normark, W.R., eds., San Gregorio-Hosgri Fault Zone, California: California Division of Mines and Geology Special Report 137, p. 25–31.

Hall, C.A., Jr., 1981, San Luis Obispo transform fault and middle Miocene rotation of the western Transverse Ranges, California: Journal of Geophysical Research, v. 86, no. B2, p. 1013–1031.

Hall, C.A., Jr., 1982, Pre-Monterey subcrop and structure contour maps, western San Luis Obispo and Santa Barbara Counties, California: U.S. Geological Survey Miscellaneous Field Studies Map MF–1384, 6 sheets, scale 1:250,000.

Hall, C.A., Jr., 1991, Geology of the Point Sur-Lopez Point region, Coast Ranges, California—A part of the southern California allochthon: Geological Society of America Special Paper 266, p. 40.

Hall, C.A., Jr., Ernst, W.G., Prior, S.W., and Wiese, J.W., 1979, Geologic map of the San Luis Obispo-San Simeon region, California: U.S. Geological Survey Miscellaneous Investigations Series Map I–1097, 3 sheets, scale 1:48,000.

Hall, N.T., Hunt, T.D., and Vaughan, P.R., 1994, Holocene behavior of the San Simeon Fault Zone, south-central coastal California, *in* Alterman, I.B., McMullen, R.B., Cluff, L.S., and Slemmons, D.B., eds., Seismotectonics of the central California Coast Ranges: Geological Society of America Special Paper 292, p. 167–189.

Hamilton, D.H., and Willingham, C.R., 1977, Hosgri Fault Zone, amount of displacement, and relation to structures of the western Transverse Ranges: Geological Society of America Abstracts with Programs, v. 9, p. 429.

Hanson, K.L., and Lettis, W.R., 1994, Estimated Pleistocene slip rate for the San Simeon Fault Zone, south-central coastal California, *in* Alterman, I.B., McMullen, R.B., Cluff, L.S., and Slemmons, D.B., eds., Seismotectonics of the central California Coast Ranges: Geological Society of America Special Paper 292, p. 133–150.

Hanson, K.L., Lettis, W.R., McLaren, M.K., Savage, W.U., and Hall, N.T., 2004, Style and rate of Quaternary deformation of the Hosgri Fault Zone, offshore south-central California, *in* Keller, M.A., ed., Evolution of sedimentary basins/onshore oil and gas investigations—Santa Maria Province: U.S. Geological Survey Bulletin 1995–BB.

Hanson, K.L., Lettis, W.R., and Mezger, L., 1987, Late Pleistocene deformation along the San Simeon Fault Zone near San Simeon, California [abs.]: Geological Society of America Abstracts with Programs, Cordilleran Section, v. 19, no. 6, p. 386.

Hanson, K.L., Lettis, W.R., Wesling, J.R., Kelson, K.I., and Mezger, L., 1992 Quaternary marine terraces, south-central coastal California—Implications for crustal deformation and coastal evolution, *in* Fletcher, C.H., and Wehmiller, J.F., eds., Quaternary coasts of the United States—Marine and lacustrine systems: Society for Sedimentary Geology Special Publication No. 48, p. 323–332.

Hanson, K.L., Wesling, J.R., Lettis, W.R., Kelson K.I., and Mezger, L., 1994, Correlation, ages, and uplift rates of Quaternary marine terraces, south-central coastal California, *in* Alterman, I.B., McMullen, R.B., Cluff, L.S., and Slemmons, D.B., eds., Seismotectonics of the central California Coast Ranges: Geological Society of America Special Paper 292, p. 45–72.

Harding, T.P., 1985, Seismic characteristics and identification of negative flower structures, positive flower structures, and positive structural inversion: American Association of Petroleum Geologists Bulletin, v. 69, no. 4, p. 582–600.

Harding, T.P., 1990, Identification of wrench faults using subsurface structural data—Criteria and pitfalls: American Association of Petroleum Geologists Bulletin, v. 74, no. 10, p. 1590–1609.

Hatton, L., Larner, K., and Gibson, B.S., 1981, Migration of seismic data from inhomogeneous media: Geophysics, v. 46, no. 5, p. 751–767.

Heck, R.G., and Mannon, R.W., 1988, Heavy oil reserves in the Monterey Formation offshore California—Geological and engineering aspects, *in* Meyer, R.F., ed., Proceedings of the third UNITAR/UNDP international conference on heavy crude and tar sands: Canada, Alberta Oil Sands Technology and Research Authority, p. 209–220.

Hoskins, E.G., and Griffiths, R.R., 1971, Hydrocarbon potential of northern and central California offshore, *in* Cram, I.H., ed., Future petroleum provinces of the United States—Their geology and potential: American Association of Petroleum Geologists Memoir 15, p. 212–228

Howie, J.M., Miller, K.C., Savage, W.U., 1993, Integrated crustal structure across the south-central California margin, Santa Lucia escarpment to the San Andreas Fault: Journal of Geophysical Research, v. 98, p. 8173–8196.

Isaacs, C.M., 1981, Porosity reduction during diagenesis of the Monterey Formation, Santa Barbara coastal area, California, *in* Garrison, R.E., and Douglas, R.G., eds., The Monterey Formation and related siliceous rocks of California: Pacific Section, Society of Economic Paleontologists and Mineralogists, p. 257–271.

Isaacs, C.M., 1982, Influence of rock compositions on kinetics of silica phase changes in the Monterey Formation, Santa Barbara area, California: Geology, v. 10, p. 304–308.

Jennings, C.W., 1977, Geologic map of California: California Division of Mines and Geology, Geologic Data Map No. 2, 1 sheet, scale 1:750,000.

Jennings, C.W., 1994, Fault activity map of California and adjacent areas: California Division of Mines and Geology, Geologic Data Map No. 6, 1 sheet, scale 1:750,000, 92 p.

Kennedy, M.P., Greene, H.G., and Clarke, S.H., 1987, Geology of the California continental margin: California Division of Mines and Geology Bulletin 207, 110 p.

Lafond, C.F., and Levander, A.R., 1993, Migration moveout analysis and depth focusing: Geophysics, v. 58, no. 1, p. 91–100.

Leighton and Associates, 1987, Geophysical investigation of potential geologic constraints, offshore Point Arguello to the Santa Maria River, northern Santa Barbara County, California: Irvine, Calif., Leighton and Associates, Inc., report for California State Lands Commission, 3 volumes.

Lemiszki, P.J., and Brown, L.D., 1988, Variable crustal structure of strike-slip fault zones as observed on deep seismic reflection sections: Geological Society of America Bulletin, v. 100, p. 655–676.

Leslie, R.B., 1981, Continuity and tectonic implications of the San Simeon-Hosgri Fault Zone, central California: U.S. Geological Survey Open-File Report 81–430, 59 p.

Lettis, W.R., DiSilvestro, L., Hanson, K.L., and Shiller, G.I., 1990, The San Simeon/Hosgri pull-apart basin—Implications for late Quaternary activity on the Hosgri Fault Zone, *in* Lettis, W.R., Hanson, K.L., Kelson, K.I., and Wesling, J.R., eds., Neotectonics of south-central coastal California: Friends of the Pleistocene, Pacific Cell, 1990 Fall Field Trip Guidebook, p. 91–138.

Lettis, W.R., and Hall N.T., 1990, The Los Osos Fault Zone, San Luis Obispo County, California, *in* Lettis, W.R., Hanson, K.L., Kelson, K.I., and Wesling, J.R., eds., Neotectonics of south-central coastal California: Friends of the Pleistocene, Pacific Cell, 1990 Fall Field Trip Guidebook, p. 299–347.

Lettis, W.R., and Hall, N.T., 1994, The Los Osos Fault Zone, San Luis Obispo County, California, *in* Alterman, I.B., McMullen, R.B., Cluff, L.S., and Slemmons, D.B., eds., Seismotectonics of the central California Coast Ranges: Geological Society of America Special Paper 292, p. 73–102.

Lettis, W.R., and Hanson, K.L., 1992, Crustal strain partitioning—Implications for seismic hazard assessment in western California: Geology, v. 19, p. 559–562.

Lettis, W.R., Hanson, K.L., Unruh, J.R., and Savage W.U., 2004, Quaternary tectonic setting of south-central California, *in* Keller, M.A., ed., Evolution of sedimentary basins/onshore oil and gas investigations—Santa Maria Province: U.S. Geological Survey Bulletin 1995–AA.

Lettis, W.R., Kelson, K.I., Wesling, J.R., Angell, M., Hanson, K.L., and Hall, N.T., 1994, Quaternary deformation of the San Luis Range, San Luis Obispo County, California, *in* Alterman, I.B., McMullen, R.B., Cluff, L.S., and Slemmons, D.B., eds., Seismotectonics of the Central California Coast Ranges: Geological Society of America Special Paper 292, p. 111–132.

Marsden, D., 1989, Layer cake depth conversion: Society of Exploration Geophysicists, The Leading Edge, v. 9, no. 1, p. 10–14.

Maruyama, Toshiaki, 2000, Middle Miocene to Pleistocene diatom stratigraphy of Leg 167, *in* Lyle, M., Koizumi, I., Richter, C., and Moore, T.C., Jr. eds., Proceedings of the Ocean Drilling Program: College Station, Tex., Texas A&M University, Ocean Drilling Program, Scientific Results, v. 167, p. 63–110.

Mayerson, D., 1997, Santa Maria-Partington basin, *in* Dunkel, C.A., and Piper, K.A., eds., 1995 National assessment of United States oil and gas resources of the Pacific Outer Continental Shelf Region: U.S. Department of the Interior Minerals Management Service, Pacific OCS Region Office of Resources Evaluation, OCS Report MMS 97–0019.

McCrory, P.A., Wilson, D.S., Ingle, J.C., Jr., and Stanley, R.G., 1995, Neogene geohistory analysis of the Santa Maria Basin, California, and its relation to transfer of central California to the Pacific Plate, in Keller, M.A., ed., Evolution of sedimentary basins/onshore oil and gas investigations—Santa Maria Province: U.S. Geological Survey Bulletin 1995–J, 38 p.

McCulloch, D.S., 1987, Regional geology and hydrocarbon potential of offshore central California, in Scholl, D.W., Grant, A., and Vedder, J., eds., Geology and resource potential of the continental margin of western North America and adjacent ocean basins, Beaufort Sea to Baja California: American Association of Petroleum Geologists, Circum-Pacific Earth Science Series, v. 6, p. 353–401.

McCulloch, D.S., and Chapman, R.H., 1977, Maps showing residual magnetic intensity along the California coast, lat. 37°30' N. to 34°30' N.: U.S. Geological Survey Open-File Report 77–79, 14 aeromagnetic maps, scale 1:250,000.

McCulloch, D.S., Greene, H.G., Heston, K.S., and Rubin, D.M., 1980, A summary of the geology and geologic hazards in proposed lease sale 53, central California outer Continental Shelf: U.S. Geological Survey Open-File Report 80–1095, 76 p.

McCulloch, D.S., Utter, P.A., and Menack, J.S., 1985, Maps showing locations of selected pre-Quaternary rock samples from 34°30' north latitude to 42° north latitude, California continental margin: U.S. Geological Survey Miscellaneous Field Investigations Series, Map MF–1719, 38 p., 4 map sheets.

McDougall, K., 2008, California Cenozoic biostratigraphy—Paleogene, in Hosford-Scheirer, A., ed., Petroleum systems and geologic assessment of oil and gas in the San Joaquin Basin Province, California: U.S. Geological Survey Professional Paper 1713, chap. 4.

McIntosh, K.D., Reed, D.L., Silver, E.A., and Meltzer, A.S., 1991, Deep structure and structural inversion along the central California continental margin from EDGE seismic profile RU-3: Journal of Geophysical Research, v. 96, no. B4, p. 6459–6473.

McLaren, M.K., and Savage, W.U., 2001, Seismicity of south-central coastal California: October 1987 through January 1997: Bulletin of the Seismological Society of America, v. 91, no. 6, p. 1629–1658.

Meltzer, A.S., and Levander, A.R., 1991, Deep crustal reflection profiling offshore southern central California: Journal of Geophysical Research, v. 96, no. B4, p. 6475–6491.

Miller, K.C., Howie, J.M., Ruppert, S.D., 1992, Shortening within underplated oceanic crust beneath the central California margin: Journal of Geophysical Research, v. 97, p. 19961–19980.

Miller, K.C., and Meltzer, A.S., 1999, Structure and tectonics of the central offshore Santa Maria and Santa Lucia basins, California—Results from the PG&E/EDGE seismic reflection survey, in Keller, M.A., ed., Evolution of sedimentary basins/onshore oil and gas investigations—Santa Maria Province: U.S. Geological Survey Bulletin 1995–Z, 12 p.

Murata, K.J., and Larson, R.R., 1975, Diagenesis of Miocene siliceous shales, Temblor Range, California: U.S. Geological Survey Journal of Research, v. 3, p. 553–556.

Namson, J.S., and Davis, T.L., 1988, Seismically active fold and thrust belt in the San Joaquin Valley, central California: Geological Society of America Bulletin, v. 100, p. 257–273.

Namson, J.S., and Davis, T.L., 1990, Late Cenozoic fold and thrust belt of the southern Coast Ranges and Santa Maria Basin, California: American Association of Petroleum Geologists Bulletin, v. 74, no. 4, p. 467–492.

Nicholson, C., Sorlien, C.C., and Luyendyk, B.P., 1992, Deep crustal structure and tectonics in the offshore southern Santa Maria Basin, California: Geology, v. 20, p. 239–242.

Nilsen, T.H., 1984, Oligocene tectonics and sedimentation, California: Sedimentary Geology, v. 38, p. 305–336.

Nur, A., and Boccaletti, M., 1990, Active and recent strike-slip tectonics: Eos, Transactions of the American Geophysical Union, v. 71, no. 35, p. 806.

Obradovich, J.D., and Naeser, C.W., 1981, Geochronology bearing on the age of the Monterey Formation and siliceous rocks in California, in Garrison, R.E., Douglas, R.G., Pisciotto, K.E., Isaacs, C.M., and Ingle, J.C., eds., The Monterey Formation and related siliceous rocks of California: Pacific Section, Society of Economic Paleontologists and Mineralogists, p. 87–95.

PG&E, 1974, Geology of the southern Coast Ranges and the adjoining offshore continental margin of California, with special reference to the geology in the vicinity of the San Luis Range and Estero Bay, in Appendix 2D, Final Safety Analysis Report for Diablo Canyon Power Plant: Pacific Gas and Electric Company (PG&E), U.S. Atomic Energy Commission Docket Nos. 50–275 and 50–323.

PG&E, 1988, Final report of the Diablo Canyon Long Term Seismic Program: Pacific Gas and Electric Company (PG&E), U.S. Nuclear Regulatory Commission Docket Nos. 50–275 and 50–323.

PG&E, 1990, Response to Nuclear Regulatory Commission questions GSG-12 and GSG-16 on the Final Report of the Diablo Canyon Long Term Seismic Program: Pacific Gas and Electric Company (PG&E), U.S. Nuclear Regulatory Commission Docket Nos. 50–275 and 50–323.

Pisciotto, K.A., 1981, Diagenetic trends in the siliceous facies of the Monterey Shale in the Santa Maria region, California: Sedimentology, v. 28, p. 547–571.

Pisciotto, K.A., and Garrison, R.E., 1983, Lithofacies and depositional environments of the Monterey Formation, California, in The Monterey Formation and related siliceous rocks of California: Society of Economic Paleontologists and Mineralogists, p. 97–122.

Pullammanappallil, S.K., and Louie, J.N., 1994, A generalized simulated-annealing optimization for inversion of first-arrival times: Bulletin of the Seismological Society of America, v. 84, no. 5, p. 1397–1409.

Richmond, W.C., Burdick, D.J., Phillips, D., and Norris, P.J., 1981, Regional geology, seismicity and potential geologic hazards and constraints, OSC lease sale 53, northern and central California: U.S. Geological Survey Open-File Report 81–318, 36 p.

Rietman, J., and Beyer, L., 1982, Bouguer gravity map of California, Santa Maria sheet: California Division of Mines and Geology, 2 sheets, scale 1:250,000.

Saucedo, G.J., Bedford, D.R., Raines, G.L., Miller, R.J., and Wentworth, C.M., 2000, Digital data for the geologic map of California: California Division of Mines and Geology, CD2000-007 (CD-ROM), scale 1:750,000.

Sauer, P.E., and Mariano, J., 1990, Isostatic residual gravity and aeromagnetic maps of the Santa Maria province, including portions of the Santa Maria, San Luis Obispo, Los Angeles, and Bakersfield quadrangles and adjacent offshore areas, California: U.S. Geological Survey Open-File Report 90–308, 2 sheets, scale 1:250,000.

Sedlock, R.L., and Hamilton, D.H., 1991, Late Cenozoic tectonic evolution of southwestern California: Journal of Geophysical Research, v. 96, no. B2, p. 2325–2351.

Sheriff, R.E., 2002, Encyclopedic dictionary of applied geophysics (4th ed.): Society of Exploration Geophysicists, Geophysical Reference Series, no. 13, 429 p.

Shih, R.C., and Levander A.R., 1994, Layer-stripping reverse-time migration: Geophysical Prospecting, v. 41, p. 211–227.

Silver, E.A., 1974, Structural interpretation of free-air gravity on the California continental margin, 35° to 40° N.: Geological Society of America Abstracts with Programs, v. 6, p. 253.

Silver, E.A., and Normark, W.R., eds., 1978, San Gregorio-Hosgri Fault Zone, California: California Division of Mines and Geology, Special Report 137, 56 p.

Snyder, W.S., 1987, Structure of the Monterey Formation—Stratigraphic, diagenetic, and tectonic influences on style and timing, in Ingersoll, R.V., and Ernst, W.G., eds., Cenozoic Basin Development of Coastal California, Rubey Volume VI: Englewood Cliffs, N.J., Prentice-Hall, Inc., p. 321–347.

Sorlien, C.C., Kamerling, M.J., and Mayerson, D., 1999a, Block rotation and termination of the Hosgri strike-slip fault, California, from three-dimensional map restoration: Geology, v. 27, no. 11, p. 1039–1042.

Sorlien, C.C., Nicholson, C., and Luyendyk, B.P., 1999b, Miocene extension and post-Miocene transpression offshore of south-central California, in Keller, M.A., ed., Evolution of sedimentary basins/onshore oil and gas investigations—Santa Maria Province: U.S. Geological Survey Bulletin 1995–Y, 38 p.

Stanley, R.G., Johnson, S.Y., Swisher, C.C., III, Mason, M.A., Obradovich, J.D., Cotton, M.L., Filewicz, M.V., and Vork, D.R., 1995, Age of the Lospe Formation (early Miocene) and origin of the Santa Maria Basin, California, in Keller, M.A., ed., Evolution of sedimentary basins/onshore oil and gas investigations—Santa Maria Province: U.S. Geological Survey Bulletin 1995–M, 37 p.

Steritz, J.W., 1986, The southern termination of the Hosgri Fault Zone, offshore south-central California: Santa Barbara, University of California, M.S. thesis, 78 p., 22 pl.

Steritz, J.W., and Luyendyk, B.P., 1994, Hosgri Fault Zone, offshore Santa Maria Basin, California, in Alterman, I.B., McMullen, R.B., Cluff, L.S., and Slemmons, D.B., eds., Seismotectonics of the central California Coast Ranges: Geological Society of America Special Paper 292, p. 191–209.

Stone, D.S., 1969, Wrench faulting and Rocky Mountain tectonics: The Mountain Geologist, v. 6, no. 2, p. 67–79.

Stone, D.S., 1989, Wrench faulting and Rocky Mountain tectonics, in Foster, N.H., and Beaumont, E.A., eds., Structural concepts and techniques II: American Association of Petroleum Geologists Treatise of Petroleum Geology Reprint Series, no. 10, p. 409–421.

Suppe, J., 1983, Geometry and kinematics of fault-bend folding: American Journal of Science, v. 283, p. 684–721.

Suppe, J., and Medwedeff, D.A., 1984, Fault-propagation folding: Geological Society of America Abstracts with Programs, v. 16, p. 670.

Sylvester, A.G., 1988, Strike-slip faults: Geological Society of America Bulletin, v. 100, no. 11, p. 1666–1703.

Tennyson, M.E., and Isaacs, C.M., 2001, Geologic setting and petroleum geology of Santa Maria and Santa Barbara basins, coastal California, in Isaacs, C.M., and Rullkötter, J., eds., The Monterey Formation from rocks to molecules: New York, N.Y., Columbia University Press, p. 206–229.

Trehu A., 1991, Tracing the subducted oceanic crust beneath the central California continental margin—Results from ocean bottom seismometers deployed during the 1986 Pacific Gas and Electric EDGE experiment: Journal of Geophysical Research, v. 96, no. B4, p. 6493–6506.

Turner, D.L., 1970, Potassium-argon dating of Pacific Coast Miocene foraminiferal stages: Geological Society of America Special Paper 124, p. 91–129.

USGS, 2007, Divisions of geologic time—Major chronostratigraphic and geochronologic units: U.S. Geological Survey Fact Sheet 2007–3015, 2 p.

Wagner, H.C., 1974, Marine geology between Cape San Martin and Point Sal, south-central California offshore: U.S. Geological Survey Open-File Report 74–252, 17 p.

Withjack, M.O., and Meisling, K.E., 1987, Seismic expression of structural styles—A modeling approach: American Association of Petroleum Geologists Bulletin, v. 71, no. 4., p. 628.

Woodring, W.P., and Bramlette, M.N., 1950, Geology and paleontology of the Santa Maria district, California: U.S. Geological Survey Professional Paper 222, 185 p.

Worden, C.B., 1992, Interactive seismic imaging on a multicomputer and application to the Hosgri fault: Pasadena, California Institute of Technology, Ph.D. dissertation.

Yilmaz, O., 1987, Seismic data processing: Society of Exploration Geophysicists, Investigations in Geophysics, no. 2, 526 p.

Yilmaz, O., 2001, Seismic data analysis: Society of Exploration Geophysicists, Investigations in Geophysics, no. 10, 2 volumes, 2027 p.

Zalan, P.V., 1987, Identification of strike-slip faults in seismic sections: American Association of Petroleum Geologists Bulletin, v. 71, no. 4, p. 629.

Zijderveld, J.D.A., Zachariasse, J.W., Verhallen, P.J.J.M., and Hilgen, F.L., 1986, The age of the Miocene-Pliocene boundary: Newsletter on Stratigraphy, v. 16, no. 3, p. 169–181.

Appendix A

Microfossil and lithology data from seven wells in the central offshore Santa Maria Basin, California

The microfossil data in this appendix are summarized from 1982 and 1983 reports by Biostratigraphics, Consulting Micropaleontologists, formerly of San Diego, California. The lithology data are from formation log descriptions prepared by well site formation logging contractors. The data listings are for wells P-0415-1, P-0415-2, P-0416-1, P-0422-1, P-0424-1, P-0430-1, and P-0435-1. The locations of the wells are shown on figure 5 and plates 2, 4, and 5 to 7. The plates indicate that the wells are generally along, or adjacent to, the crest of two anticlinal structures in the area offshore Point Sal to Purisima Point: the Purisima structure (wells P-0415-1, P-0415-2, P-0416-1, P-0422-1, and P-0435-1) and the Lompoc structure (wells P-0424-1 and P-0430-1). Partial well logs for wells P-0415-1, P-0422-1, P-0424-1, and P-0435-1 are shown on plate 3. Figure A1 shows the relations we used in the central offshore Santa Maria Basin for ages in million years (Ma), epochs and subepochs, formation names, diatom zones, and benthic foraminiferal stages.

Appendix tables A1 to A7 summarize the data for the seven wells. Specific data categories and listing formats vary between the wells depending on data available in our files and proprietary ownership releases. Detailed background lithology and siliceous microfossil data are provided for wells P-0424-1 and P-0435-1 in tables A6 and A7, respectively.

The microfossil data were originally referenced to depths (ft) below the Kelly bushings. We converted the depths to meters (m) below mean lower low water (MLLW), the subsea reference elevation used in this paper. The diatom zones and ages (Ma) are based on our comparison of the sample descriptions to the late Miocene to Quaternary North Pacific Diatom Zones (NPDZ) and ages listed in Maruyama (2000). The benthic foraminiferal stages are the responsibility of the authors and the associated ages are based on McDougall (2008). The radiolarian and calcareous nannoplankton data are from Biostratigraphics, but the age assignments are by the authors.

Table A1.   Interpreted Summary of Data From Well P-0415-1. A blank in the Age (Ma) column indicates insufficient information for age determination.

Siliceous Microfossils

Age (Ma)	Depth (m)	Siliceous microfossil zones
3.5	283 to 365	Indeterminate, possibly Pliocene
	365 to 502	*Thalassiosira oestrupii*, upper part, early Pliocene
	502 to749	*T. oestrupii*, middle and lower part, early Pliocene
	749 to 859	Indeterminate

Benthic Foraminifers

Depth (m)	Foraminiferal stages
283 to 383	Upper Wheelerian, Provincial late Pliocene
383 to 685	Delmontian, early Pliocene, possibly late Miocene
685 to 1426	Delmontian, late Miocene
1,426 to 1,581	Upper Mohnian, late Miocene
1,581 to 2,029	Possibly lower Mohnian, late Miocene, Baggina californica
2,029 to 2,058	Luisian, middle Miocene, Valvulineria californica
2,058 to 2,139	Possibly upper Saucesian to Relizian, early Miocene
2,139 to 2,770	Indeterminate and repeated Miocene age units due to faulting
2,770 to 2,852	Possibly Eocene (repeat zone)

Radiolarian Stages

Age (Ma)	Depth (m)	Radiolarian stages
3.5 to 5.3	283 to 365	Indeterminate
	365 to 667	Early Pliocene, *Sphaeropyle langii*
	667 to 859	Indeterminate

Formation Names

Depth (m)	Formation
128 to 365	Unnamed offshore units
365 to 412	Upper Sisquoc Formation
412 to 1382	Lower Sisquoc Formation
1,382 to 2,058	Monterey Formation
2,058 to 2,898	Obispo and younger Miocene strata repeated due to faulting
2,898 to 3,000	Franciscan Complex

Table A2.   Interpreted Summary of Data From Well P-0415-2.

Siliceous Microfossils

Age (Ma)	Depth (m)	Siliceous microfossil zones
3.5 to 5.3	279 to 466	*T. oestrupii*, lower to middle part, early Pliocene
	466 to 630	Indeterminate

Benthic Foraminifers

Depth (m)	Foraminiferal stages
379 to 1078	Delmontian, late Miocene, *Virgulina californiensis*
1,078 to 1,225	Upper Mohnian, late Miocene
1,225 to 1,435	Lower Mohnian, late Miocene, *Globigerina spp.*
1,435 to 1,618	Relizian to lower Mohnian, middle to late Miocene
1,618 to 1,627	Probably Relizian to Luisian, middle Miocene, *Baggina cancriformis, Pullenia aff. Miocenica, Valvulineria californica var., and V. californica obesa*
1,627 to 1,654	Upper Saucesian to Relizian equivalent, based on lithology, early to middle Miocene
1,654 to 1,792	Oligocene and older, based on lithology

Radiolarian Stages

Age (Ma)	Depth (m)	Radiolarian stages
ca 38	1,682 to 1,792	Eocene to possibly Oligocene, *Braarudosphaera bigelowi, Coccolithus pelagicus, Cyclicargolithus sp., C. floridanus, C. neogammation and Dictyococcites bisectus*

Formation Names

Depth (m)	Formation
116 to 279	Unnamed offshore units
279 to 466	Upper Sisquoc Formation
466 to 1057	Lower Sisquoc Formation
1,057 to 1,627	Monterey Formation
1,627 to 1,792	Point Sal Formation and Older units
1,792 to 1,951	Franciscan Complex

Table A3.   Interpreted Summary of Data From Well P-0416-1

Siliceous Microfossils

Age (Ma)	Depth (m)	Siliceous microfossil zones
3.5 to 5.3	271 to 298	*T. oestrupii*, early Pliocene
	298 to 572	Early Miocene, transition to Opal-CT between 298 and 353 m

Benthic Foraminifers

Depth (m)	Foraminiferal stages
271 to 764	Late Miocene, Delmontian to possibly Mohnian based on lithology and sparse faunal remains
764 to 899	Late Miocene, upper Mohnian
899 to 1148	Late Miocene, probably lower Mohnian
1,148 to 1,252	Middle to late Miocene, probably Relizian to lower Mohnian
1,252 to 1,261	Early to middle Miocene, probably upper Saucesian to Relizian based on lithology

Formation Names

Depth (m)	Formation
134 to 298	Unnamed offshore units, possibly upper Sisquoc Formation
298 to 727	Lower Sisquoc Formation
727 to 1,252	Monterey Formation
1,252 to 1,307	Pre-Monterey Units
1,307 to 1,807	Franciscan Complex

Table A4.   Interpreted Summary of Data From Well P-0422-1

Table A5.   Interpreted Summary of Data From Well P-0430-1.

Siliceous Microfossils

Age (Ma)	Depth (m)	Siliceous microfossil zones
3.5 to 5.5	267 to 579	*T. oestrupii*, upper part, early Pliocene
5.5 to 6.0	579 to 789	Indeterminate, possibly late Miocene
	789 to 899	Indeterminate

Benthic Foraminifers

Depth (m)	Foraminiferal stages
267 to 579	Delmontian, possibly early Pliocene
579 to 1585	Delmontian, possibly late Miocene, *Virgulinella miocenica*
1,585 to 1,823	Upper Mohnian, late Miocene, based on lithology
1,823 to 2,225	Lower Mohnian, late Miocene, based on lithology
2,225 to 2,390	Relizian to lower Mohnian, middle to late Miocene, based on lithology
2,390 to 2,435	Early Miocene
2,435 to 2,469	Possibly Paleocene?, *Silicosigmoilina californica*
2,469 to 2,499	Late Cretaceous, *Inoceramus prisms*, radiolaria

Calcareous Nannoplankton Zones

Age (Ma)	Depth (m)	Radiolarian stages
	1,896 to 2,024	Indeterminate
11.5 to 15.5	2,024 to 2,051	Middle Miocene or older, *Cyclicargolithus floridanus*
	2,051 to 2,417	Indeterminate
49 to 55	2,417 to 2,469	Early Eocene, *Discoaster lodoensis*
65 +	2,469 to 2,508	Late Cretaceous, *Cretarhabdus angustiforatus, Tetralithus trifidus*

Formation Names

Depth (m)	Formation
105 to 249	Unnamed offshore units
249 to 579	Upper Sisquoc Formation
579 to 1,585	Lower Sisquoc Formation
1,585 to 2,390	Monterey Formation
2,390 to 2,499	Point Sal and Obispo(?) Formations
2,499 to 2,508	Franciscan Complex

Siliceous Microfossils

Age (Ma)	Depth (m)	Siliceous microfossil zones
3.5 to 5.49	249 to 469	*T. oestrupii*, early Pliocene
5.1 to 5.49	469 to 496	Possible *T. oestrupii*, possibly early Pliocene
	496 to 1,246	Indeterminate

Benthic Foraminifers

Depth (m)	Foraminiferal stages
249 to 469	Indeterminate
469 to 569	Indeterminate
569 to 1517	Indeterminate, probable late Miocene based on lithology
1,517 to 1,539	Middle Miocene undifferentiated
1,539 to 1,593	Early to middle Miocene, upper Relizian

Radiolarian Stages and Ages

Age (Ma)	Depth (m)	Radiolarian stages
3.5 to 5.1	249 to 441	Early Pliocene, *Lamprocyrtis heteroporos, Stichocorys peregrina*
5.3 +	441 to 496	Possible late Miocene, *Lychnocanoma grande*

Formation Names

Depth (m)	Formation
99 to 249	Unnamed offshore units
249 to 496	Upper Sisquoc Formation
496 to 1,091	Lower Sisquoc Formation
1,091 to 1,539	Monterey Formation
1,539 to 1,593	Point Sal Formation
1,593 to 1,740	Franciscan Complex

Table A6.   Interpreted Summary of Data From Well P-0424-1

Siliceous Microfossils

Age (Ma)	Depth (m)	Siliceous microfossil zones
	326 to 335	Indeterminate, Quaternary by superposition
1.01–1.46 to 2.0	335 to 359	Quaternary to late Pliocene, probably *A. oculatus* Zone, North Pacific Diatom Zone 10 (NPDZ10)
2.0 to 2.61–2.68	359 to 417	Late Pliocene, *N. koizumii* Zone, NPDZ 9
2.61–2.68 to 3.53–3.59	417 to 426	Late Pliocene to early Pliocene, *N. koizumii–N. kamtschatica* Zone, NPDZ 8
3.53–3.59 to no older than 3.7	426 to 545	Early Pliocene, *N. kamtschatica*-b Subzone, NPDZ 7Bb
3.53–3.59 to no older than 5.49	545 to 600	Early Pliocene to late Miocene, *N. kamtschatica*-b Subzone, NPDZ 7Bb
5.49 to 5.9	600 to 636	Late Miocene, *N. kamtschatica*-a Subzone, NPDZ 7Ba
5.49 to 6.65	636 to 646	Late Miocene, *N. kamtschatica*-a Subzone, NPDZ 7Ba

Benthic Foraminifers

Depth (m)	Foraminiferal stages
326 to 353	Wheelerian, Provincial late Pliocene, *Cassidulina californica*
353 to 408	Transitional from Venturian to Wheelerian, middle Pliocene to late Pliocene, *Uvigerina peregrina, Cassiudlina translucens*
408 to 975	Indeterminate, probable early Pliocene to late Miocene
975 to 1,024	Mohnian, late Miocene
1,024 to 1,076	Indeterminate
1,076 to 1,201	Franciscan Complex, based on lithology

Formation Names

Depth (m)	Formation
156 to 405	Unnamed offshore units
405 to 610	Upper Sisquoc Formation
610 to 911	Lower Sisquoc Formation
911 to 1,024	Monterey Formation
1,024 to 1,071	Point Sal Formation
1,071 to 1,200	Franciscan Complex

Well P-0424-1

Summary of the lithology and siliceous microfossils in the depth interval 326 m to 646 m

[Detailed listings of the sample lithology and diatom content are on the following pages]

Sample 1: 326 m to 335 m, soft clay and sand; **age:** indeterminate, Quaternary by superposition.

Samples 2, 3, and 4 (upper part): 335 m to 359 m, soft clay and sand; **age:** Quaternary to late Pliocene, probable *A. oculatus* Zone, NPDZ 10, 1.01–1.46 Ma to 2.0 Ma.

Samples 4 to 10: 359 m to 417 m, soft clay, sand and siltstone, volcanic, shell, and chert fragments; **age:** late Pliocene, *N. koizumi* Zone, NPDZ 9, 2.0 Ma to 2.61-2.68 Ma.

Sample 11: 417 m to 426 m, clay, siltstone and limestone; **age:** late Pliocene, probable *N. koizumii– N. kamtschatica* Zone, NPDZ 8, 2.61 –2.68 Ma to 3.53–3.59 Ma.

Samples 12 to 22: 426 m to 527 m, clay, siltstone and limestone; **age:** early Pliocene, *N. kamtschatica*-b Subzone, NPDZ 7Bb, 3.53–3.59 Ma to no older than 3.7 Ma.

Samples 23 to 30: 527 m to 600 m, clay, siltstone and limestone; **age:** early Pliocene, *N. kamtschatica*-b Subzone, NPDZ 7Bb, 3.53–3.59 Ma to no older than 5.4 Ma.

Samples 31 to 34: 600 m to 636 m, clay, siltstone, limestone, and shale; **age:** early Pliocene to late Miocene, *N. kamtschatica*-a Subzone, NPDZ 7Ba, 5.49 Ma to no older than 5.9 Ma.

Sample 35: 636 m to 646 m, clay, limestone, siltstone, and shale; **age:** late Miocene, *N. kamtschatica*-a Subzone, NPDZ 7Ba, 5.49 Ma to 6.65 Ma.

Below 646 m: no preserved siliceous microfossils due to diagenetic alteration of the host rocks.

The individual samples are 9 m (30 ft) composites of well cuttings. The lithology descriptions are from well site formation logging contractors. Preparation and identification of diatoms was by Biostratigraphics in 1983. Their terms for the frequency of observed diatoms in a sample are common (200–900), frequent (9–200), rare (4–8), and very rare (1–3). The assignment of North Pacific Diatom Zones (NPDZ) and ages is by the authors based on zones in Maruyama (2000). Depths are subsea (MLLW). The casing shoe was at 313 m (1,026 ft).

Sample 1: 326 m (1,068 ft) to 335 m (1,089 ft); **lithology**: soft clay and unconsolidated sand; **siliceous microfossils**: none; **age**: indeterminate, Quaternary by superposition.

Sample 2: 335 m (1,089 ft) to 344 m (1,128 ft); **lithology**: soft clay and unconsolidated sand; **siliceous microfossils**: very rare *Melosira sol*; **age**: Quaternary to late Pliocene, probable *A. oculatus* Zone, NPDZ 10, 0.30 to 1.01–1.46 to 2.0 Ma.

Sample 3: 344 m (1,128 ft) to 356 m (1,158 ft); **lithology**: soft clay, unconsolidated sand, trace siltstone with indurated calcite; **siliceous microfossils**: very rare *Actinocyclus ehrenbergii v. tenella, Coscinodiscus marginatus, Thalassionema nitzschioides*; **age**: Quaternary to late Pliocene, probable *A. oculatus* Zone, NPDZ 10, 1.01–1.46 Ma to 2.0 Ma.

An unconformity at approximately 356 m is noted in the seismic reflection data in the vicinity of this well. This unconformity may represent the late Pliocene-Pleistocene unconformity shown in figure 6.

Last occurrence of *N. koizumii* is in Sample 4.

Sample 4: 356 m (1,158 ft) to 362 m (1,188 ft); **lithology**: soft clay, unconsolidated sand, at 359 m (1,178 ft) lithology changes from 70% sand to 20% sand with the first occurrence of traces of shell fragments, argillaceous chert fragments, volcanic fragments, limestone fragments; **siliceous microfossils**: rare M. sol, *C. marginatus*; very rare *T. nitzschioides*, last occurrence *Neodenticula koizumii* (formerly *Neodenticula seminae v. fossilis*), *Thalassiosira oestrupii*; very rare reworked *C. marginatus f. fossilis*; **age**: from 356 m (1,158 ft) to 359 m (1,178 ft), Quaternary to late Pliocene, *A. oculatus* Zone, NPDZ 10, from 359 m (1,178 ft) to 362 m (1,188 ft), late Pliocene, *N. koizumii* Zone, NPDZ 9, 2.0 Ma to 2.61–2.68 Ma.

Sample 5: 362 m (1,188 ft) to 371 m (1,218 ft); **lithology**: soft clay, sand, siltstone, volcanic, shell and chert fragments; **siliceous microfossils**: frequent *N. koizumii*; rare *C. marginatus, N. seminae, Thalassiosira excentrica*; very rare *M. sol, T. nitzschioides, Coscinodiscus robustus, Diploneis bombus, Hemidiscus cuneiformis, Stephanopyxis turris, Thalassiosira lineata*, very rare reworked *Thalassiosira antiqua, C. marginatus f. fossilis*; **age**: late Pliocene, *N. koizumi* Zone, NPDZ 9, 2.0 Ma to 2.61–2.68 Ma.

Sample 6: 371 m (1,218 ft) to 380 m (1,248 ft); **lithology**: clay, sand and siltstone, trace shell fragments; **siliceous microfossils**: frequent *N. koizumii, D. seminae*; rare *M. sol, C. marginatus, T. nitzschioides, A. ehrenbergii v. tenella, C. marginatus f. fossilis, Actinoptychus senarius*; very rare *A. ehrenbergii, T. oestrupii, S. turris, Actinoptychus undulatus, Bachteriastrum spp., Bidulphia auria, Cocconeis costata, Cocconeis dirupta, Coscinodiscus nodulifer, Grammatophora spp. Melosira sulcata, Nitzschia reinholdi, Porosira glacialis, Rhaponeis cocconeides*; **age**: probable late Pliocene, *N. koizumii* Zone, NPDZ 9, 2.0 Ma to 2.61–2.68 Ma.

Sample 7: 380 m (1,248 ft) to 390 m (1,278 ft); **lithology**: clay, sand and siltstone, shell fragments, change from 30% sand to zero sand at 387 m (1,268 ft); **siliceous**

microfossils: frequent *M. sol, C. marginatus*; rare *C. marginatus f. fossilis, N. koizumii, C. robustus;* very rare *T. nitzschioides, T. oestrupii, N. seminae, S. turris, T. antiqua, T. excentrica, A. senarius, Grammatophora spp., Porosira glacialis, Actinocyclus oculatus, Endicta oceanica, Navicula lyra, Stephnopyxis dimorpha*; **age**: 380 m to 387 m, late Pliocene, *N. koizumii* Zone, NPDZ 9, 2.0 Ma to 2.61–2.68 Ma.

Sample 8: 390 m (1,278 ft) to 399 m (1,308 ft); **lithology**: clay and siltstone; **siliceous microfossils**: rare *C. marginatus v. fossilis, N. koizumii, T. antique*; very rare *M. sol, A. ehrenbergii, C. marginatus, T. nitzschioides, C. robustus, S. turris, T. lineata, A. senarius, C. nodulifer, Grammatophora spp., M. sulcata, P. glacialis, N. lyra, Actinoptychus splendens, Coscinodiscus radius*; **age**: late Pliocene, *N. koizumii* Zone, NPDZ 9, 2.0 Ma to 2.61–2.68 Ma.

Sample 9: 399 m (1,308 ft) to 408 m (1,338 ft); **lithology**: clay and siltstone; **siliceous microfossils**: rare *M. sol, C. marginatus*, first occurrence of *N. koizumii, T. antiqua, Rhizosolenia barboi, Thalassiosira nativa*; very rare *A. ehrenbergii, T. nitzschioides, C. marginatus v. fossilis, D. bombus, H. cuneiformis, S. turris, T. excentrica, A. senarius, B. aurita, C. dirupta, C. costata, C. nodulifer, Grammatophora spp., N. lyra, Actinocyclus curvulatus, Actinocyclus ochotensis, Cocconeis scutellum, T. excentrica*; **age**: late Pliocene, *N. koizumii* Zone, NPDZ 9, 2.0 Ma to 2.61–2.68 Ma.

Sample 10: 408 m (1,338 ft) to 417 m (1,368 ft); **lithology**: clay (change at 413 m from 50% clay to 80% clay) and siltstone, trace limestone; **siliceous microfossils**: frequent *C. marginatus, T. nitzschioides, C. marginatus f. fossilis, T. antiqua, Thalassiothrix longissima*; rare *C. nodulifer, M. sulcata, Delphineis sachalinensis*; very rare *M. sol, A. ehrenbergii, A. ehrenbergii v. tenella, N. rheinholdi, C. radiatus, A. curvatulus, A. divisus, R. barboi, T. nativa, Actinoptychus biformus, Thalassiosira leptopus, Coscinodiscus oculus-iridis, Liradiscus ellipticus, Lithodesmium cornigerum*; **age**: late Pliocene, *N. koizumii* Zone, NPDZ 9, 2.0 Ma to 2.61–2.68 Ma.

Regional early-late Pliocene unconformity is between 408 m and 417m (1,338 to 1,368 ft) in this well based on electric log data (pl. 3) and mapping of the unconformity from seismic reflection data.

Last occurrence of *N. kamtschatica* is in Sample 11.

Sample 11: 417 m (1,368 ft) to 426 m (1,398 ft); **lithology**: clay and siltstone; **siliceous microfossils**: frequent *C. marginatus, T. nitzschioides, C. marginatus f. fossilis, T. antiqua, M. sulcata, T. longissima*; rare *M. sol, A. ehrenbergii, A. ehrenbergii v. tenella, H. cuneiformis, C. nodulifer, A. minutus, C. oculus-iridis*; very rare *C. dirupta, S. dimorpha, T. excentrica, D. sachalinensis, Actinoptychus bismarckii, Campyloneis grevillei, Coscinodiscus denarius*, last occurrence *Neodenticula kamtschatica* (formerly *Denticulopsis kamtschatica*), *Lithodesmium minisculum, Rhaphoneis amphiceros angularis, Rhaphoneis amphiceros* *elongata, Rhizosolenia styliformis*; **age**: probable late Pliocene, probable *N. koizumii-N. kamtschatica* Zone, NPDZ 8, 2.61–2.68 Ma to 3.53–3.59 Ma.

Sample 12: 426 m (1,398 ft) to 435 m (1,428 ft); **lithology**: clay and siltstone; **siliceous microfossils**: common *T. antique*; frequent *A. ehrenbergii, C. marginatus, T. nitzschioides, C. marginatus v. fossilis, M. sulcata, C. oculus iridis, T. longissima*; rare *A. ehrenbergii v. tennella, A. bismarckii, C. stellaris*; very rare *M. sol, T. oestrupii, H. cuneiformis, Bacteriastrum spp., C. nodulifer, N. reinholdii, R. barboi, T. nativa, R. sachalinensis, L. minisculum, R. amphiceros elongata, R. styliformis, Lithodesmium californicum, Melosira granulate, Pseudopyxilla americana, Delphineis simbirskiana, Triceratium cinnamomeum*; **age**: early Pliocene, *N. kamtschatica*-b Subzone, NPDZ 7Bb, 3.53–3.59 Ma to no older than 3.7 Ma.

Sample 13: 435 m (1,428 ft) to 444 m (1,458 ft); **lithology**: clay and siltstone; **siliceous microfossils**: common *C. marginatus, C. marginatus f. fossilis, T. antique; frequent A. ehrenbergii, H. cuneiformis, R. barboi*; rare *M. sol, A. ehrenbergii v. tenella, N. reinholdii, A. curvalatulus, A. divisus, A. minutus, C. denarius, L. minisculum, Rhizolenia hebetata f. semispina*; very rare *C. dirupta, C. nodulifer, Grammatophora spp., S. dimorpha, C. radiutus, T. excentrica, T. nativa, A. bismarckii, R. styliformis, R. curvirostris v. inermis, Navicula pennata*; **age**: early Pliocene, *N. kamtschatica*-b Subzone, NPDZ 7Bb, 3.53–3.59 Ma to no older than 3.7 Ma.

Sample 14: 444 m (1,458 ft) to 454 m (1,488 ft); **lithology**: clay, 10% siltstone, 10% limestone, trace shell fragments; **siliceous microfossils**: common *C. marginatus; frequent A. ehrenbergii, T. nitzschioides, C. marginatus f. fossilis, H. cuneiformis, T. antiqua, M. sulcata*; rare *M. sol, A. ehrenbergii v. tenella, M. sulcata, N. reinholdii, A. curvatulus, A. divisus, C. denarius, L. minisculum*; very rare *D. bombus, C. dirupta, C. nodulifer, S. dimorpha, C. radiatus, T. excentrica, T. nativa, A. bismarckii, R. styliformis, R. curvirostris v. inermis*; **age**: early Pliocene, *N. kamtschatica*-b Subzone, NPDZ 7Bb, 3.53–3.59 Ma to no older than 3.7 Ma.

Sample 15: 454 m (1,488 ft) to 463 m (1,518 ft); **lithology**: clay, 10% siltstone, 10% limestone; **siliceous microfossils**: common *C. marginatus*; frequent *A. ehrenbergii, T. nitzschioides, C. marginatus v. fossilis, H. cuneiformis, T. antiqua, Bacteriastrum spp., M. sulcata, T. longissima*; very rare *M. sol, C. dirupta, C. nodulifer, N. reinholdii, A. curvatulus, A. ochotensis, R. barboi, T. nativa, A. minutus, C. lineatus, C. oculus-iridis, D. sachalinensis, A. bismarckii, C. denarius, L. minisculum, R. amphiceros angularis, R. hebetata f. semispina*; **age**: early Pliocene, *N. kamtschatica*-b Subzone, NPDZ 7Bb, 3.53–3.59 Ma to no older than 3.7 Ma.

Sample 16: 463 m (1,518 ft) to 472 m (1,548 ft); **lithology**: 90% clay with minor siltstone and limestone beds; **siliceous microfossils**: frequent *C. marginatus, T. nitzschioides, A. ehrenbergii v. tenella, H. cuneiformis, T.*

antiqua, M. sulcata, T. longissima; rare *M. sol, A. ehrenbergii, S. turris, T. excentrica, C. nodulifer, R. barboi, A. minutus, C. oculus-iridis, C. denarius, L. minisculum*; very rare *C. robustus, Bacteriastrum spp., S. dimorpha, A. divisus, T. nativa, T. leptopus, L. cornigerum, A. bismarckii, C. grevillei, N. kamtschatica, R. amphiceros angularis, R. amphiceros elongata, D. simbirskiana, Rhaphoneis amphiceros*; **age**: early Pliocene, *N. kamtschatica*-b Subzone, NPDZ 7Bb, 3.53–3.59 Ma to no older than 3.7 Ma.

Sample 17: 472 m (1,548 ft) to 481 m (1,578 ft); **lithology**: 80% clay, 10% limestone and 10% siltstone, trace lignite; **siliceous microfossils**: common *C. marginatus, C. marginatus v. fossilis, T. antique*; frequent *T. nitzschioides, M. sulcata, T. longissima*; rare *A. ehrenbergii, S. turris, N. reinholdii, A. minutus*; very rare *M. sol, A. ehrenbergii v. tenela, T. oestrupii, H. cuneiformis, C. nodulifer, A. curvulatus, C. excentricus, R. barboi, T. leptopus, D. sachalinensis, A. bismarckii, C. denarius, L. minisculum, R. amphiceros angularis, R. styliformis, T. cinnamomeum, N. pennata, R. hebetata f. semispina, R. amphiceros, Rhaphoneis elegans*; **age**: early Pliocene, *N. kamtschatica*-b Subzone, NPDZ 7Bb, 3.53–3.59 Ma to no older than 3.7 Ma.

Sample 18: 481 m (1,578 ft) to 490 m (1,608 ft); **lithology**: 80% clay, 10% limestone and 10% siltstone; **siliceous microfossils**: common *C. marginatus, C. marginatus v. fossilis; frequent A. ehrenbergii, T. nitzschioides, T. antiqua, C. oculus-iridis, T. longissim*; rare *S. turris, M. sulcata, A. divisus, R. barboi, C. denarius, C. asteromphalus*; very rare *M. sol, A. ehrenbergii v. tenella, T. oestrupii, C. robustus, C. costata, C. nodulifer, Grammatophora spp., A. curvulatus, Actinoptychus biformis, A. minutus, T. leptopus, D. sachalinensis, A. bismarckii, L. minisculum, P. americana*; **age**: early Pliocene, *N. kamtschatica*-b Subzone, NPDZ 7Bb, 3.53–3.59 Ma to no older than 3.7 Ma.

Sample 19: 490 m (1,608 ft) to 499 m (1,638 ft); **lithology**: 80% clay, 10% limestone, 10% siltstone; **siliceous microfossils**: common *C. marginatus, C. marginatus f. fossilis, T. antique; frequent A. ehrenbergii, T. nitzschioides, S. turris, M. sulcata, C. oculus-iridis, T. longissima*; rare *A. ehrenbergii v. tenella, T. oestrupii, S. dimorpha, T. excentrica, A. divisus, R. barboi, C. grevillei, R. amphiceros angularis, R. amphiceros elongata, R. styliformis, C. stellaris, Thalassiosira undulosa*; **age**: early Pliocene, *N. kamtschatica*-b Subzone, NPDZ 7Bb, 3.53–3.59 Ma to no older than 3.7 Ma.

Sample 20: 499 m (1,638 ft) to 508 m (1,668 ft); **lithology**: 70% clay, 20% limestone, 10% siltstone; **siliceous microfossils**: common *C. marginatus, C. marginatus v. fossilis; frequent A. ehrenbergii, T. nitzschioides, S. turris, T. antiqua, M. sulcata, C. oculus-iridis, T. longissima, C. denarius*; rare *A. ehrenbergii v. tenella, T. oestrupii, H. cuneiformis, C. nodulifer, A. curvulatus, R. barboi, L. minisculum*; very rare *A. undulatus, Bacteriastrum spp., B. aurita, S. dimorpha, A. divisus, T. excentrica, A. minutus, T. leptopus, L. cornigerum, A. bismarckii, R.*

amphiceros angularis, R. amphiceros elongata, C. stellaris, T. cinnamomeum, C. asteromphalus, N. pennata, R. hebetata f. semispina, Asteromphalus darwinii, Rhaphoneis surirella; **age**: early Pliocene, N. kamtschatica-b Subzone, NPDZ 7Bb, 3.53–3.59 Ma to no older than 3.7 Ma.

Sample 21: 508 m (1,668 ft) to 518 m (1,698 ft); **lithology**: 70% clay, 20% limestone, 10% siltstone; **siliceous microfossils**: common *C. marginatus, C. marginatus v. fossilis*; frequent *A. ehrenbergii, T. nitzschioides, S. turris, M. sulcata, A. curvatulus, R. barboi, T. longissima*; rare *A. biformis, R. amphiceros angulari*; very rare *M. sol, A. undulatus, C. nodulifer, N. reinholdii, A. divisus, A. ochotensis, T. nativa, A. minutus, ,T. leptopus, L. cornigerum, A. bismarckii, P. americana, Asteromphalus robustus*; **age**: early Pliocene, *N. kamtschatica-b* Subzone, NPDZ 7Bb, 3.53–3.59 Ma to no older than 3.7 Ma.

Sample 22: 518 m (1,698 ft) to 527 m (1,728 ft); **lithology**: 80% clay, 20% limestone; **siliceous microfossils**: frequent *C. marginatus, T. nitzschioides, C. marginatus f. fossilis, T. antiqua, , M. sulcata, C. oculus-iridis, T. longissima*; rare *M. sol, C. nodulifer, A. curvatulus, R. barboi, A. biformis, L. cornigerum, C. denarius*; very rare *A. ehrenbergii v. tenella, T. oestrupii, H. cuneiformis, N. reinholdii, N. lyra, S. dimorpha, C. radiatus, A. divisus, T. excentrica, A. minutus, D. sachalinensis, C. grevillei, L. minisculum, R. amphiceros angularis, C. stellaris, L. californicum, P. americana, C. asteromphalus, R. amphiceros, Thalassiosira manifesta*; **age**: early Pliocene, *N. kamtschatica-b* Subzone, NPDZ 7Bb, 3.53–3.59 Ma to no older than 3.7 Ma.

Sample 23: 527 m (1,728 ft) to 536 m (1,758 ft); **lithology**: 80% clay, 20% limestone; **siliceous microfossils**: common *C. marginatus*; frequent *A. ehrenbergii, T. nitzschioides, C. marginatus v. fossilis, S. turris, T. antiqua, M. sulcata, C. oculus-iridis, T. longissima, C. denarius*; rare *M. sol, A. ehrenbergii v. fossilis, H. cuneiformis, N. reinholdii, R. barboi, A. biformis, L. cornigerum, C. asteromphalus, Coscinodiscus temperei*; **age**: early Pliocene, *N. kamtschatica-b* Subzone, NPDZ 7Bb, 3.53–3.59 Ma to 3.7 Ma.

First occurrence of *S. dimorpha* in sample 24 is 3.7 Ma (Barron, 1992).

Sample 24: 536 m (1,758 ft) to 545 m (1,788 ft); **lithology**: 90% clay, 10% limestone; **siliceous microfossils**: common *T. antique*; frequent *A. ehrenbergii, C. marginatus, T. nitzschioides, C. marginatus f. fossilis, H. cuneiformis, S. turris, M. sulcata, C. oculus-iridis, A. biformis, L. cornigerum, T. longissima, C. denarius*; rare *M. sol, A. ehrenbergii v. tenella, C. nodulifer, N. reinholdii A. curvulatus, A. divisus, T. excentrica, D. sachalinensis, A. bismarckii, L. minisculum, R. amphiceros angularis*; very rare *T. oestrupii, Bacteriastrum spp., S. dimorpha, R. barboi, T. nativa, A. minutus, T. leptopus, N. kamtschatica, R. styliformis, C. stellaris, C. asteromphalus, A. darwinii, C. temperei,*; **age**: early Pliocene, *N. kamtschatica-b* Subzone, NPDZ 7Bb, 3.53–3.59 Ma to 3.7 Ma.

Sample 25: 545 m (1,788 ft) to 554 m (1,818 ft); **lithology**: 70% clay, 20% siltstone, 10% limestone; **siliceous microfossils**: common *T. antique*; frequent *A. ehrenbergii, C. marginatus, T. nitzschioides, C. marginatus v. fossilis, A. ehrenbergii v. tenella, S. turris, M. sulcata, L. cornigerum, T. longissima, C. denarius*; rare *M. sol, C. nodulifer, N. reinholdii, R. barboi, T. nativa, A. biformis, A. minutus, C. oculus-iridis*; very rare *T. oestrupii, Bacteriastrum spp., A. splendens, A. divisus, T. excentrica, D. sachalinensis, A. bismarckii, L. minisculum, R. amphiceros angularis, R. amphiceros elongata, R. styliformis, L. californicum, R. hebetata f. semispina, T. leptopus, Cocconeis antiqua*; **age**: early Pliocene, *N. kamtschatica-b* Subzone, NPDZ 7Bb, 3.53–3.59 Ma to 5.49 Ma.

Sample 26: 554 m (1,818 ft) to 563 m (1,848 ft); **lithology**: 60% clay, 20% siltstone, 20% limestone; **siliceous microfossils**: frequent *A. ehrenbergii, C. marginatus, T. nitzschioides, C. marginatus f. fossilis, H, cuneiformis, S. turris, T. antiqua, M. sulcata, T. longissima, C. denarius*; rare *M. sol, A. undulatus, C. nodulifer, N. reinholdii, R. barboi, A. biformis, A. minutus, C. oculus-iridis, L. cornigerum, D. sachalinensis*; very rare *A. ehrenbergii v. tenella, D. bombus, Bacteriastrum spp., C. radiatus, A. curvulatus, A. divisus, T. excentrica, T. nativa, T. leptopus, N. kamtschatica, R. amphiceros angularis, R. amphiceros elongata, R. styliformis, C. asteromphalus, A. darwinii, R. surirella, C. leptopus*; **age**: early Pliocene, *N. kamtschatica-b* Subzone, NPDZ 7Bb, 3.53–3.59 Ma to 5.49 Ma.

Sample 27: 563 m (1,848 ft) to 572 m (1,878 ft); **lithology**: 70%clay, 20% siltstone, 10% limestone; **siliceous microfossils**: frequent *C. marginatus, T. nitzschioides, C. marginatus f. fossilis, T. antiqua, C. oculus-iridis, T. longissima*; rare *M. sol, A. ehrenbergii, S. turris, A. undulatus, M. sulcata, N. reinholdii, R. barboi, A. biformis, L. cornigerum, C. denarius*; very rare *A. ehrenbergii v. tenella, T. oestrupii, H. cuneiformis, C. nodulifer, A. curvulatus, A. divisus, T. excentrica, T. leptopus, A. bismarckii, L. minisculum, C. stellaris, C. asteromphalus, R. hebetata f. semispina*; **age**: early Pliocene, *N. kamtschatica-b* Subzone, NPDZ 7Bb, 3.53–3.59 Ma to 5.49 Ma.

Sample 28: 572 m (1,878 ft) to 582 m (1,908 ft); **lithology**: 60% clay, 20% siltstone, 20% limestone; **siliceous microfossils**: frequent *A. ehrenbergii, C. marginatus, T. nitzschioides, C. marginatus f. fossilis, T. antiqua, M. sulcata, L. cornigerum, T. longissima, C. denarius*; rare *M. sol, S. turris, N. reinholdii, A. minutus, C. oculus-iridis, D. sachalinensis, C. asteromphalus*; very rare *H. cuneiformis, A. undulatus, Bacteriastrum spp., B. aurita, C. nodulifer, A. curvulatus, A. divisus, T. excentrica, R. barboi, T. nativa, A. biformis, C. lineatus, A. bismarckii, L. minisculum, L. californicum, T. cinnamomeum, R. curvirostris v. inermis, Lithodesmium asketogonium, Cladogramma californica, Nitzschia fossilis, Rhizosolenia hebetata var.*; **age**: early Pliocene, *N. kamtschatica-b* Subzone, NPDZ 7Bb, 3.53–3.59 Ma to 5.49 Ma.

Sample 29: 582 m (1,908) ft) to 591 m (1,938 ft); **lithology**: 70% clay, 20% siltstone, 10% limestone; **siliceous**

microfossils: frequent *A. ehrenbergii, C. marginatus, T. nitzschioides, C. marginatus f. fossilis, T. antiqua, M. sulcata, T. longissima*; rare *S. turris, N. reinholdii, C. denarius*; very rare *M. sol, A. ehrenbergii v. tenella, T. oestrupii, H. cuneiformis, S. dimorpha, C. radiatus, A. curvulatus, T. excentrica, R. barboi, T. nativa, A. biformis, A. minutus, C. oculus-iridis, L. cornigerum, D. sachalinensis, A. bismarckii, L. minisculum, C. stellaris*; **age**: early Pliocene, *N. kamtschatica*-b Subzone, NPDZ 7Bb, 3.53–3.59 Ma to 5.49 Ma.

Sample 30: 591 m (1,938 ft) to 600 m (1,968 ft); **lithology**: 60% clay, 40% siltstone; **siliceous microfossils**: frequent *M. sol, A. ehrenbergii, C. marginatus, T. nitzschioides, C. marginatus f. fossilis, T. antiqua, M. sulcata, T. longissima*; rare *S. turris, N. reinholdii, L. cornigerum, C. denarius*; very rare *A. ehrenbergii v. tenella, H. cuneiformis, A. undulatus, A. splendens, C. nodulifer, C. radiatus, A. curvulatus, A. divisus, R. barboi, T. nativa, A. biformis, C. oculus-iridis, D. sachalinensis, A. bismarckii, L. minisculum, R. amphiceros angularis, C. stellaris, T. cinnamomeum*; **age**: early Pliocene, *N. kamtschatica*-b Subzone, NPDZ 7Bb, 3.53–3.59 Ma to 5.49 Ma.

Regional top of Miocene unconformity is at about 600 m in this well based on mapping seismic reflection data.

First occurrence of Thalassiosira oestrupii is in Sample 31

Sample 31: 600 m (1,968 ft) to 609 m (1,998 ft); **lithology**: 30% clay, 10 % limestone, 60% siltstone and shale; **siliceous microfossils**: common *C. marginatus*; frequent *T. nitzschioides, C. marginatus f. fossilis, T. antiqua, N. reinholdii, T. longissima, C. denarius*; rare *S. turris, A. curvulatus, A. divisus, T. excentrica, A. minutus, C. oculus-iridis, L. minisculum, N. fossilis*; very rare *M. sol, A. ehrenbergii v. tenella*, first occurrence of *T. oestrupii, D. bombus, C. nodulifer, T. nativa, A. biformis, R. amphiceros angularis, R. amphiceros elongata, R. styliformis, R. amphiceros*; **age**: early Pliocene to Late Miocene, *N. kamtschatica*-b Zone, NPDZ 7Bb, 3.53–3.59 Ma to 5.49 Ma to, *N. kamtschatica*-a Subzone, NPDZ 7Ba, 5.49 Ma to 5.9 Ma.

Sample 32: 609 m (1,998 ft) to 618 m (2,028 ft); **lithology**: 30% clay, 10% limestone, 60% siltstone

and shale with argillaceous chert fragments; **siliceous microfossils**: common *C. marginatus, T. nitzschioides, C. marginatus f. fossilis, T. longissima*; frequent *S. turris, N. reinholdii, R. barboi, C. denarius*; rare *H. cuneiformis, C. nodulifer, C. excentricus, L. cornigerum, L. californicum, C. californica*; very rare *A. ehrenbergii, A. ehrenbergii v. tenella, Bacteriastrum spp., M. sulcata, C. radiatus, A. curvulatus, A. divisus, A. biformis, A. minutus, C. oculus-iridis, A. bismarckii, L. minisculum, R. amphiceros angularis, T. cinnamomeum, Diploneis smithii*; **age**: late Miocene, *N. kamtschatica*-a Subzone, NPDZ 7Ba, 5.49 Ma to 5.9 Ma.

Sample 33: 618 m (2,028 ft) to 627 m (2,058 ft); **lithology**: 30% clay, 10% limestone, 60% siltstone and shale; **siliceous microfossils**: frequent *A. ehrenbergii, C. marginatus, T. nitzschioides, C. marginatus f. fossilis, T. antiqua*; rare *A. ehrenbergii v. tenella, S. turris, T. longissima, C. denarius*; very rare *M. sol, H. cuneiformis, A. undulatus, Bacteriastrum spp., C. nodulifer, M. sulcata, A. curvulatus, A. divisus, T. excentrica, T. nativa, A. biformis, A. minutus, C. oculus-iridis, D. sachalinensis, L. minisculum, L. californicum, R. hebetata f. semispina*; **age**: late Miocene, *N. kamtschatica*-a Subzone, NPDZ 7Ba, 5.49 Ma to 5.9 Ma.

Sample 34: 627 m (2,058 ft) to 636 m (2,088 ft); **lithology**: 30% clay, 70% siltstone and shale; **siliceous microfossils**: frequent *C. marginatus, T. nitzschioides, S. turris, T. antiqua, N. reinholdii, C. denarius*; rare *A. ehrenbergii v. tenella, C. marginatus f. fossilis, M. sulcata, A. divisus, D. sachalinensis, T. longissima*; very rare *A. ehrenbergii, D. bombus, H. cuneiformis, A. undulatus, C. nodulifer, C. radiatus, A. curvulatus, C. excentricus, R. barboi, T. nativa, A. biformis, A. minutus, T. leptopus, A. bismarckii, C. oculus-iridis, L. cornigerum, L. minisculum, R. amphiceros angularis, R. amphiceros elongata, C. asteromphalus, R. hebetata f. semispina, Aulocodiscus spp.*; **age**: late Miocene, *N. kamtschatica*-a Subzone, NPDZ 7Ba, 5.49 Ma to 5.9 Ma.

Sample 35: 636 m (2,088 ft) to 646 m (2,118 ft); **lithology**: 20-30% clay, 60% siltstone and shale, 0-10% limestone; **siliceous microfossils**: frequent *T. antiqua*; rare *M. sol, C. marginatus, C. marginatus f. fossilis*; very rare *A. ehrenbergii v. tenella, C. robustus, S. turris, C. nodulifer, N. reinholdii, A. divisus, A. bismarckii, R. hebetata f. semispina*; **age**: late Miocene, *N. kamtschatica*-a Subzone, NPDZ 7Ba, 5.49 Ma to 6.65 Ma

Table A7.   Interpreted Summary of Data From Well P-0435-1

Siliceous Microfossils

Age (Ma)	Depth (m)	Siliceous microfossil zones
2.0 to 2.61–2.68	242 to 297	*Neodenticula koizumii* Zone, NPDZ 9, late Pliocene
3.53–3.59 to 5.49	297 to 462	*Neodenticula kamtschatica* Subzone b, NPDZ 7Bb, early Pliocene to late Miocene
5.49 to 6.65	462 to 489	*N. kamtschatica* Subzone a, NPDZ 7Ba, late Miocene

Benthic Foraminifers

Depth (m)	Foraminiferal stages
242 to 333	Indeterminate
333 to 470	Early Pliocene, Repettian, *Uvigerina peregrina, Pulvinulinella pacifica*
470 to 644	Indeterminate
644 to 1,488	Probable late Miocene, upper Mohnian to Delmontian, *Virginulina californiensis*
1,488 to 1,903	Probable late Miocene, upper Mohnian to middle Miocene lower Mohnian, based on lithology
1,903 to 2,074	Franciscan Complex, based on lithology

Formation Names

Depth (m)	Formation
75 to 297	Unnamed offshore units
297 to 461	Upper Sisquoc Formation
461 to 1,360	Lower Sisquoc Formation
1,360 to 1,903	Monterey Formation
1,903 to 2,074	Franciscan Complex

Well P-0435-1

Summary of the lithology and siliceous microfossils In the depth interval 242 meters to 489 meters

Samples 1 and 2: 242 m to 297 m, clay, sand and siltstone; **age:** late Pliocene, *N. koizumii* Zone, NPDZ 9, 2.0 Ma to 2.61–2.68 Ma.

Samples 3 to 6: 297 m to 407 m, clay siltstone; **age:** early Pliocene, *N. kamtschatica*-b Subzone, NPDZ 7Bb, 3.53–3.59 Ma to 5.49 Ma.

Samples 7 and 8: 407 m to 462 m, clay, claystone, siltstone, and shale; **age:** early Pliocene, *N. kamtschatica*-b Subzone, NPDZ 7Bb, 3.53–3.59 Ma to 5.49 Ma.

Sample 9: 462 m to 489 m, clay, claystone, siltstone and shale; **age:** late Miocene, *N. kamtschatica*-b Subzone, NPDZ 7Ba, 5.49 Ma to 6.65 Ma.

Below 489 m there are no preserved siliceous microfossils due to diagenetic alteration of the host rocks.

Detailed listings of the sample lithology and diatom content are below.

Well P-0435-1, Sample Descriptions—Lithology and Siliceous Microfossils

The individual samples are 27 m (90 ft) composites of well cuttings. The lithology descriptions are from well site formation logging contractors. Preparation and identification of diatoms was by Biostratigraphics in 1982. Their terms for the frequency of observed diatoms in a sample are common (200–900), frequent (9–200), rare (4–8), and very rare (1–3). The assignment of North Pacific Diatom Zones (NPDZ) and ages is by the authors based on zones in Maruyama (2000). Depths are subsea (MLLW). The casing shoe was at 230 m (755 ft).

Sample 1: 242 m (794 ft) to 269 m (884 ft); **lithology**: 80% soft clay, 10% unconsolidated sand, 10% siltstone; **siliceous microfossils**: frequent *Coscinodiscus marginatus*; rare *Thalassiosira convexa, Thalassiosira antiqua, Melosira sol, Melosira sulcata*; very rare *Xanthiopyxis ovalis, Thalassiothrix longissima, Thalassiosira excentrica, Rhizosolenia curvirostris v. inermis, Raphoneis cocconeides, Pseudopodasira elegans, Diploneis smithii, Neodenticula koizumii, Coscinodiscus stellaris, Coscinodiscus nodulifer, Coscinodiscus marginatus f. fossilis, Coscinodiscus excentricus, Actinoptychus undulatus, Actinocyclus oculatus, Actinocyclus curvatulus*; **age**: late Pliocene, *N. koizumii* Zone, NPDZ 9, 2.0 Ma to 2.61–2.68 Ma.

Sample 2: 269 m (884 ft) to 297 m (974 ft); **lithology**: 80% clay, 10% unconsolidated sand, 10% siltstone; **siliceous microfossils**: frequent *C. marginatus*; rare *T. antiqua, M. sulcata, C. excentricus, Thalassiosira nitzschioides, Diploneis bombus*; *very rare* X. ovalis, T. longissima, T. excentrica, T. convexa, R. curvirostris v. inermis, P. elegans, D. smithii, N. koizumii (first occurrence), C. stellaris, C. nodulifer, C. marginatus f. fossilis, A. oculatus, Stephanopyxis turris, Rhizosolenia hebetata f. semispina, Rhaponeis surirella, Hemidiscus cuneiformis, Endictya oceanica, Actinocyclus ochotensis, Actinocyclus ehrenbergii; **age**: late Pliocene, *N. koizumii* Zone, NPDZ 9, 2.0 Ma to 2.61–2.68 Ma.

Early-late Pliocene unconformity is at approximately 297 m based on mapping of seismic reflection data (pl. 7).

Sample 3: 297 m (974 ft) to 324 m (1,064 ft); **lithology**: 80% clay, 20% siltstone; **siliceous microfossils**: frequent *T. antiqua, C. marginatus, Rhizosolenia barboi*; rare *M. sol, M. sulcata, C. marginatus f. fossilis*; very rare *X. ovalis, T. convexa, R. curvirostris v. inermis, C. nodulifer, S. turris, H. cuneiformis, D. bombus, A. ehrenbergii, Thalassiosira oestrupii* (first occurrence), *Thalassiosira nativa, Delphineis sachalinensis, Rhaphoneis amphiceros elongata, Pseudopyxilla americana, Melosira granulata, Lithodesmium cornigerum, Coscinodiscus oculus-iris, Cladogramma californica, Actinocyclus ehrenbergii v. tenella*; **age**: early Pliocene, *N. kamtschatica*-b Subzone, NPDZ 7Bb, 3.53–3.59, Ma to 5.49 Ma.

Sample 4: 324 m (1,064 ft) to 352 m (1,154 ft); **lithology**: 80% clay, 20% siltstone, occasional streaks of sand; **siliceous microfossils**: frequent *C. excentricus, R. barboi*; rare *C. marginatus v. fossilis*; very rare *T. convexa, M. sol, M. sulcata, S. turris, H. cuneiformis, D. bombus, A. ehrenbergii, T. oestrupii, T. nativa, C. californica, A. ehrenbergii v. tenella, C. robustus, A. minutus, A. biformis*; **age**: early Pliocene, *N. kamtschatica*-b Subzone, NPDZ 7Bb, 3.53–3.59 Ma to 5.49 Ma.

Sample 5: 352 m (1,154 ft) to 379 m (1,244 ft); **lithology**: 80% clay, 20% siltstone, trace dolomite detritus; **siliceous microfossils**: frequent *T. antiqua, M. sulcata, C. marginatus f. fossilis, C. marginatus, A. ehrenbergii, R. barboi*; rare *T. longissima M. sol, S. turris*; very rare *R. curvirostris v. inermis, A. curvulatus, T. nitzschioides, H. cuneiformis, A. ochotensis, T. oestrupii, T. nativa, P. americana, C. oculus-iridis, C. californica, A. ehrenbergii v. tenella, C. robustus, A. minutus, A. biformis, Nitzschia princeps, Coscinodiscus vetustissimus, Thalassiosira leptopus, Actinoptychus splendens*; **age**: early Pliocene, *N. kamtschatica*-b Subzone, NPDZ 7Bb, 3.53–3.59 Ma to 5.49 Ma.

Sample 6: 379 m (1,244 ft) to 407 m (1,344 ft); **lithology**: 80% clay, 10 to 20% siltstone, 0 to 10% indurated silt to granular size conglomerate; **siliceous microfossils**: frequent *C. marginatus*; rare *T. antiqua, M. sol, C. marginatus f. fossilis, R. barboi*; very rare *T. longissima, M. sulcata, T. excentrica, S. turris, A. ehrenbergii, T. oestrupii, C. robustus, Cocconeis costata*; **age**: early Pliocene, *N. kamtschatica*-b Subzone, NPDZ 7Bb, 3.53–3.59 Ma to 5.49 Ma.

Sample 7: 407 m (1,344 ft) to 434 m (1,424 ft); **lithology**: 80% clay to claystone, 20% siltstone and shale; **siliceous microfossils**: frequent *C. marginatus*; rare *T. antiqua, M. sol, M. sulcata, C. marginatus f. fossilis, T. nitzschioides, A. ehrenbergii, R. barboi*; very rare *T. excentrica, T. convexa, C. nodulifer, T. excentrica, S. turris, A. ehrenbergii, T. oestrupii, T. nativa, A. ehrenbergii v. tenella, A. minutus, A. biformis, Thalassiosira undulosa, Navicula pennata, Lithodesmium minisculum, Campyloneis grevillei*; **age**: early Pliocene, *N. kamtschatica*-b Subzone, NPDZ 7Bb, 3.53–3.59 Ma to 5.49 Ma.

Sample 8: 434 m (1,424 ft) to 462 m (1,514 ft); **lithology**: 80% clay to claystone, 20% siltstone and shale; **siliceous microfossils**: frequent *C. marginatus*; rare *M. sol, M. sulcata, T. nitzschioides, R. barboi*; very rare *T. convexa, T. antiqua, C. stellaris, C. marginatus f. fossilis, T. excentrica, S. turris, R. surirella, A. ehrenbergii, T. oestrupii* (first occurrence) *, A. ehrenbergii v. tenella, A. biformis, C. vetustissimus, T. leptopus, A. splendens, C. grevillei, Nitzschia reinholdii, Chaetocerus sp.*; **age**: early Pliocene, *N. kamtschatica*-b Subzone, NPDZ 7Bb, 3.53–3.59 Ma to 5.49 Ma.

Regional top of Miocene unconformity is at 461 m based on mapping of seismic reflection data (pl. 6).

Sample 9: 462 m (1,514 ft) to 489 m (1,604 ft), **lithology**: 80% clay to claystone, 20% siltstone and shale; **siliceous microfossils**: rare *T. excentrica, R. barboi, Thalassiosira gravida, Denticulopsis hyalina, Actinocyclus ingens*; very rare *T. longissima, T. antiqua, M. sol, M. sulcata, C. marginatus, A. curvulatus, T. nitzschioides, D. bombus, D. sachalinensis, A. ehrenbergii v. tenella, T. undulosa, Thalassiosira miocenica, Thalassiosira cf. burckliana, Opephora schwartzii, Navicula lyra, Endicta japonica, Dicladia capreolis, Diploneis crabro, Denticulopsis hustedii*; **age**: late Miocene, *N. kamtschatica*-a Subzone, NPDZ 7Ba, 6.0 Ma to 6.65 Ma.

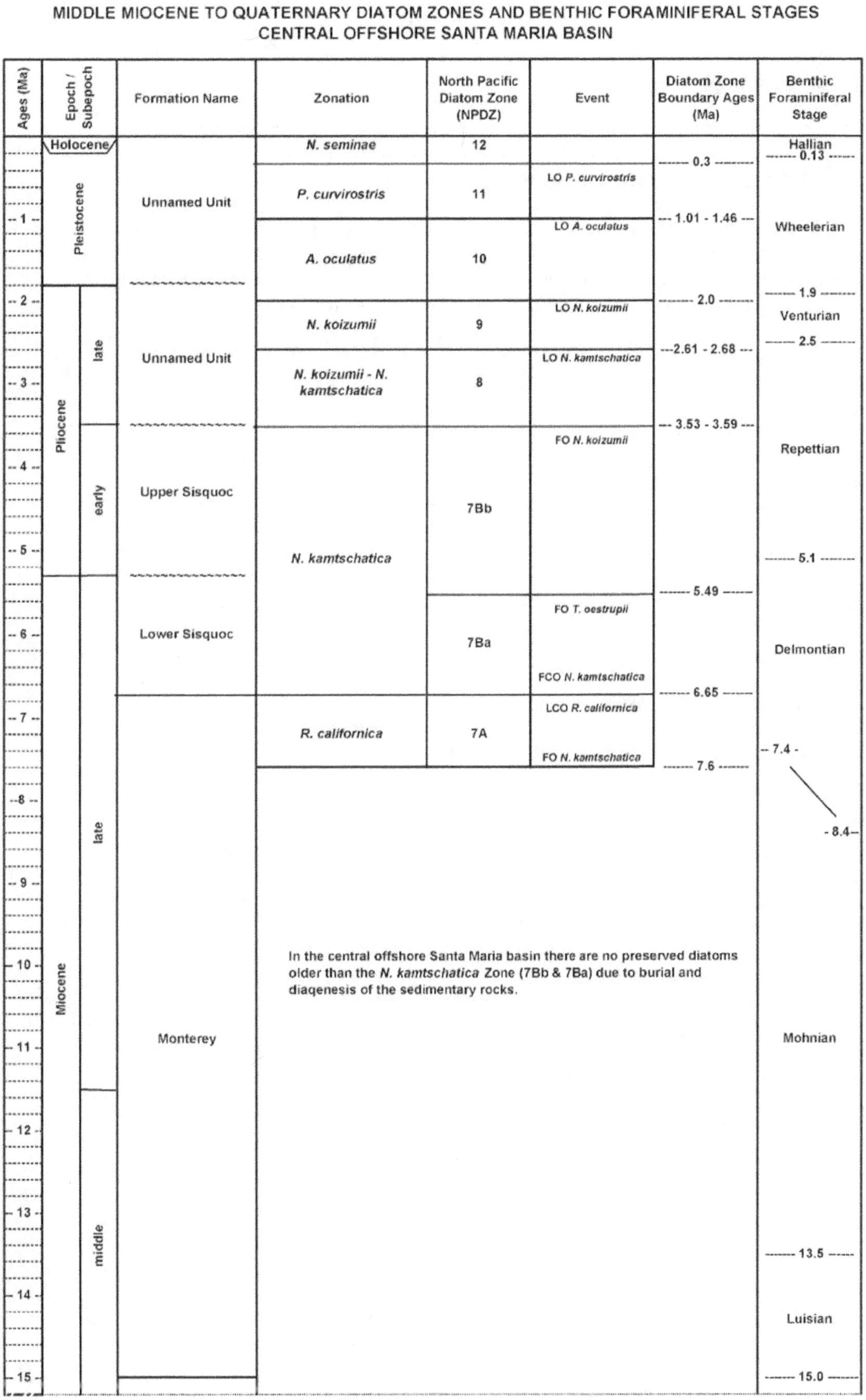

MIDDLE MIOCENE TO QUATERNARY DIATOM ZONES AND BENTHIC FORAMINIFERAL STAGES
CENTRAL OFFSHORE SANTA MARIA BASIN

Figure A1. The figure shows diatom zones and benthic foraminiferal stages for the middle Miocene to Quaternary sedimentary units in the central offshore Santa Maria Basin. Geologic formation names and ages are the same as shown in figure 6 and described in the text. Unconformities are shown as wavy lines. The diatom zone names, NPDZ designations, event occurrences, and diatom zone boundary ages (Ma) are from Maruyama (2000). Event occurrences are labeled as FO (first occurrence), FCO (first common occurrence), LO (last occurrence), and LCO (last common occurrence). Ages for the epochs, subepochs, and benthic foraminiferal stages are from McDougall (2008) and follow recent revisions of the time scale (Gradstein and others, 2004; USGS, 2007).

Ages (Ma)	Epoch / Subepoch	Formation Name	Zonation	North Pacific Diatom Zone (NPDZ)	Event	Diatom Zone Boundary Ages (Ma)	Benthic Foraminiferal Stage
	Holocene		*N. seminae*	12			Hallian
						0.3	0.13
	Pleistocene	Unnamed Unit	*P. curvirostris*	11	LO *P. curvirostris*		
1						1.01 - 1.46	Wheelerian
			A. oculatus	10	LO *A. oculatus*		
2	Pliocene late	Unnamed Unit	*N. koizumii*	9	LO *N. koizumii*	2.0	1.9
							Venturian
3			*N. koizumii - N. kamtschatica*	8	LO *N. kamtschatica*	2.61 - 2.68	2.5
					FO *N. koizumii*	3.53 - 3.59	Repettian
4	Pliocene early	Upper Sisquoc	*N. kamtschatica*	7Bb			
5							5.1
						5.49	
6		Lower Sisquoc		7Ba	FO *T. oestrupii*		Delmontian
					FCO *N. kamtschatica*	6.65	
7		*R. californica*	7A		LCO *R. californica*		7.4
8	Miocene late				FO *N. kamtschatica*	7.6	8.4
9		Monterey					
10							Mohnian
11							
12							
13	Miocene middle					13.5	
14							Luisian
15						15.0	

In the central offshore Santa Maria basin there are no preserved diatoms older than the *N. kamtschatica* Zone (7Bb & 7Ba) due to burial and diagenesis of the sedimentary rocks.

Appendix B

Uninterpreted seismic sections

This appendix contains uninterpreted copies of the seismic sections illustrated in this paper and the companion paper by Hanson and others (2004). These 20 seismic sections are identical to the interpreted seismic section figures included in the papers, except the interpretive markings of faults and unconformities have been removed.

PROFILE PB1-PB1', NORTH OF RAGGED POINT

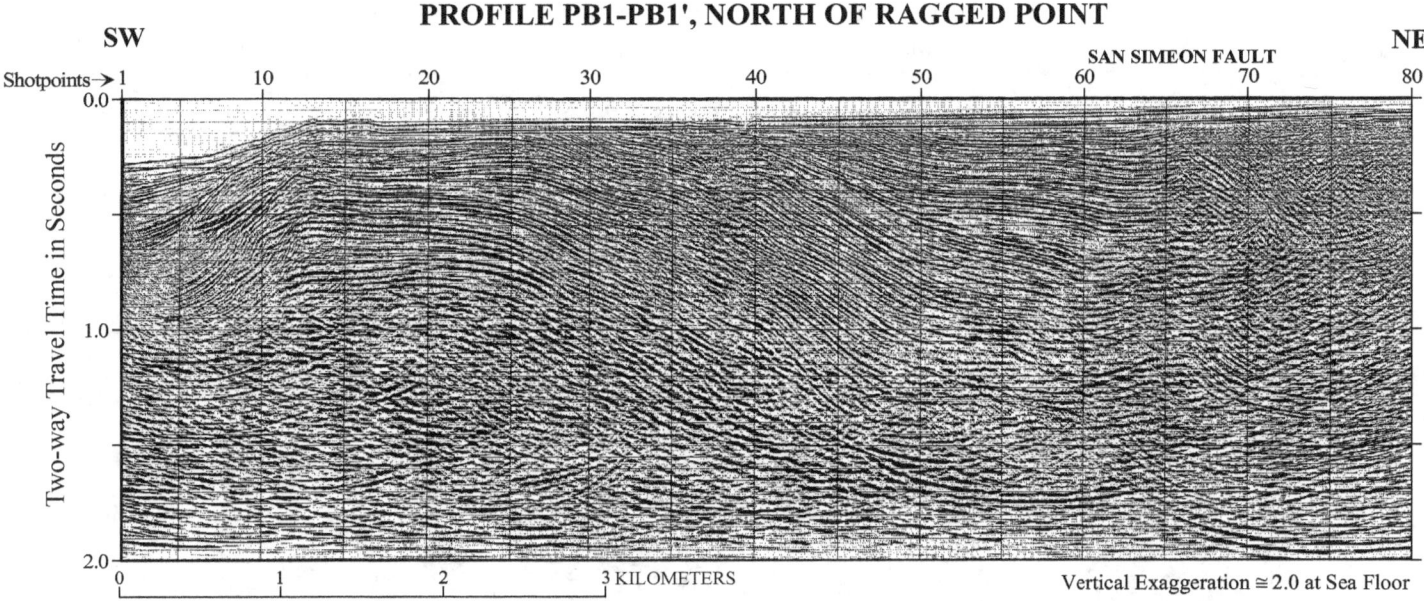

Figure B1.   Seismic profile PB1–PB1', north of Ragged Point.

PROFILE PB2-PB2', OFFSHORE POINT PIEDRAS BLANCAS

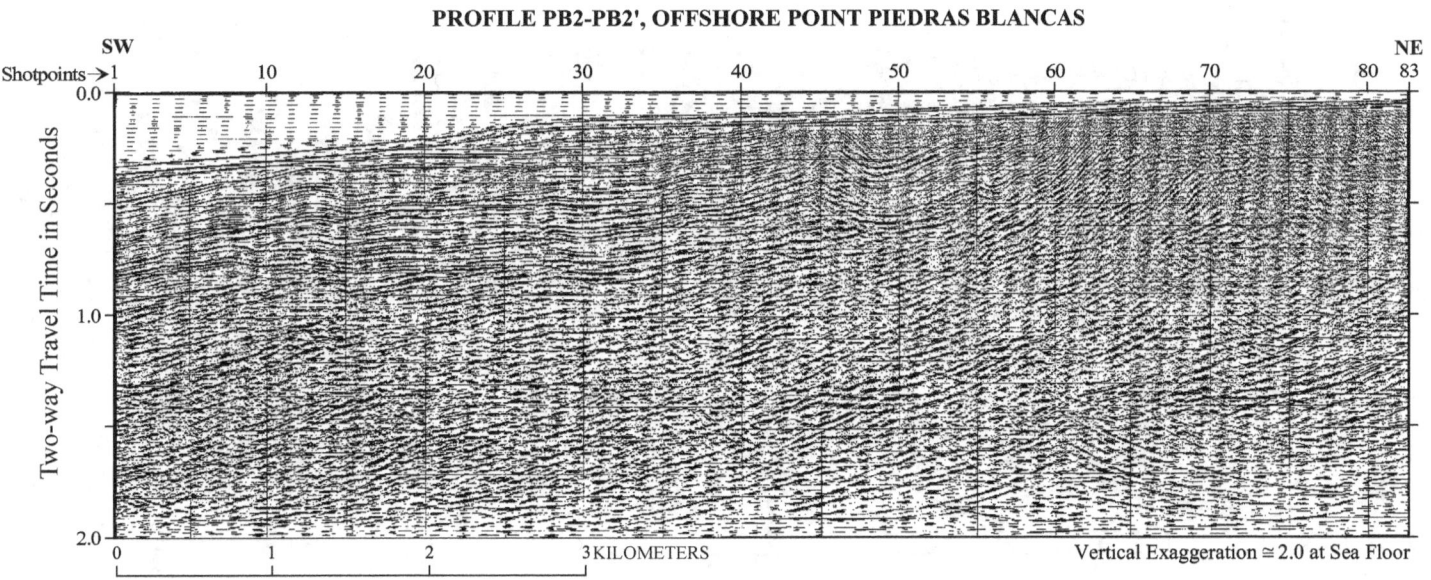

Figure B2.   Seismic profile PB2–PB2', offshore Point Piedras Blancas.

PROFILE SS-SS', OFFSHORE SAN SIMEON POINT

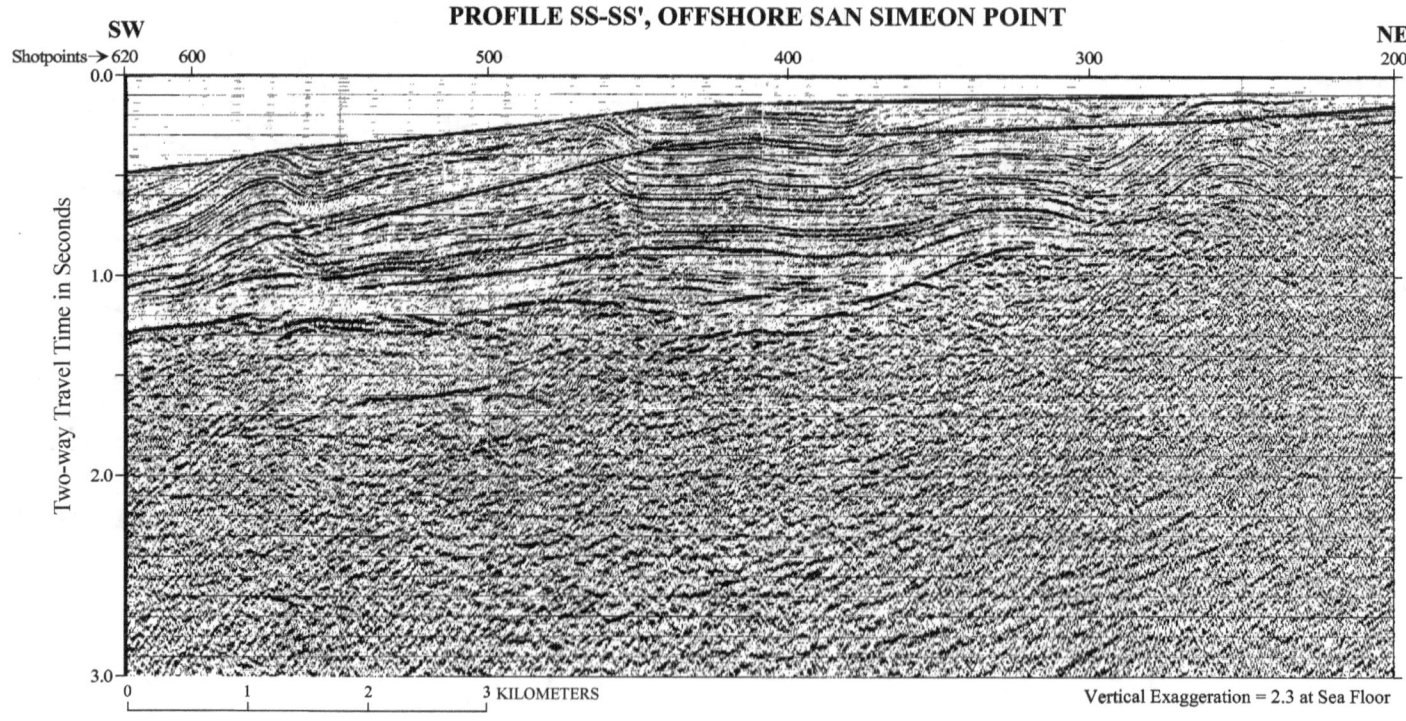

Figure B3.   Seismic profile SS–SS', offshore San Simeon Point.

PROFILE NT-NT', NORTHERN TERMINATION AREA

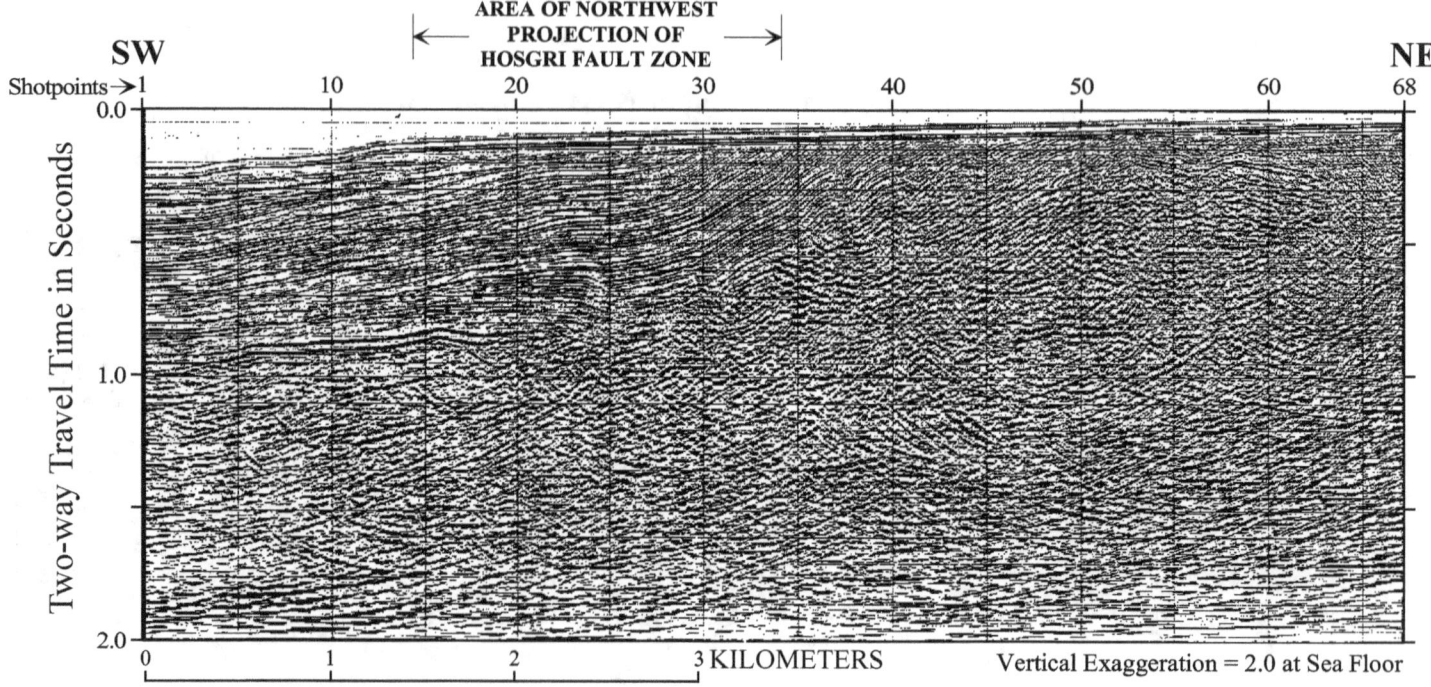

Figure B4.   Seismic profile NT–NT', northern termination area.

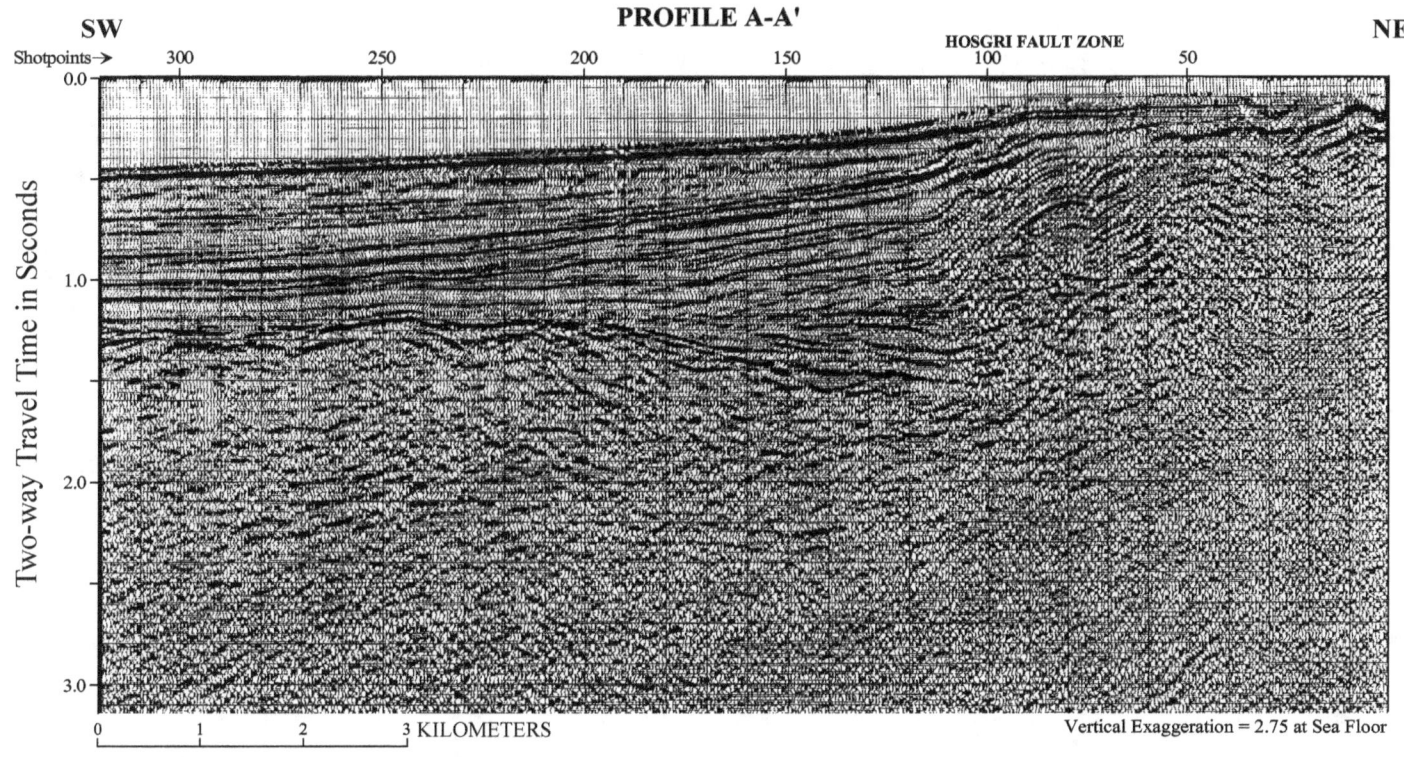

PROFILE A-A'

SW

Shotpoints →   300   250   200   150   HOSGRI FAULT ZONE 100   50   NE

Two-way Travel Time in Seconds

0   1   2   3 KILOMETERS

Vertical Exaggeration = 2.75 at Sea Floor

Figure B5.   Seismic profile A–A'.

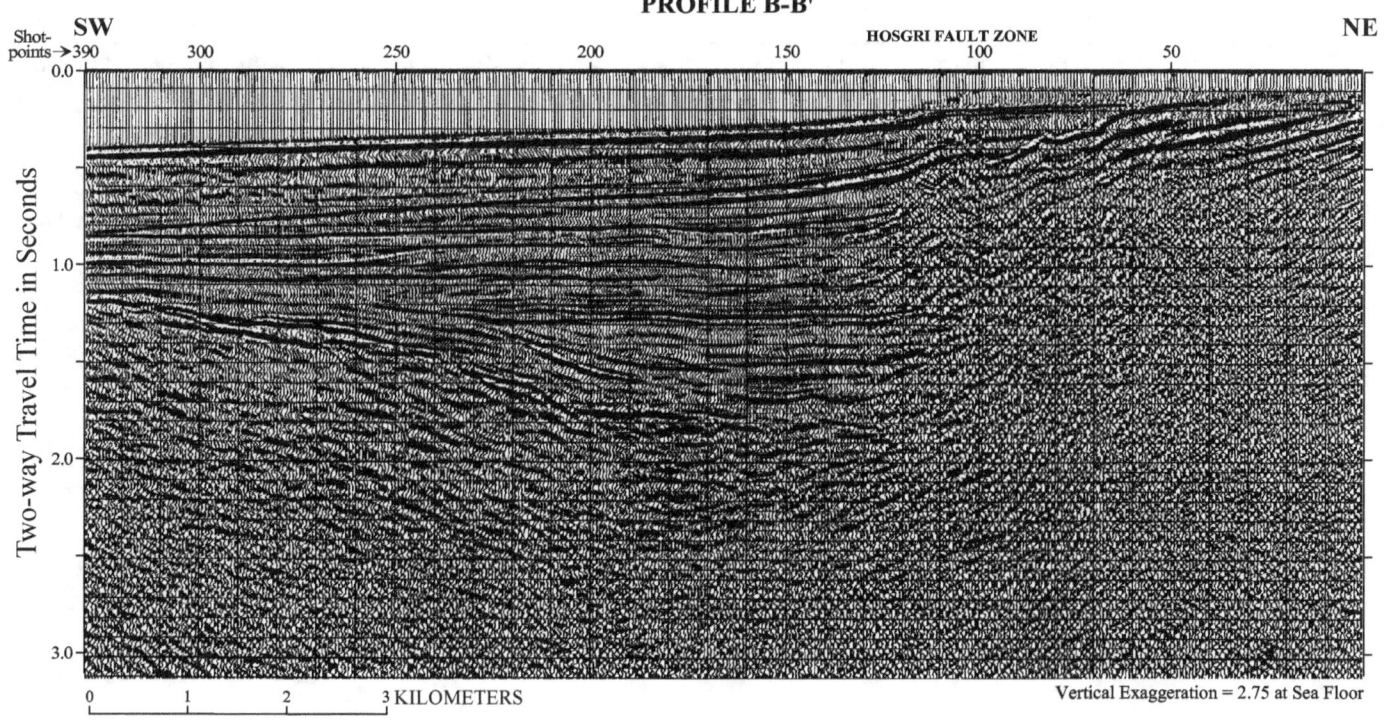

PROFILE B-B'

SW

Shot-points → 390   300   250   200   150   HOSGRI FAULT ZONE   100   50   NE

Two-way Travel Time in Seconds

0   1   2   3 KILOMETERS

Vertical Exaggeration = 2.75 at Sea Floor

Figure B6.   Seismic profile B–B'.

PROFILE C''-C'''

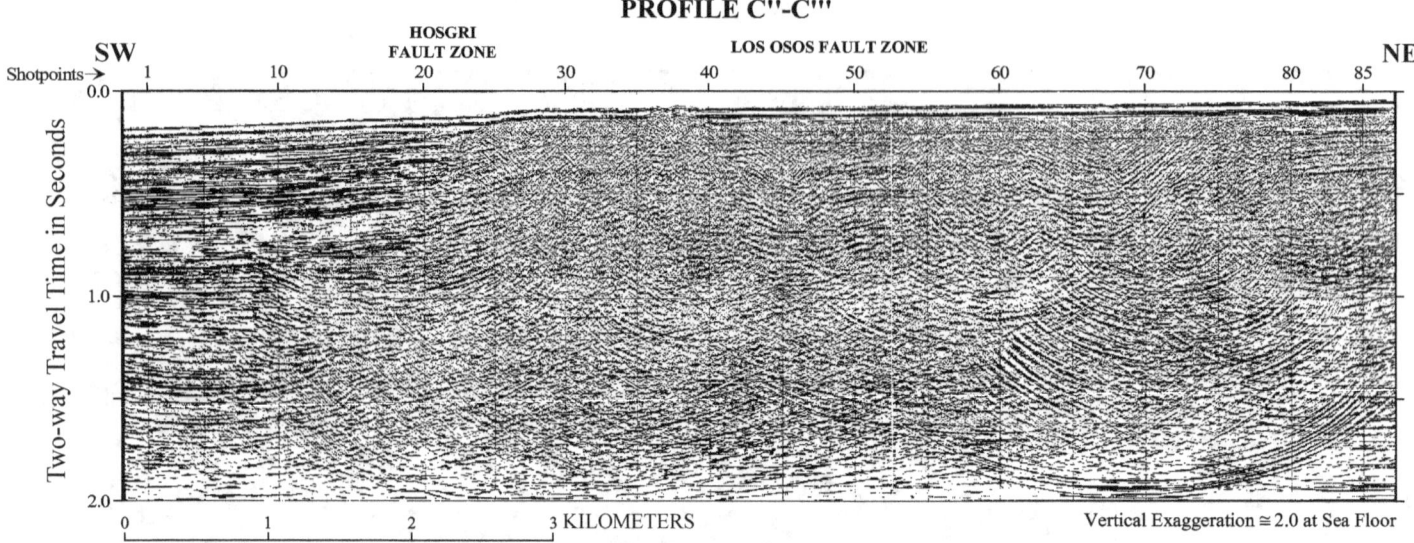

Figure B7.   Seismic profile CC''–CC''.

PROFILE C-C'

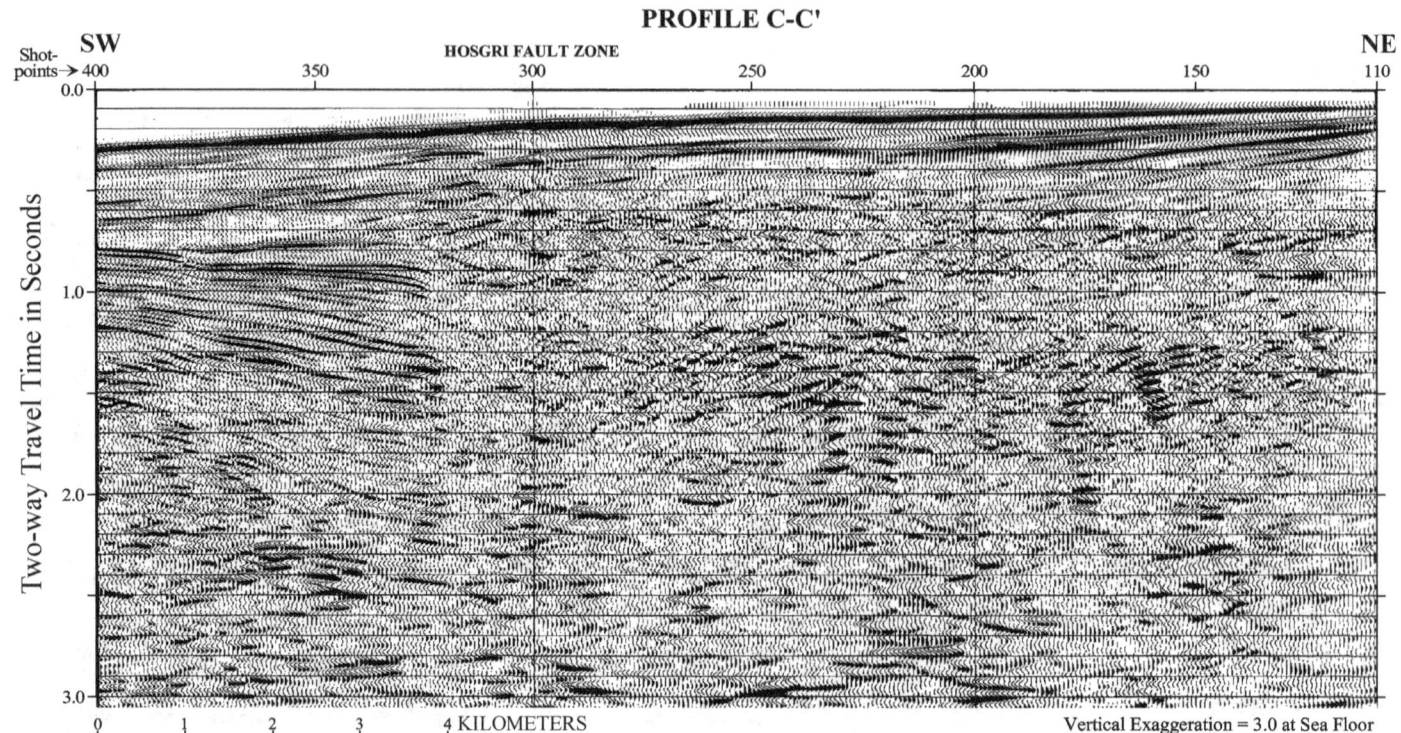

Figure B8.   Seismic profile C–C'.

PROFILE D-D'

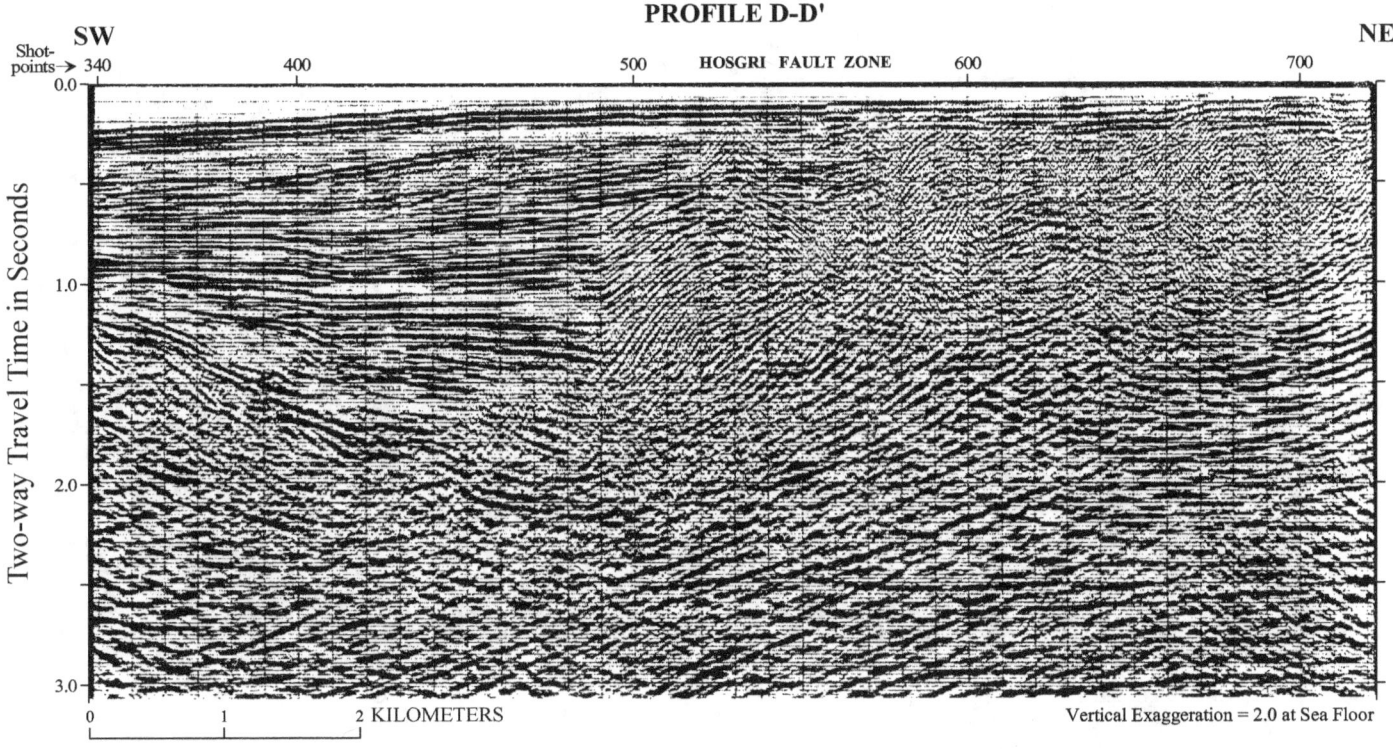

Figure B9.   Seismic profile D–D'.

PROFILE E-E'

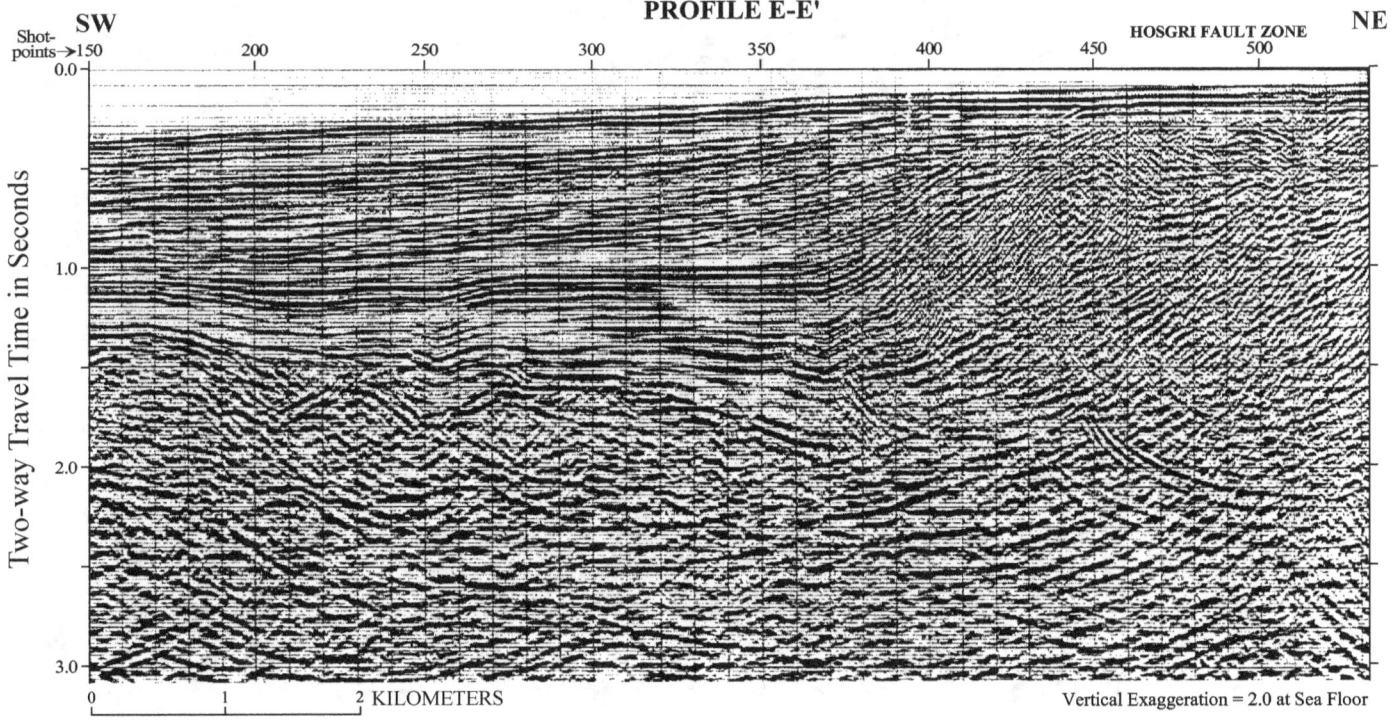

Figure B10.   Seismic profile E–E'.

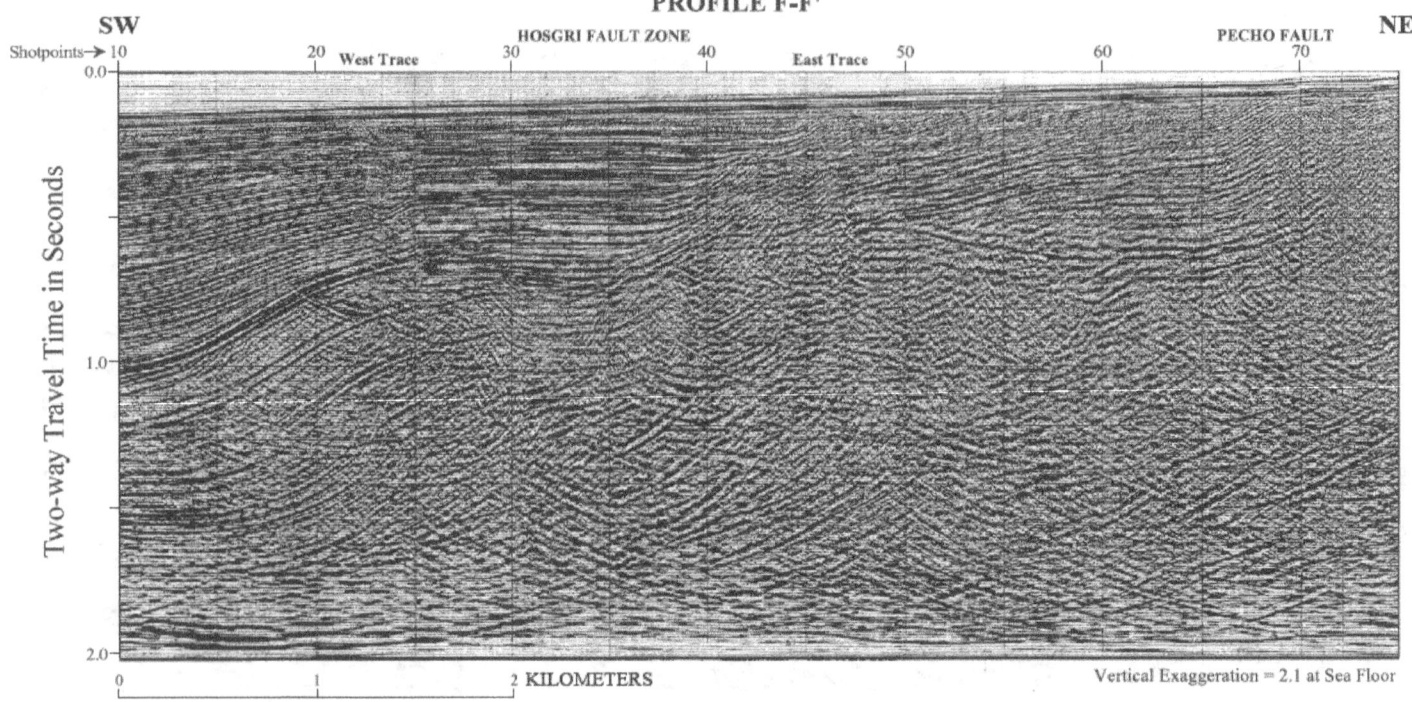

Figure B11.   Seismic profile F–F'.

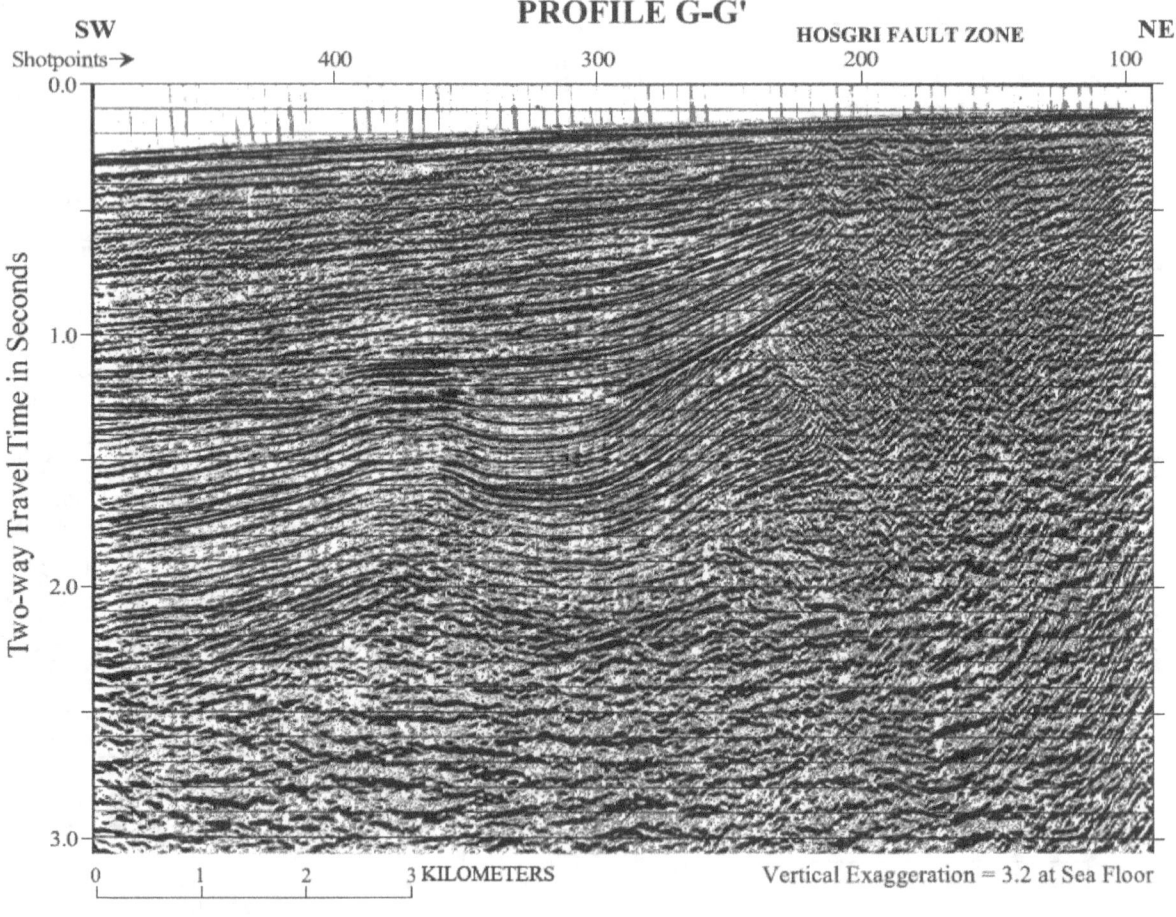

Figure B12.   Seismic profile G–G'.

PROFILE H-H'

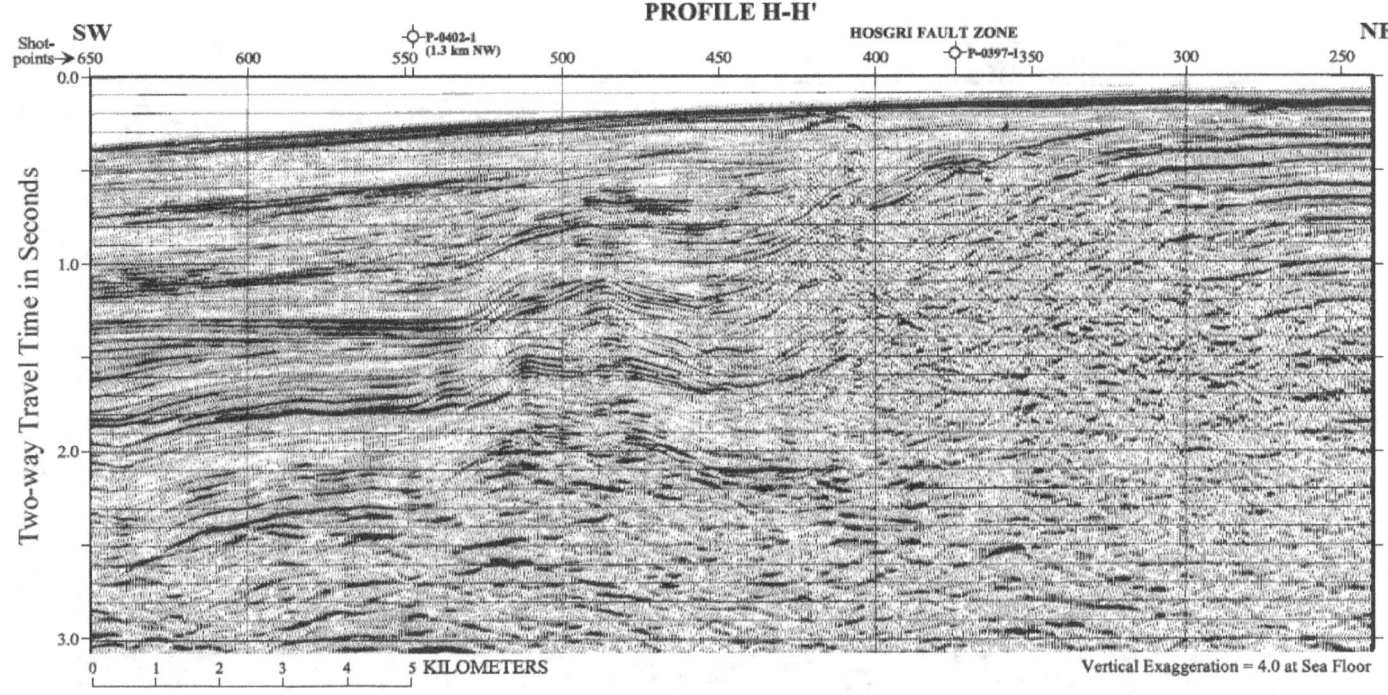

Figure B13.   Seismic profile H–H'.

PROFILE I-I'

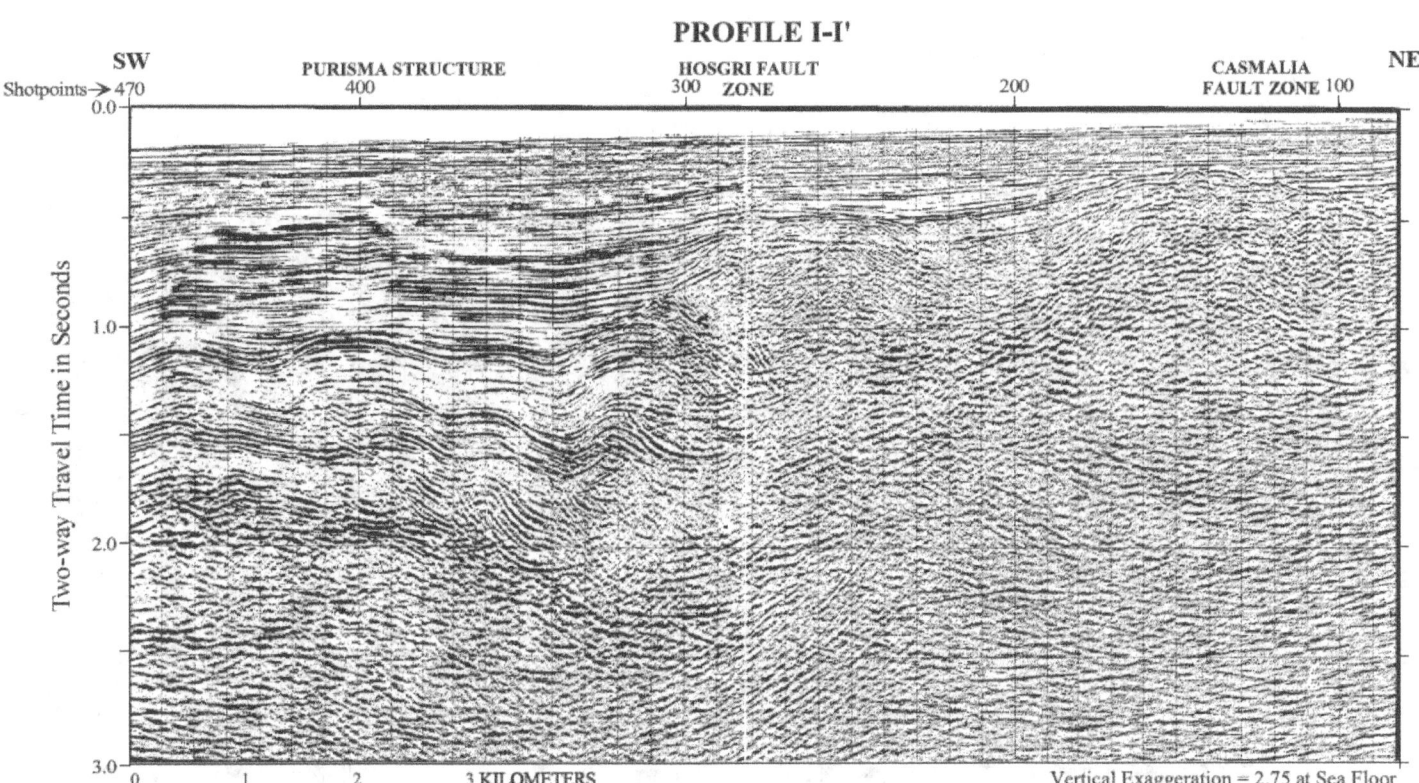

Figure B14.   Seismic profile I–I'.

PROFILE J-J'

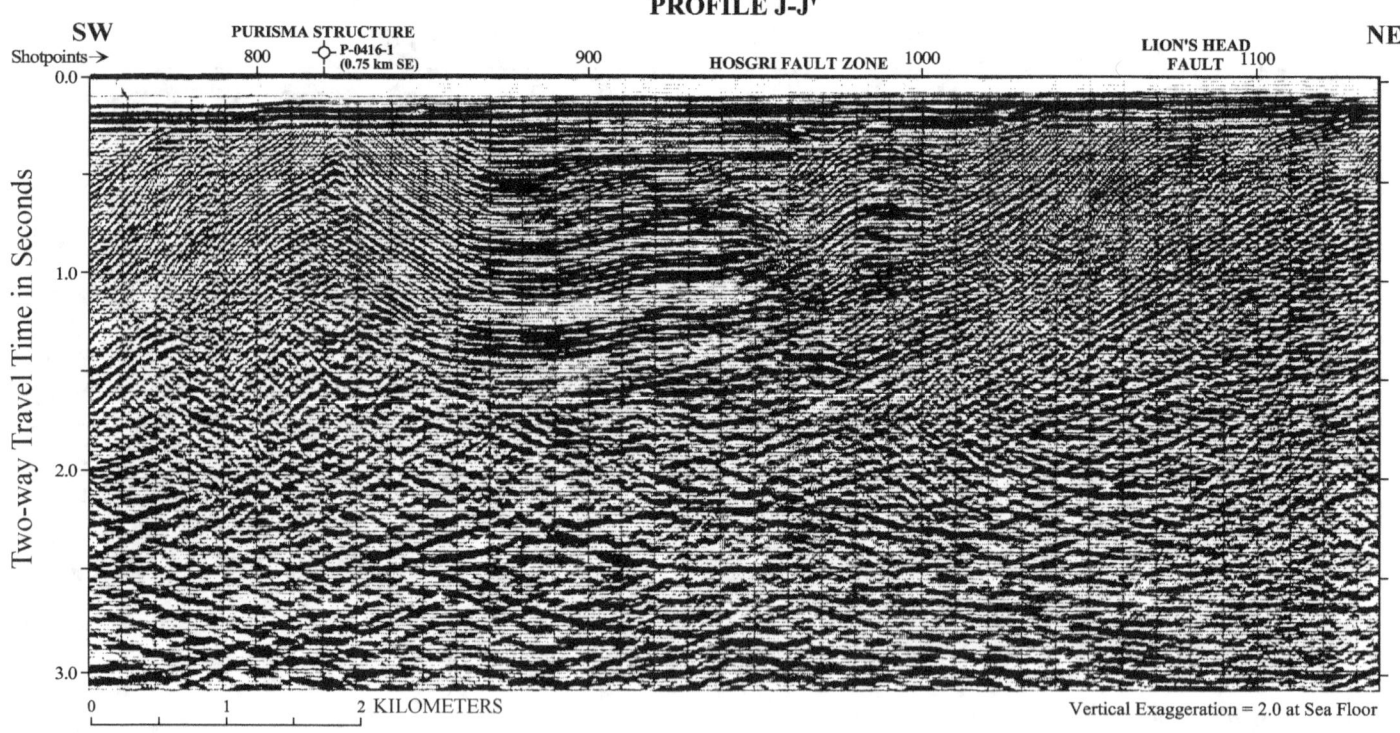

Figure B15. Seismic profile J–J'.

PROFILE K-K'

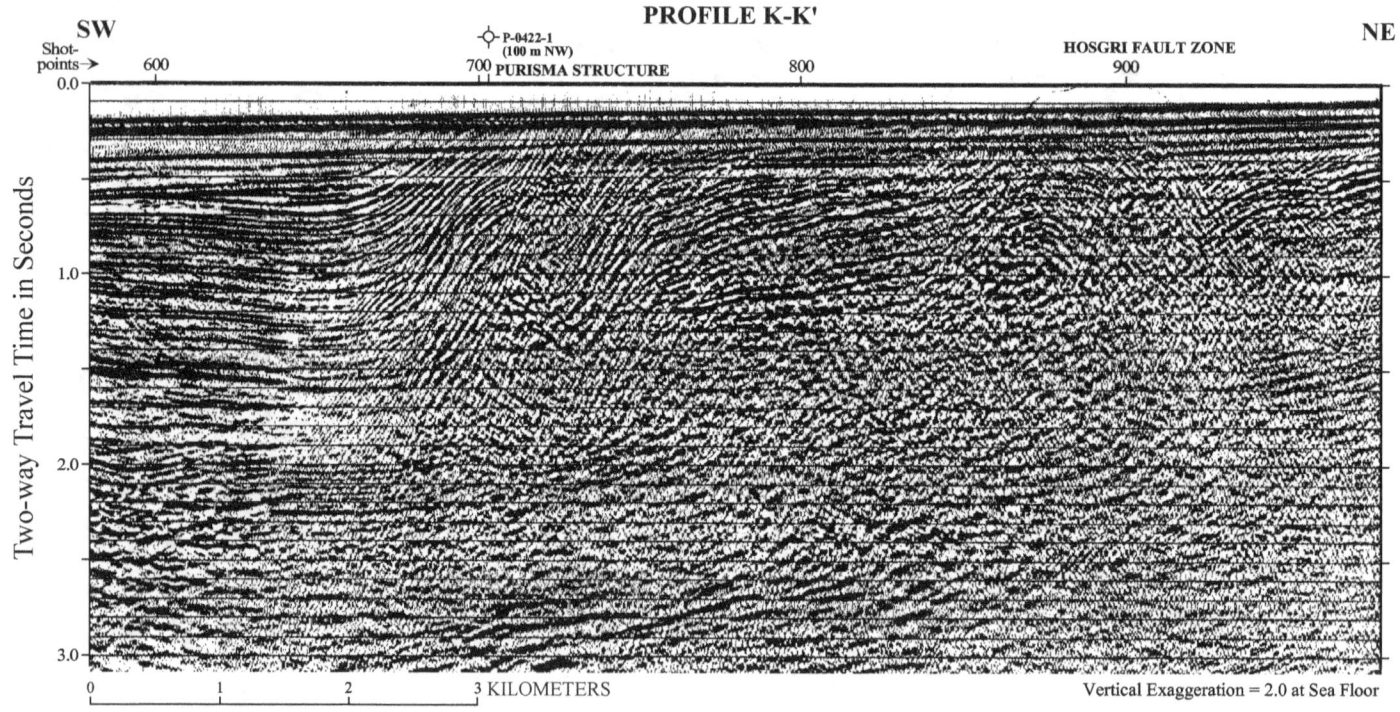

Figure B16. Seismic profile K–K'.

PROFILE L-L'

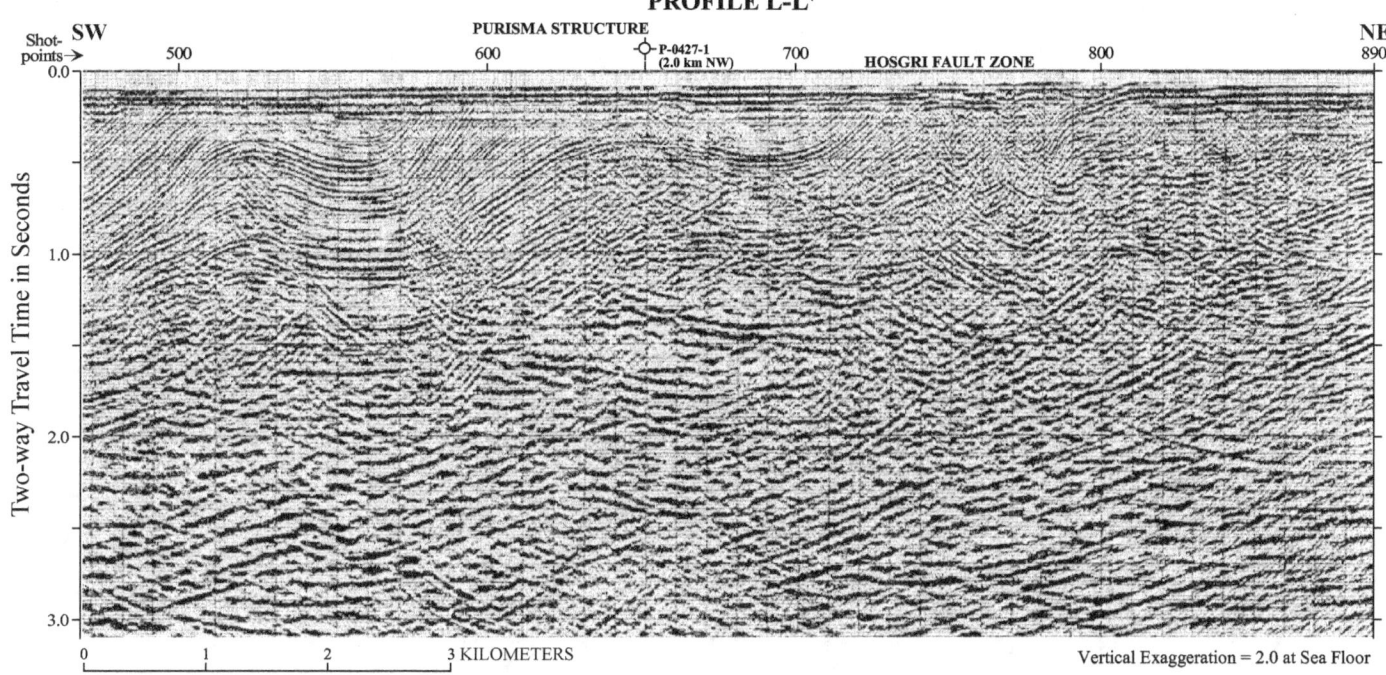

Figure B17. Seismic profile L–L'.

PROFILE M-M'

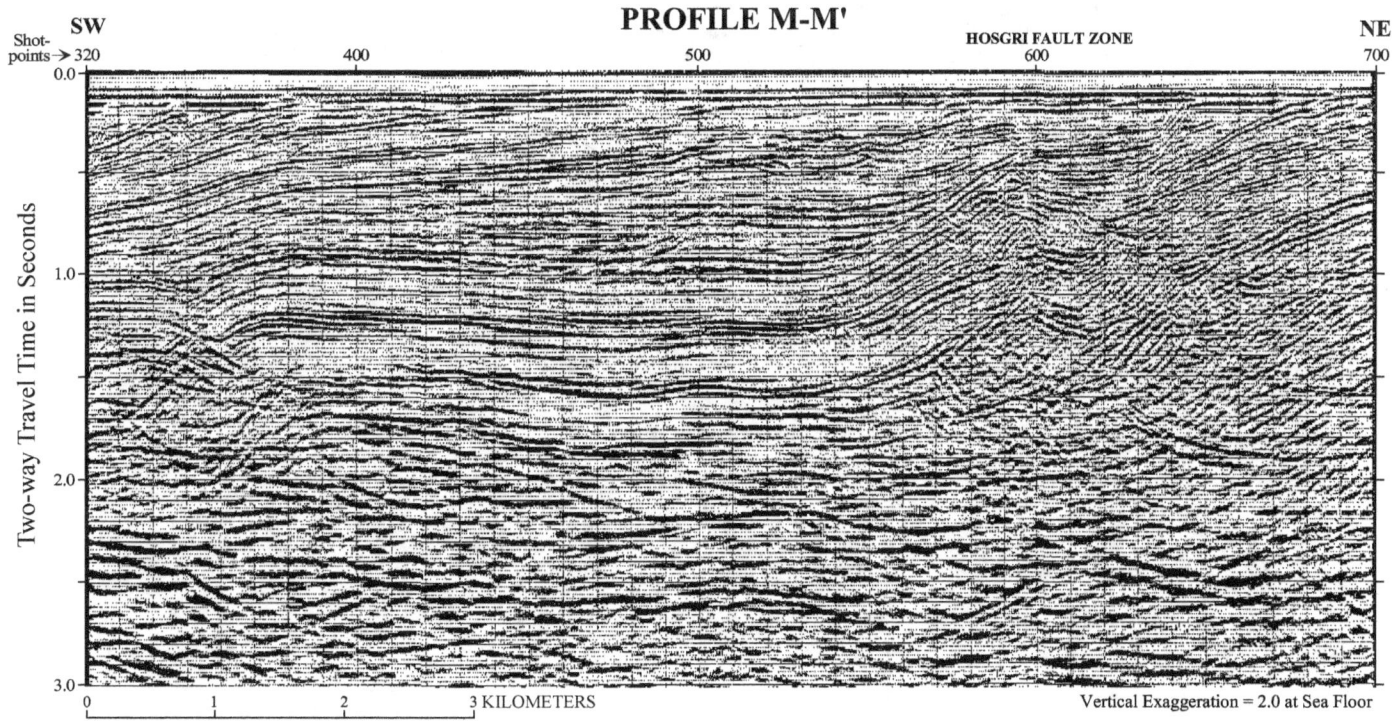

Figure B18. Seismic profile M–M'.

PROFILE CM-47

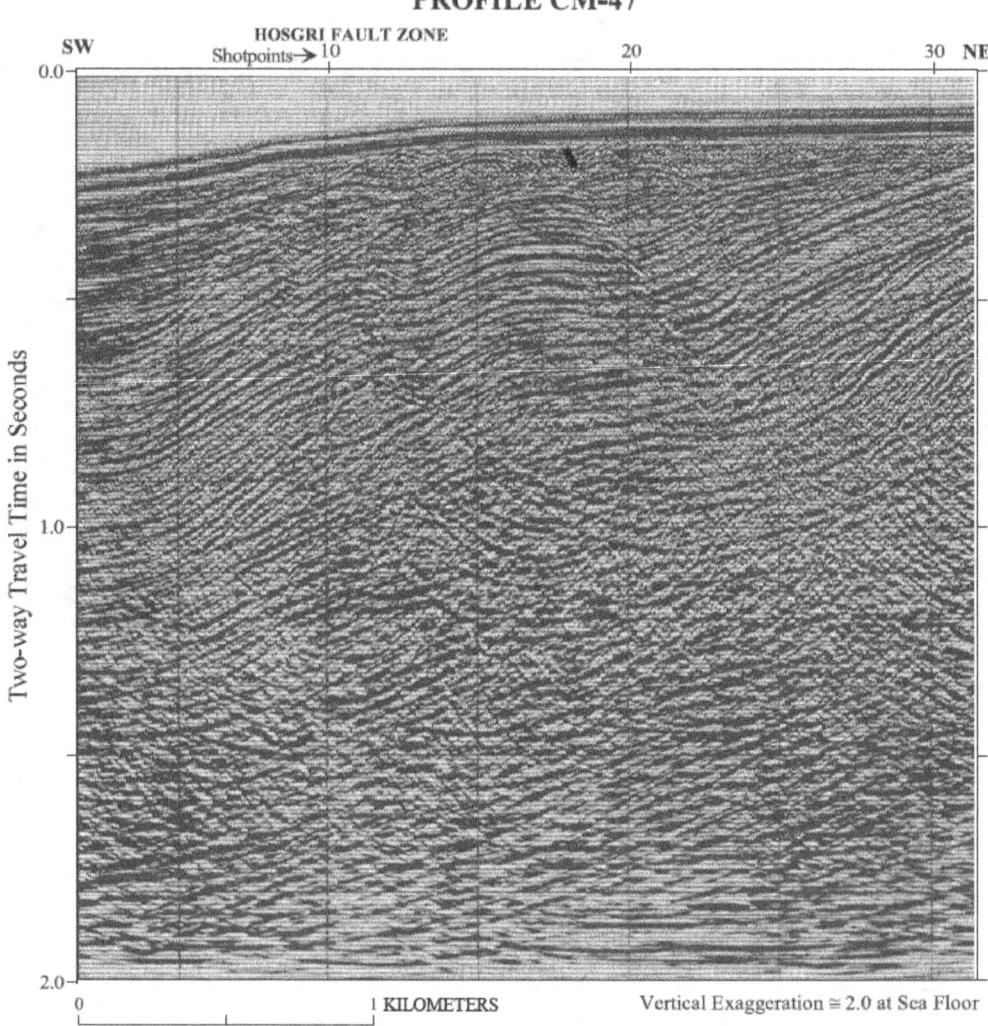

Figure B19.   Seismic profile CM-47.

PROFILE GSI-100

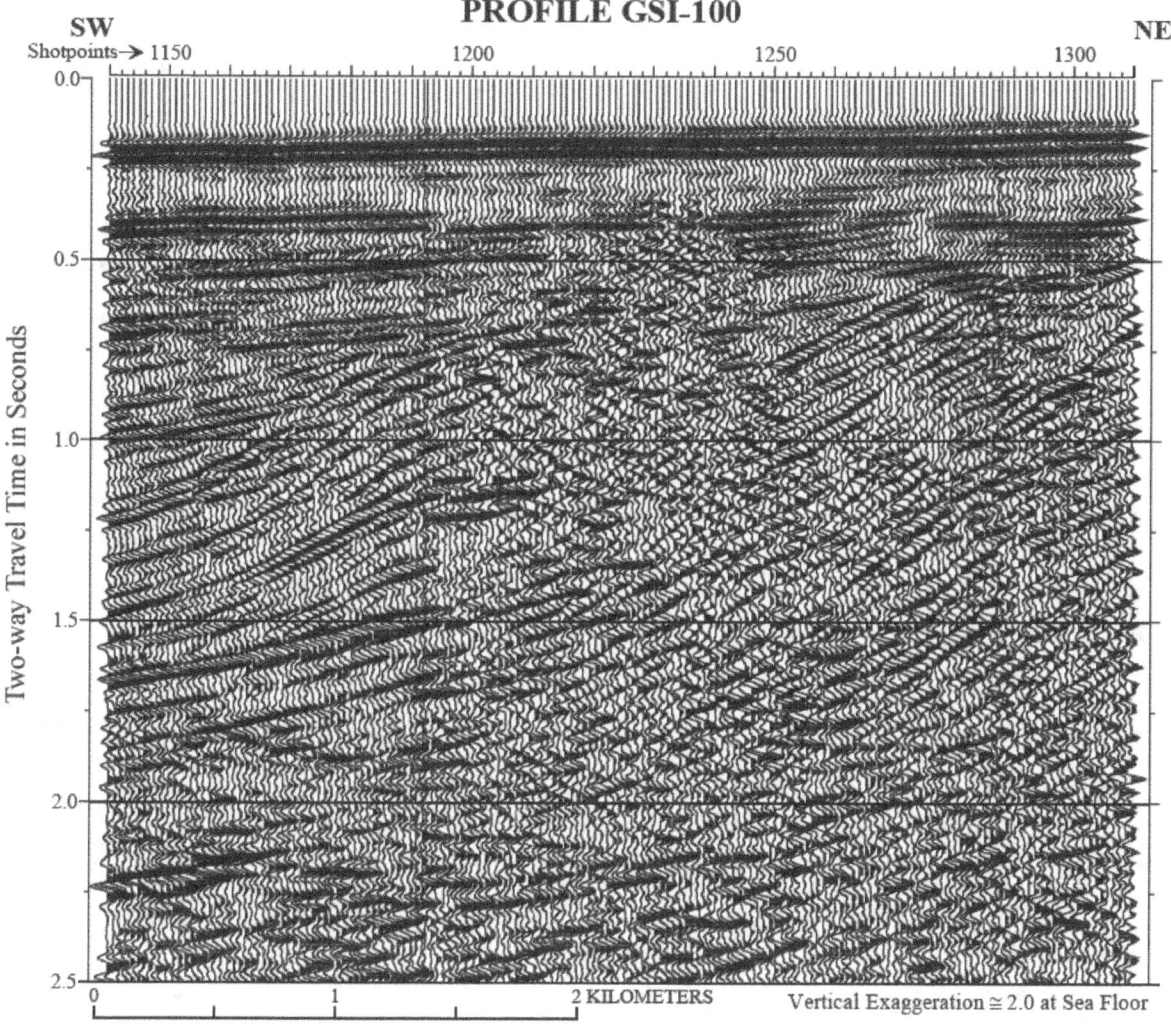

Figure B20.   Seismic profile GSI-100.

Menlo Park Publishing Service Center, California
Manuscript approved for publication, December 12, 2012
Edited by J.L. Zigler
Design and layout by Jeanne S. DiLeo